the MODERN

AIR FRYER
COOKBOOK

---
500 HEALTHY, EASY & DELICIOUS RECIPES

FOR AIR FRYING **PERFECTION**

Patricia June

© Copyright 2021 By **Patricia June** - All rights reserved.

The content contained within this book may not be reproduced, duplicated or transmitted without direct writ- ten permission from the author or the publisher. Under no circumstances will any blame or legal responsibility be held against the publisher, or author, for any damages, reparation, or monetary loss due to the information contained within this book. Either directly or indirectly.

Legal Notice:

This book is copyright protected. This book is only for personal use. You cannot amend, distribute, sell, use, quote or paraphrase any part, or the content within this book, without the consent of the author or publisher.

Disclaimer Notice:
Please note the information contained within this document is for educational and entertainment purposes only. All effort has been executed to present accurate, up to date, and reliable, complete information. No warranties of any kind are declared or implied. Readers acknowledge that the author is not engaging in the rendering of legal, financial, medical or professional advice. The content within this book has been derived from various sources. Please consult a licensed professional before attempting any techniques outlined in this book. By reading this document, the reader agrees that under no circumstances is the author responsible for any losses, direct or indirect, which are incurred as a result of the use of information contained within this document, including, but not limited to, errors, omissions, or inaccuracies.

INSIDE THIS BOOK

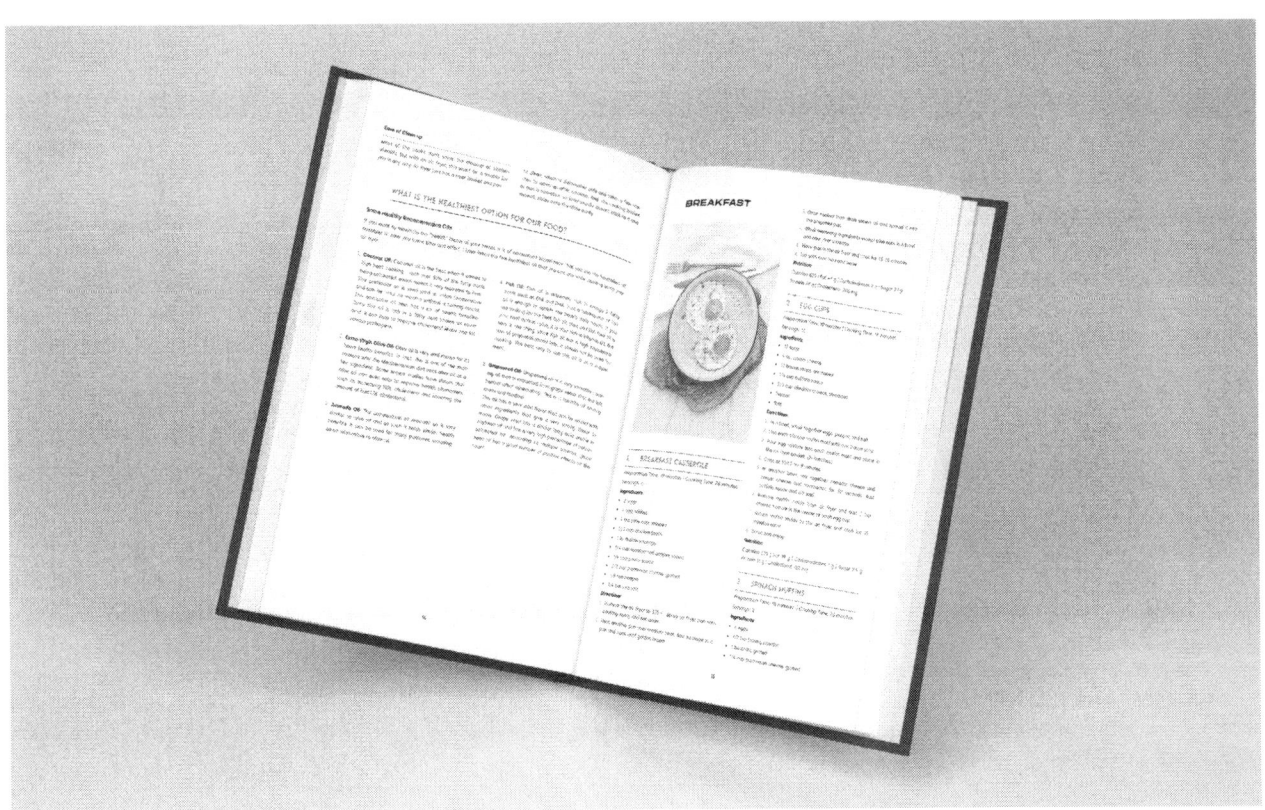

Table of Content

INTRODUCTION 11

HOW DOES AN AIR FRYER WORK? 13

ADVANTAGES OF AIR FRYING 13

WHAT IS THE HEALTHIEST OPTION FOR OUR FOOD? 14

Breakfast 15

1. Breakfast Casserole 15
2. Egg Cups 15
3. Spinach Muffins 15
4. Broccoli Muffins 16
5. Zucchini Gratin 16
6. Breakfast Egg Muffins 16
7. Cheese Pie 17
8. Parmesan Breakfast Casserole 17
9. strawberry French toast 17
10. Apple Roll-Ups 17
11. Pepper Egg Bites 18
12. Crunchy Nut Granola 18
13. Breakfast Pizza 18
14. Veggie Frittata 19
15. Spicy Hash Brown Potatoes 19
16. Sage and Pear Sausage Patties 20
17. Bacon Bombs 20
18. Morning Potatoes 20
19. Breakfast Pockets 20
20. Avocado Flautas 21
21. Cheese Sandwiches 21
22. Sausage Cheese Wraps 21
23. Bacon, Mushroom & Tomato Frittata 22
24. Sausage, Spinach & Broccoli Frittata 22
25. Sausage & Scallion Frittata 22
26. Trout Frittata 23
27. Tasty Cinnamon Toast 23
28. Delicious Potato Hash 23
29. Turkey Burrito 24
30. Biscuits Casserole 24
31. Cheese Air Fried Bake 24
32. Oatmeal Casserole 24
33. Chicken Omelet 25
34. Sausage Burritos 25
35. Sausage Patties 25
36. Spicy Sweet Potato Hash 25
37. Cinnamon Cream Doughnuts 26
38. Sausage Frittata 26
39. Potato Jalapeno Hash 26
40. Bread Rolls 27
41. Spinach Egg Breakfast 27
42. Vegetable Quiche 27
43. Breakfast Egg Tomato 28
44. Mushroom Leek Frittata 28
45. Perfect Breakfast Frittata 28
46. Indian Cauliflower 28
47. Banana Oats 29
48. Zucchini Salad 29
49. Cinnamon Buns 29
50. Egg Cheddar Muffins 29
51. Go-to Easy Cornbread 30
52. Exotic Cornbread 30
53. Mozzarella Bread & Eggs 30
54. Vanilla Flavoured Strawberry Porridge 31
55. Creamy Mushroom Porridge 31
56. Scrambled Eggs with Pesto & Cheese 31
57. Mango and Lime Bowl 31
58. Carrot Small Cakes 31
59. Creamy Scrambled Eggs 32
60. Rosti with Salmon 32
61. Vegetarian tofu Omelet 32
62. Banana Bread with Walnuts 33
63. Cinnamon Donuts 33
64. Coffee Favoured Muffins 33
65. Fruity Bacon Slices+Yogurt Dip 34
66. Vanilla & Berries French toast 34
67. Healthy Angel Cake 34
68. Cheesy Cinnamon Pancake 35
69. Delicious Cinnamon Pancake 35
70. Cinnamon French Toast 35

Appetizer 36

71. Sweet Cinnamon Peaches 36
72. Roasted Grapes with Yogurt 36
73. Garlic Edamame 36
74. Baked Sardines with Sauce 37
75. Cheesy Baked Potatoes 37
76. Sausage and Onion Rolls 37
77. Green Chiles Nachos 38
78. Parmesan Cauliflower 38
79. Cheesy Jalapeño Poppers 38
80. Salty Baked Almonds 38
81. Lemon-Pepper Wings 39
82. Spicy and Sweet Roasted Nuts 39
83. Paprika Deviled Eggs 39
84. Sausage Balls with Cheese 39
85. Mozzarella Pepperoni Pizza Bites 40
86. Air Fry Bacon 40
87. Crunchy Bacon Bites 40
88. Easy Jalapeno Poppers 40
89. Perfect Crab Dip 41
90. Spinach Dip 41
91. Sweet Potato Tots 41
92. Herb Zucchini Slices 41

#	Item	Page
93.	Ranch Kale Chips	42
94.	Curried Sweet Potato Fries	42
95.	Roasted Almonds	42
96.	Pepperoni Chips	42
97.	Crispy Eggplant	43
98.	Steak Nuggets	43
99.	Cabbage Chips	43
100.	Healthy Broccoli Tots	43
101.	Classic French Fries	44
102.	Olive Oil Sweet Potato Chips	44
103.	Low-Carb Cheese-Stuffed Jalapeño Poppers	44
104.	Vidalia Onion Blossom	44
105.	Spiced Nuts	45
106.	Pigs in a Blanket	45
107.	Crunchy Pork Egg Rolls	45
108.	Spinach and Artichoke Dip Wontons	46
109.	Loaded Disco Fries	46
110.	Fried Olives	47

LUNCH 48

#	Item	Page
111.	Garlic Duck Breasts	48
112.	Healthy Chicken Thighs	48
113.	Chili Sauce Chicken	48
114.	Exotic Duck Breasts	49
115.	Peachy Chicken	49
116.	Tea Flavoured Chicken	49
117.	Healthy Ratatouille	50
118.	Veggy Egg Rolls	50
119.	Red Lentils English Muffins	50
120.	Italian Flag English Muffin	50
121.	Veggy Pita	51
122.	Vegan Falafel	51
123.	Stuffed Tomatoes	51
124.	Tasty Small Potatoes	52
125.	Vegetables Quiche	52
126.	Healthy Beans Pizza	52
127.	Pork Bites with Yogurt Sauce	53
128.	Baby Spinach Nutty Lamb	53
129.	Creamy Beef Strips	53
130.	Mustard Lamb Bites	53
131.	Aromatic Lamb Bites	53
132.	Za'atar Lamb Loin Bites	54
133.	Honey Minty Lamb	54
134.	Lamb & Brussels Sprout	54
135.	Garlic Cheesy Meatballs	55
136.	Chili Beef	55
137.	Sage Daikon	55
138.	Parmesan Spinach	55
139.	Parmesan Sticks	56
140.	Buttery Snow Peas	56
141.	Sesame Seed Okra	56
142.	Chili Fennel Wedges	56
143.	Chili Bamboo Shoots	57
144.	Buttery Rosmary Mushrooms	57
145.	Spinach Quiche	57
146.	Aromatic Baby Potatoes	57

DINNER 59

#	Item	Page
147.	Tumeric Indian Wrap	59
148.	Lemony Lentils	59
149.	Delicious Daily Bean	60
150.	Taco Salad	60
151.	BBQ Lime Nachos	60
152.	Aromatic Garlic Eggplants	61
153.	Exotic Eggplant Recipe	61
154.	Tomato Filled Eggplants	62
155.	Sesame Bok Choy	62
156.	Cheesy Pork Rinds	62
157.	Salty Green Beans	62
158.	Salty Grilled Corn	63
159.	Mozzarella Bean Bake	63
160.	Maple Brisket	63
161.	Cheesy Beef Sandwiches	63
162.	Chicken Meatball Wraps	64
163.	Paprika Whole Chicken	64
164.	Coco Curry Rice Plate	64
165.	Soy Sauce Egg Roll	65
166.	Korean Lamb Bites	65
167.	Air Fried Chicken Kabobs	65
168.	Panko Breaded Cheesy Chicken	66

Main Course 67

#	Item	Page
169.	Vegetable Egg Rolls	67
170.	Veggies on Toast	67
171.	Jumbo Stuffed Mushrooms	67
172.	Mushroom Pita Pizzas	68
173.	Spinach Quiche	68
174.	Yellow Squash Fritters	68
175.	Pesto Gnocchi	69
176.	English Muffin Tuna Sandwiches	69
177.	Tuna Zucchini Melts	69
178.	Shrimp and Grilled Cheese Sandwiches	69
179.	Shrimp Croquettes	70
180.	Crispy Salt and Pepper Tofu	70
181.	Crispy Indian Wrap	70
182.	Easy Peasy Pizza	71
183.	Eggplant Parmigiana	71
184.	Luscious Lazy Lasagna	72
185.	Pasta With Creamy Cauliflower Sauce	72
186.	Lemony Lentils With "Fried" Onions	73
187.	Our Daily Bean	73
188.	Taco Salad with Creamy Lime Sauce	74
189.	Bbq Jackfruit Nachos	74
190.	10-Minute Chimichanga	74
191.	Mexican Stuffed Potatoes	75

#	Recipe	Page
192.	Kids' Taquitos	75
193.	Immune-Boosting Grilled Cheese Sandwich	75
194.	Tamale Pie With Cilantro Lime Cornmeal Crust	76
195.	Garlic Parmesan Chicken Wings	76
196.	Buffalo Cauliflower Bites	77
197.	Spicy Dry-Rubbed Chicken Wings	77
198.	Air Fryer Steak Bites and Mushrooms	78
199.	Pecan Crusted Chicken	78
200.	Chicken Tikka Kebab	78
201.	Air Fryer Brussels sprouts	79
202.	Crispy Air Fried Tofu	79
203.	Buttermilk Fried Mushrooms	79
204.	Crispy Baked Avocado Tacos	79
205.	Buttery Cod	80
206.	Creamy Chicken	80
207.	Mushroom and Turkey Stew	80
208.	Basil Chicken	81
209.	Eggplant Bake	81
210.	Meatball Casserole	81
211.	Herbed Lamb Rack	81
212.	Baked Beef	82
213.	Crispy Pork Chops	82
214.	Turkey Pillows	82
215.	Chicken Wings	82
216.	Chicken Cordon Bleu	83
217.	Fried Chicken	83
218.	Chicken and Potatoes	83
219.	Coconut-Crusted Chicken Tenders	83
220.	Crispy Chicken Sliders	84
221.	Garlic Herb Turkey Breast	84
222.	Honey-Lime Chicken Wings	84
223.	Rotisserie-Style, Whole Chicken	84
224.	Tarragon Chicken	85
225.	Beef and Potato	85
226.	Beef Roll-Ups	85
227.	Breaded Beef Schnitzel	85
228.	Lemon Chicken Breast	86
229.	Parmesan Chicken Meatballs	86
230.	Oregano Chicken Meatballs	86
231.	Honey and Chicken Drumsticks	87
232.	Lemon and Chicken Pepper	87
233.	Chicken Curry on Edamame and Asparagus	87
234.	Cheeseburger 'Mini' Sliders	87
235.	Quick and Easy Rib Eye Steak	88
236.	Roast Beef	88
237.	Air Fryer Chicken Wings	88
238.	Sweet and Spicy Montreal Steak	88
239.	Bacon-Wrapped Pork Tenderloin	89
240.	Bratwurst and Veggies	89
241.	Dutch Pancake With Shrimp Salsa	89
242.	Steamed Scallops With Dill	89
243.	Chicken Pita Sandwiches	90
244.	Chicken À La King	90
245.	Perfect Pork chops	90
246.	Tasty meatballs	91
247.	Good'ol steak	91
248.	Chicken Curry	91
249.	Roasted Brussels Sprouts	92
250.	Sesame Chicken	92
251.	Pepper Flakes Pork	92
252.	Marinated Pork Shoulder	92
253.	Asian Style Pork	93
254.	Mussels & Sausages	93
255.	Chicken Thighs in Soy Sauce	93
256.	Lemon Drumsticks	93
257.	Chicken In Salsa Verde	94
258.	Madeira Beef Cubes	94
259.	Juicy BBQ Tofu	94
260.	Veggie Plate	94
261.	Corned Beef	95
262.	Creamy Pork Chops	95
263.	Spicy Pork Belly	95
264.	Cinnapple Pork Tenderloins	95
265.	Juicy Beef & Mushrooms	96
266.	Beef Liver	96
267.	Real Wiener Beef Schnitzel	96
268.	Bacon Wrapped Pork	96

POULTRY 98

#	Recipe	Page
269.	Asian Chicken Wings	98
270.	Healthy Chicken & Asparagus	98
271.	Sweet Duck Breasts	98
272.	Lemony Turkey	99
273.	Mustard Chicken Thighs	99
274.	Mozzarella Chicken Bake	99
275.	Pesto & Tomato Chicken	99
276.	Simple Grilled Chicken	100
277.	Chestnut Turkey Meatballs	100
278.	Orangy Spicy Chicken	100
279.	Breaded Chicken bites	101
280.	Buffalo Yogurt Chicken	101
281.	Barbecue Lemon Chicken	101
282.	Chicken Popcorn	102
283.	Delicious Rotisserie Chicken	102
284.	Asian Style Teriyaki Chicken	102
285.	Mozzarella Rolls	103
286.	Sage Turkey rolls	103
287.	Moroccan Style Chicken	103

Fish Dishes 104

#	Recipe	Page
288.	Spicy Shrimp	104
289.	Lemon Tuna	104
290.	Lemony & Spicy Coconut Crusted Prawns	104
291.	Tuna Stuffed Potatoes	105
292.	Packet Lobster Tail	105

#	Title	Page
293.	Shrimp and Green Beans	105
294.	Crab Dip	105
295.	Buttered Shrimp Skewers	106
296.	Sesame Shrimp	106
297.	Salmon and Cauliflower Rice	106
298.	Tilapia and Salsa	106
299.	Garlic Tilapia	107
300.	Trout and Mint	107
301.	Salmon and Coconut Sauce	107
302.	Simple Salmon	107
303.	Cajun Spiced Salmon	108
304.	Tangy Salmon	108
305.	Sesame Seeds Coated Fish	108
306.	Parsley Catfish	108
307.	Seasoned Salmon	109
308.	Ranch Fish Fillets	109
309.	Montreal Fried Shrimp	109
310.	Shrimp Scampi	110
311.	Buttered Scallops	110
312.	Ham Wrapped Prawns	110
313.	Nacho Chips Crusted Prawns	110
314.	Fish Tacos	111
315.	Grilled Tilapia with Portobello Mushrooms	111
316.	Authentic Mediterranean Calamari Salad	111
317.	Shrimp Scampi Linguine	112
318.	Sunday Fish with Sticky Sauce	112
319.	Tasty Air Fried Cod	112
320.	Delicious Catfish	113
321.	Cod Fillets with Fennel and Grapes Salad	113
322.	Tabasco Shrimp	113
323.	Asian Salmon	113
324.	Asian Coconut Shrimp	114
325.	Mahi Mahi with Herby Buttery Drizzle	114
326.	Classic Lemon Pepper Haddock	114
327.	Fried Scallops with Saffron Cream Sauce	114
328.	Easy Crab Cakes	115
329.	Sweet Asian Style Salmon	115
330.	Zesty Ranch Fish Fillets	115
331.	Dill Fish Chops	116
332.	Easy Fish Sticks with Chili Ketchup Sauce	116
333.	Basil Cod	116
334.	Lime Baked Salmon	117
335.	Sea Bass and Fennel.	117
336.	Snapper and Spring Onions	117
337.	Herbed Trout and Asparagus	117
338.	Coco Shrimp	118
339.	Shrimp and Zucchinis	118
340.	Trout and Zucchinis	118
341.	Flounder Fillets	118
342.	Garlic Lemon Shrimp	118
343.	Crab Cakes	119
344.	Remarkable Fish and Chips with Sauce	119
345.	Grand Air-Fried Coconut Shrimp	120
346.	Splendid Salmon Patties	120
347.	Japanese-Style Fried Prawns	120
348.	Great Air-Fried Soft-Shell Crab	120
349.	Stunning Air-Fried Clams	121
350.	Mind-Blowing Air-Fried Crawfish with Cajun Dipping Sauce	121
351.	Southern-Air-Fried Catfish	121
352.	Wondrous Creole Fried Shrimp with Sriracha Sauce	122
353.	Lemon & Orange Grilled Branzini	122
354.	Creamy Breaded Salmon	122
355.	Buttery Pesto Salmon	123
356.	Breaded Cod Bites	123
357.	Tasty Lobster Tail	123
358.	Pecan-Crusted Catfish Fillets	123
359.	Creamy Pesto Scallops	124
360.	Lemony Parmesan Shrimp	124
361.	Honey & Vinegar Salmon	124

Vegetables _____ 125

#	Title	Page
362.	Carrot Sticks	125
363.	Cheesy Broccoli	125
364.	Fried bananas	125
365.	Tasty Wrapped Asparagus	125
366.	Balsamic Brussels Sprouts	126
367.	Healthy Thyme Mushrooms	126
368.	Jicama Fries	126
369.	Eggplant stacks	126
370.	Juicy Spaghetti Squash	127
371.	Blue Cheese & Beets Salad	127
372.	Avocado chips	127
373.	Italian Spaghetti Squash	127
374.	Cinnamon flavoured Fries	128
375.	Broccoli & Sweet Potato	128

SOUPS & STEWS _____ 129

#	Title	Page
376.	Chicken Soup	129
377.	Cheesy Potato Soup	129
378.	Split Pea Soup	130
379.	Veggy Corn Soup	130
380.	Aromatic Butternut Squash Cream	130
381.	Beef Soup with Rice	131
382.	Noodle Soup with Chicken	131
383.	Original Tuscan Soup	131
384.	Italian Minestrone	132
385.	Wild Rice Soup with Chicken	132
386.	Celery and Tomato Soup	132
387.	Delicious Tomato Soup	133
388.	Sriracha Carrot Soup	133
389.	Cabbage & Celery Soup	133
390.	Creamy Chicken Asparagus Soup	134
391.	Vegan Noodle Soup	134
392.	Carrot Soup with Cashew Sour Cream	134

#	Recipe	Page
393.	Vegan Soup	135
394.	Mushroom Tofu Soup	135
395.	Sweet Potato & Tomato Stew	135
396.	Fresh Veggy Stew	136
397.	Creamy Celery Soup	136
398.	Buttery Garlic Cauliflower Soup	137
399.	Low-Sodium Pumpkin Soup	137
400.	Spaghetti Chicken Soup	137
401.	Simple Balsamic Onion Soup	138
402.	Buttery Apple & Broccoli Soup	138
403.	Swiss Chard Cumin Stew	138
404.	Chili Lentil Soup	139
405.	Galric Fish Balls Soup	139
406.	Coconut Chicken Breast Soup	139
407.	Shredded Chicken Stew	140
408.	Ginger Kale Soup	140
409.	Avocado Flavoured Leek and Salmon Soup	140
410.	Asian Coconut Soup	140
411.	Ginger Soup	141
412.	Onion Salmon Soup	141
413.	Chicken Curry Soup	141
414.	Healthy Salmon Stew	141
415.	Coco Tilapia Soup	142
416.	Egg Soup	142
417.	Kale Soup & Chicken	142
418.	Asparagus Soup	143
419.	Broccoli Creamy Soup	143
420.	Turkey and Turmeric Soup	143

Desserts 144

#	Recipe	Page
421.	Mini Cheesecakes	144
422.	Vanilla Cheesecake	144
423.	Ricotta Cheesecake	145
424.	Pecan Pie	145
425.	Fruity Crumble	145
426.	Cherry Clafoutis	146
427.	Apple Bread Pudding	146
428.	Raisin Bread Pudding	147
429.	Donuts Pudding	147
430.	Orange Sponge Cake	148
431.	Apricot Crumble With Blackberries	148
432.	Apple & Cinnamon Pie	148
433.	Chocolate Cake	148
434.	Berry Crumble With Lemon	149
435.	Vanilla-Lemon Cupcakes With Lemon Glaze	149
436.	Handmade Donuts	149
437.	Apple Treat With Raisins	150
438.	Almond Cookies With Dark Chocolate	150
439.	Air Fried Banana With Sesame Seeds	150
440.	Vanilla Brownies With Chocolate Chips	150
441.	Cinnamon & Honey Apples With Hazelnuts	151
442.	Pan-Fried Bananas	151
443.	Delicious Banana Pastry With Berries	151
444.	Easy Mocha Cake	151
445.	Choco Lava Cakes	152
446.	Mouthwatering Chocolate Soufflé	152
447.	Maple Pecan Pie	152
448.	Tangerine Cake	152
449.	Blueberry Pudding	153
450.	Blackberries Cobbler	153
451.	Glazed Bananas	153
452.	Banana Muffins	154
453.	Chocolate Muffins	154
454.	Banana-Choco Brownies	154
455.	Blueberry & Lemon Cake	155
456.	Bread Pudding with Cranberry	155
457.	Cocoa And Almond Bars	155
458.	Chocolate And Pomegranate Bars	156
459.	Tomato Cake	156
460.	Berries Mix	156
461.	Passion Fruit Pudding	156
462.	Air Fried Apples	156
463.	Pumpkin Cookies	157
464.	Figs And Coconut Butter Mix	157
465.	Lemon Bars	157
466.	Pears And Espresso Cream	157
467.	Sweet Squares	158
468.	Cashew Bars	158
469.	Brown Butter Cookies	158
470.	Sweet Potato Cheesecake	158
471.	Peach Pie	159
472.	Special Brownies	159
473.	Coffee Cheesecakes	159
474.	Carrot Cake	159
475.	Delicious Maple Plantains	160
476.	Coco Bananas	160
477.	Cinnamon & Maple Apples	160
478.	Vanilla-Choco Bars	160
479.	Coco-Berry Bars	161
480.	Sweet Chocolate Pudding	161
481.	Crispy Blueberry Crackers	161
482.	Cinnamon Cauli-Rice Pudding	161
483.	Avocado & Pineapple Pudding	161
484.	Raspberry Jam	162
485.	Plum Jam	162
486.	Pumpkin Plate	162
487.	Apple Jam	162
488.	Vanilla Pumpkin Cream	163
489.	Sweet Coconut Rice	163
490.	Vanilla Pears	163
491.	Lemon Bars	163
492.	Vanilla Sweet Pears	163
493.	Coconut Apple Compote	164
494.	Cinnamon Apple & Dates	164

495.	Choco Rice	164
496.	Vanilla Cinnamon Peaches	164
497.	Original Mug Cake	164
498.	Sweet Buttery Peaches	165
499.	Basic Apple Recipe	165
500.	Sweet Dried Mango Slices	165
501.	Fried Lemony Raspberries	165

TIPS AND TRICKS 167

CONCLUSION 168

index _____ 169

Introduction

An air fryer uses the convection mechanism in cooking food. It circulates hot air through the use of a mechanical fan to cook the ingredients inside the fryer.

The process was named after the person who first explained it in 1912, French chemist Louis-Camille Maillard. The effect gives a distinctive flavor to browned foods, such as bread, biscuits, cookies, pan-fried meat, seared steaks, and many more. The air fryer requires only a thin layer of oil for the ingredients to cook. It circulates hot air up to 392 degrees Fahrenheit. It's an innovative way of eliminating up to 80 percent of the oil that is traditionally used for frying different foods and preparing pastries.

You can find a dose of friendly features in air fryers, depending on the brand you're using. Most brands include a timer adjustment and temperature control setting to make cooking easier and precise. An air fryer comes with a cooking basket where you'll place the food. The basket is placed on top of a drip tray. Depending on the model you're using, you will either be prompted to shake the basket to distribute the oil evenly, or it automatically does the job via a food agitator.

This is perfect for home use, but if you're cooking for many people and you want to apply the same cooking technique, you can put your food items in specialized air crisper trays and cook them using a convection oven. An air fryer and convection oven apply the same technique in cooking, but an air fryer has a smaller built and produces less heat.

Uses of Air Fryer

Here are some of the cooking techniques that you can do with this single appliance:

- **Fry**: You can actually omit oil in cooking, but a little amount adds crunch and flavor to your food. You can add oil to the ingredients while mixing or lightly spray the food with oil before cooking. You can use most kinds of oils, but many users prefer peanut, olive, sunflower, and canola oils.

- **Roast**: You can produce the same quality of roasted foods as the ones cooked in a conventional roaster in a faster manner. This is recommended to people who need to come up with a special dish but do not have much time to prepare.

- **Bake**: There are baking pans suited for this appliance that you can use to bake bread, cookies, and other pastries. It only takes around 15 to 30 minutes to get your baked goods done.

- **Grill**: It effectively grills your food easily and without a mess. You only need to shake the basket halfway through the cooking process or flip the ingredients once or twice, depending on the instructions. To make it easier, you can put the ingredients in a grill pan or grill layer with a handle, which other models include in the package, or you can also buy one as an added accessory.

There are many kinds of foods that you can cook using an air fryer, but there are also certain types that are not suited for it. Avoid cooking ingredients, which can be steamed, like beans and carrots. You also cannot fry foods covered in heavy batter in this appliance.

Aside from the above mentioned, you can cook most kinds of ingredients using an air fryer. You can use it for cooking foods covered in light flour or bread crumbs. You can cook a variety of vegetables in the appliance, such as cauliflower, asparagus, zucchini, kale, peppers, and corn on the cob. You can also use it for cooking frozen foods and home-prepared meals by following a different set of instructions for these purposes.

An air fryer also comes with another useful feature - the separator. It allows you to cook multiple dishes at a time. Use the separator to divide ingredients in the pan or basket. You have to make sure that all ingredients have the same temperature setting so that everything will cook evenly at the same time.

How Does an Air Fryer Work?

The secret of the air fryer is the unique cooking technology that uses hot-air that circulates inside the fryer. It works no differently than any other thermic-processing method, but without all the detrimental side-effects you get when you eat deep-fried foods, for example. Depending on the model, you may be able not only to fry but also to bake, broil, roast, rotisserie, and steam things as well. An air fryer can also be a great substitute for your microwave, oven, or stove. Except it's much healthier, easier, and faster to use.

On top of that, you can use an air fryer to prepare batters and marinades. The only thing that you should never put in there is generally speaking liquids. That means that things like broth or other soups are not coming at play here. Remember, safety comes first. But given the wide variety of other things you can do with it - it's a tiny con.

The Basic Features of an Air Fryer

Again, different brands of air fryers tend to add something special regarding their functionality in order to make their device stand out. However, the following features are common to almost all air fryers.

1. Automated Temperature Control System: This is one of the more crucial and essential elements of an air fryer. The automated temperature control system plays a great role in determining how the final product turns out.

2. Digital Screen and Touch Panel: In our modern "digitized" generation, touch screen and digital controls are generating all the buzz! If you don't have a device with a touch screen panel, then you might as well be living in the past! Air fryer manufacturers are fully aware of this trend and have recently added a fully functional touchscreen interface into many fryers! This allows the users to seamlessly control the device without any hassle.

3. A Convenient Buzzer: Most air fryers come with a buzzer that makes it extremely simple for users to know whenever their meals are ready. When cooking with an air fryer, you won't have to stand in front of the device all day just to make sure that your meals aren't burnt! All you have to do is set the timer, and your air fryer will let you know once the cooking is done!

Advantages of Air Frying

Air fryers have many perks to offer when it comes to improving quality of life.

Healthier Cooking

With an air fryer, frying your food is healthy. How? Air fryer only needs just a tiny sprit of oil or no oil at all to cook your cook. You can easily cook fries, chicken wings, onion rings and much more and still get crispy foods without the extra oil. And, compared to oven and deep-frying cooking, the foods from the air fryer, especially fries, are crispier and not dried out, making the food even more impressive.

Quicker Meals

Since the air fryer is smaller than the oven, it circulates hot air around its fan quickly that cooks the food faster. Air fryer takes less time to reach the cooking temperature compare to an oven, which may take 20 minutes or more to properly preheat and begin cooking. So, if you need to make your meals in a hurry, you will love the air fryer time-saving features.

Versatility

The air fryer doesn't only just do the frying. You can do so much more cooking with it! The air fryer can also roast, grill, stir-fry, broil and bakes, even cakes. You can make fresh or frozen food in it, or reheat the leftovers. Make use of air fryer additional accessories like a cake pan, pizza pan, rotisserie rack, frill pan, steamer inserts to cook a variety of foods.

Space Saver

If you live in a dorm, share a house, or have a small kitchen, then you will definitely appreciate the small size of the air fryer. The air fryer comes in different sizes, but its small size can be of a coffee maker size, which won't take too much room on your kitchen counter. Hence, an air fryer is easy to move or store away. The air fryer is also handy to take it on your travel ventures and placing it in your office kitchen to cook fresh food.

Ease of Clean up

Most of the cooks don't enjoy the cleanup of kitchen utensils, but with an air fryer, this won't be a trouble for you in any way. Air fryer just has a fryer basket and pan to clean, which is dishwasher safe and takes a few minutes to wash up after cooking. And, the cooking basket or pan is non-stick, so food usually doesn't stick to it and instead, slides onto the plate easily.

What Is The Healthiest Option For Our Food?

Some Healthy Recommended Oils

If you want to maximize the "health" factor of your meals, it is of paramount importance that you use the healthiest oil possible! To save you some time and effort, I have listed the five healthiest oil that you can use while cooking using your air fryer.

1. **Coconut Oil:** Coconut oil is the best when it comes to high heat cooking, with over 90% of the fatty acids being saturated, which makes it very resistant to heat. This particular oil is semi-solid at room temperature and can be used for months without it turning rancid. This particular oil also has a lot of health benefits! Since this oil is rich in a fatty acid known as lauric acid, it can help to improve cholesterol levels and kill various pathogens.

2. **Extra-Virgin Olive Oil:** Olive oil is very well known for its heart health benefits. In fact, this is one of the main reasons why the Mediterranean diet uses olive oil as a key ingredient. Some recent studies have shown that olive oil can even help to improve health biomarkers such as increasing HDL cholesterol and lowering the amount of bad LDL cholesterol.

3. **Avocado Oil:** The composition of Avocado oil is very similar to olive oil and as such it holds similar health benefits. It can be used for many purposes including as an alternative to olive oil.

4. **Fish Oil:** Fish oil is extremely rich in omega-3 fatty acids such as EPA and DHA. Just a tablespoon of fish oil is enough to satisfy the body's daily needs. If you are looking for the best fish oil, then cod fish liver oil is your best option—plus, it is also rich in Vitamin D3. But here is the thing, since fish oil has a high concentration of polyunsaturated fats, it should not be used for cooking. The best way to use this oil is as a supplement.

5. **Grapeseed Oil:** Grapeseed oil is a very versatile cooking oil that is extracted from grape seeds that are left behind after winemaking. This is a favorite oil among chefs and foodies! This oil has a very mild flavor that can be added with other ingredients that give a very strong flavor to meals. Grape seed has a similar fatty acid profile to soybean oil and has a very high percentage of polyunsaturated fat. According to multiple sources, grape seed oil has a good number of positive effects on the heart.

BREAKFAST

1. Breakfast Casserole

Preparation Time: 10 minutes | Cooking Time: 28 minutes
Servings: 4

Ingredients:
- 2 eggs
- 4 egg whites
- 4 tsp pine nuts, minced
- 2/3 cup chicken broth
- 1 lb. Italian sausage
- 1/4 cup roasted red pepper, sliced
- 1/4 cup pesto sauce
- 2/3 cup parmesan cheese, grated
- 1/8 tsp pepper
- 1/4 tsp sea salt

Directions:
1. Preheat the air fryer to 370 F. Spray air fryer pan with cooking spray and set aside.
2. Heat another pan over medium heat. Add sausage in a pan and cook until golden brown.
3. Once cooked then drain excess oil and spread it into the prepared pan.
4. Whisk remaining ingredients except pine nuts in a bowl and pour over sausage.
5. Place pan in the air fryer and cook for 25-28 minutes.
6. Top with pine nuts and serve.

Nutrition:
Calories 625 | Fat 49 g | Carbohydrates 2 g | Sugar 2.1 g Protein 39 g | Cholesterol 200 mg

2. Egg Cups

Preparation Time: 10 minutes | Cooking Time: 18 minutes
Servings: 12

Ingredients:
- 12 eggs
- 4 oz. cream cheese
- 12 bacon strips, uncooked
- 1/4 cup buffalo sauce
- 2/3 cup cheddar cheese, shredded
- Pepper
- Salt

Directions:
1. In a bowl, whisk together eggs, pepper, and salt.
2. Line each silicone muffin mold with one bacon strip.
3. Pour egg mixture into each muffin mold and place in the air fryer basket. (In batches)
4. Cook at 350 F for 8 minutes.
5. In another bowl, mix together cheddar cheese and cream cheese and microwave for 30 seconds. Add buffalo sauce and stir well.
6. Remove muffin molds from air fryer and add 2 tsp cheese mixture in the center of each egg cup.
7. Return muffin molds to the air fryer and cook for 10 minutes more.
8. Serve and enjoy.

Nutrition:
Calories 225 | Fat 19 g | Carbohydrates 1 g | Sugar 0.4 g Protein 11 g | Cholesterol 180 mg

3. Spinach Muffins

Preparation Time: 10 minutes | Cooking Time: 20 minutes
Servings: 8

Ingredients:
- 4 eggs
- 1/2 tsp baking powder
- 1 zucchini, grated
- 1/4 cup parmesan cheese, grated

- 1/2 cup feta cheese, crumbled
- 4 onion spring, chopped
- 1/3 cup coconut flour
- 1/4 cup butter, melted
- 4 tbsp parsley, chopped
- 1/2 tsp nutmeg
- 1/4 cup water
- 1/2 cup spinach, cooked
- 1/4 tsp pepper
- 1/4 tsp salt

Directions:
1. Preheat the air fryer to 370 F.
2. In a bowl, whisk together eggs, water, butter, and salt.
3. Add baking soda and coconut flour and mix well.
4. Add onions, nutmeg, parsley, spinach, and zucchini. Mix well.
5. Add parmesan cheese and feta cheese and stir well. Season with pepper and salt.
6. Pour batter into the silicone muffin molds and place in the air fryer basket.
7. Cook muffins for 20 minutes.
8. Serve and enjoy.

Nutrition:

Calories 235 | Fat 18.1 g | Carbohydrates 4.2 g | Sugar 1.1 g | Protein 16 g | Cholesterol 135 mg

4. Broccoli Muffins

Preparation Time: 10 minutes | Cooking Time: 24 minutes
Servings: 6

Ingredients:
- 2 large eggs
- 1 cup broccoli florets, chopped
- 1 cup unsweetened almond milk
- 2 cups almond flour
- 1 tsp baking powder
- 2 tbsp nutritional yeast
- 1/2 tsp sea salt

Directions:
1. Preheat the air fryer to 325 F.
2. Add all ingredients into the large bowl and mix until well combined.
3. Pour mixture into the silicone muffin molds and place into the air fryer basket.
4. Cook muffins for 20-24 minutes.
5. Serve and enjoy.

Nutrition:

Calories 260 | Fat 21.2 g | Carbohydrates 11 g | Sugar 1.7 g Protein 12 g | Cholesterol 62 mg

5. Zucchini Gratin

Preparation Time: 10 minutes | Cooking Time: 24 minutes
Servings: 4

Ingredients:
- 1 large egg, lightly beaten
- 1 1/4 cup unsweetened almond milk
- 3 medium zucchinis, sliced
- 1 tbsp Dijon mustard
- 1/2 cup nutritional yeast
- 1 tsp sea salt

Directions:
1. Preheat the air fryer to 370 F.
2. Arrange zucchini slices in the air fryer baking dish.
3. In a saucepan, heat almond milk over low heat and stir in Dijon mustard, nutritional yeast, and sea salt. Add beaten egg and whisk well.
4. Pour sauce over zucchini slices.
5. Place dish in the air fryer and cook for 20-24 minutes.
6. Serve and enjoy.

Nutrition:

Calories 120 | Fat 3.4 g | Carbohydrates 14 g | Sugar 2 g Protein 13 g | Cholesterol 47 mg

6. Breakfast Egg Muffins

Preparation Time: 10 minutes | Cooking Time: 20 minutes
Servings: 12

Ingredients:
- 6 eggs
- 1 lb ground pork sausage
- 3 tbsp onion, minced
- 1/2 red pepper, diced
- 1 cup egg whites
- 1/2 cup mozzarella cheese
- 1 cup cheddar cheese

Directions:
1. Preheat the air fryer to 325 F.
2. Brown sausage over medium-high heat until meat is no pink.
3. Divide red pepper, cheese, cooked sausages, and onion into each silicone muffin mold.
4. In a large bowl, whisk together egg whites, egg, pepper, and salt.
5. Pour egg mixture into each muffin mold and place into the air fryer basket in batches.
6. Cook muffins in the air fryer for 20 minutes.
7. Serve and enjoy.

Nutrition:

Calories 189 | Fat 13.6 g | Carbohydrates 2 g | Sugar 0.7 g

Protein 13 g | Cholesterol 115 mg

7. Cheese Pie

Preparation Time: 10 minutes | Cooking Time: 16 minutes

Servings: 4

Ingredients:

- 8 eggs
- 1 1/2 cups heavy whipping cream
- 1 lb cheddar cheese, grated
- Pepper
- Salt

Directions:

1. Preheat the air fryer to 325 F.
2. In a bowl, whisk together cheese, eggs, whipping cream, pepper, and salt.
3. Spray air fryer baking dish with cooking spray.
4. Pour egg mixture into the prepared dish and place in the air fryer basket.
5. Cook for 16 minutes or until the egg is set.
6. Serve and enjoy.

Nutrition:

Calories 735 | Fat 63 g | Carbohydrates 3 g | Sugar 1.3 g Protein 40.2 g | Cholesterol 505 mg

8. Parmesan Breakfast Casserole

Preparation Time: 10 minutes

Cooking Time: 20 minutes

Servings: 3

Ingredients:

- 5 eggs
- 2 tbsp heavy cream
- 3 tbsp chunky tomato sauce
- 2 tbsp parmesan cheese, grated

Directions:

1. Preheat the air fryer to 325 F.
2. In mixing bowl, combine together cream and eggs.
3. Add cheese and tomato sauce and mix well.
4. Spray air fryer baking dish with cooking spray.
5. Pour mixture into baking dish and place in the air fryer basket.
6. Cook for 20 minutes.
7. Serve and enjoy.

Nutrition:

Calories 185 | Fat 14 g | Carbohydrates 2 g | Sugar 1.2 g
Protein 13.6 g | Cholesterol 290 mg

9. strawberry French toast

Preparation Time: 15 minutes

Cooking Time: 8 minutes

Servings: 4

Ingredients:

- 4 (1-inch-thick) slices French bread
- 2 tablespoons strawberry jam
- ⅓ cup fresh strawberry
- 2 egg yolks
- ⅓ cup 2% milk
- 1 tablespoon sugar
- ½ teaspoon vanilla extract
- 3 tablespoons sour cream

Directions:

1. Cut a pocket into the side of each bread slice, making sure you don't cut through to the other side.
2. In a small bowl, combine the raspberry jam and raspberries and crush the raspberries into the jam with a fork.
3. In a shallow bowl, beat the egg yolks with the milk, sugar, and vanilla until combined.
4. Spread some of the sour cream in the pocket you cut in the bread slices, then add the raspberry mixture. Squeeze the edges of the bread slightly to close the opening.
5. Dip the bread in the egg mixture, letting the bread stand in the egg for 3 minutes. Flip the bread over and let stand on the other side for 3 minutes.
6. Set or preheat the air fryer to 375°F. Arrange the stuffed bread in the air fryer basket in a single layer.
7. Air fry for 5 minutes, then carefully flip the bread slices and cook for another 3 to 6 minutes, until the French toast is golden brown.

Nutrition:

Calories: 278 | Total fat: 6g | Saturated fat: 3g

Cholesterol: 99mg | Sodium: 406mg | Carbohydrates: 46g Fiber: 2g | Protein: 9g

10. Apple Roll-Ups

Preparation Time: 20 minutes

Cooking Time: 20 minutes

Servings: 8

Ingredients:

- 3 tablespoons ground cinnamon
- 3 tablespoons granulated sugar
- 2 teaspoons ground nutmeg
- 1 teaspoon ground cardamom
- ½ teaspoon ground allspice
- 2 large Granny Smith apples, peeled and cored
- 10 tablespoons butter, melted, divided

- 2 tablespoons light brown sugar
- 8 thin slices white sandwich bread, crusts cut off.

Directions:

1. In a 7-inch springform pan that has been wrapped in foil to prevent leaks, combine the olive oil, cherry tomatoes, plum tomatoes, tomato sauce, scallions, garlic, honey, salt, and cayenne.
2. Set or preheat the air fryer to 375°F. Set the pan in the air fryer basket. Cook the tomato mixture for 15 to 20 minutes, stirring twice during the cooking time, until the tomatoes are soft.
3. Use a fork to mash some of the tomatoes right in the pan, then stir the mashed tomatoes into the sauce.
4. Break the eggs into the sauce. Return the pan to the air fryer.
5. Cook for about 2 minutes or until the egg whites start to set. Remove the pan from the air fryer and gently stir the eggs into the sauce, marbling them through the sauce. Don't mix them in completely.
6. Continue cooking the mixture until the eggs are just set, 4 to 8 minutes more.
7. Cool for 10 minutes, then serve.

Nutrition:

Calories: 232 | Total fat: 15g | Saturated fat: 9g

Cholesterol: 38mg | Sodium: 249mg | Carbohydrates: 21g

Fiber: 4g | Protein: 4g

11. Pepper Egg Bites

Preparation Time: 15 minutes

Cooking Time: 15 minutes

Servings: 7

Ingredients:

- 5 large eggs, beaten
- 3 tablespoons 2% milk
- ½ teaspoon dried marjoram
- ⅛ teaspoon salt
- Pinch freshly ground black pepper
- ⅓ cup minced bell pepper, any color
- 3 tablespoons minced scallions
- ½ cup shredded Colby or Muenster cheese

Directions:

1. In a medium bowl, combine the eggs, milk, marjoram, salt, and black pepper; mix until combined.
2. Stir in the bell peppers, scallions, and cheese. Fill the 7 egg bite cups with the egg mixture, making sure you get some of the solids in each cup. Set or preheat the air fryer to 325°F.
3. Make a foil sling: Fold an 18-inch-long piece of heavy-duty aluminum foil lengthwise into thirds. Put the egg bite pan on this sling and lower it into the air fryer.
4. Leave the foil in the air fryer, but bend down the edges so they fit in the appliance.
5. Bake the egg bites for 10 to 15 minutes or until a toothpick inserted into the center comes out clean.
6. Use the foil sling to remove the egg bite pan. Let cool for 5 minutes, then invert the pan onto a plate to remove the egg bites. Serve warm.

Nutrition:

Calories: 87 | Total fat: 6g | Saturated fat: 3g

Cholesterol: 141mg | Sodium: 149mg

Carbohydrates: 1g | Fiber: 0g | Protein: 7g

12. Crunchy Nut Granola

Preparation Time: 10 minutes

Cooking Time: 15 minutes

Servings: 6

Ingredients:

- 2 cups old-fashioned rolled oats
- ¼ cup pistachios
- ¼ cup chopped pecans
- ¼ cup chopped cashews
- ¼ cup honey
- 2 tablespoons light brown sugar
- 3 tablespoons butter
- ½ teaspoon ground cinnamon
- Nonstick baking spray (containing flour)
- ½ cup dried cherries

Directions:

1. In a medium bowl, combine the oats, pistachios, pecans, and cashews and toss.
2. In a small saucepan, combine the honey, brown sugar, butter, and cinnamon. Cook over low heat, stirring frequently, until the butter melts and the mixture is smooth, about 4 minutes. Pour over the oat mixture and stir.
3. Spray a 7-inch springform pan with baking spray. Add the granola mixture.
4. Set or preheat the air fryer to 325°F. Set the pan in the air fryer basket. Cook for 7 minutes, then remove the pan and stir. Continue cooking for 6 to 9 minutes or until the granola is light golden brown. Stir in the dried cherries.
5. Remove the pan from the air fryer and let cool, stirring a couple of times as the granola cools. Store in a covered container at room temperature up to 4 days.

Nutrition:

Calories: 446 | Total fat: 18g | Saturated fat: 5g

Cholesterol: 15mg | Sodium: 51mg | Carbohydrates: 64g

Fiber: 7g | Protein: 11g

13. Breakfast Pizza

Preparation Time: 10 minutes

Cooking Time: 15 minutes

Servings: 4

Ingredients:

- 4 (½-inch-thick) slices French bread, cut on a diagonal
- 6 teaspoons butter, divided
- 4 large eggs
- 2 tablespoons light cream
- ½ teaspoon dried basil
- ¼ teaspoon sea salt
- ⅛ teaspoon freshly ground black pepper
- 4 bacon slices, cooked until crisp and crumbled
- ⅔ cup shredded Colby or Muenster cheese

Directions:

1. Spread each slice of bread with 1 teaspoon of butter and place in the air fryer basket.
2. Set or preheat the air fryer to 350°F. Toast the bread for 2 to 3 minutes or until it's light golden brown. Remove from the air fryer and set aside on a wire rack.
3. Melt the remaining 2 teaspoons of butter in a 6-inch cake pan in the air fryer for 1 minute. Remove the basket from the air fryer.
4. In a medium bowl, beat together the eggs, cream, basil, salt, and pepper and add to the melted butter in the pan. Return the basket to the air fryer. Cook for 3 minutes, then stir. Cook for another 3 to 5 minutes or until the eggs are just set. Remove the eggs from the pan and put them in a bowl.
5. Top the bread with the scrambled eggs mixture, bacon, and cheese. Put back in the air fryer basket. Cook for 4 to 8 minutes or until the cheese is melted and starting to turn brown in spots.
6. Let cool for 5 minutes and serve.

Nutrition:

Calories: 425 | Total fat: 23g | Saturated fat: 11g

Cholesterol: 233mg | Sodium: 947mg

Carbohydrates: 34g | Fiber: 1g | Protein: 21g

---

14. Veggie Frittata

Preparation Time: 15 minutes | Cooking Time: 25 minutes

Servings: 4

Ingredients:

- ¼ cup chopped red bell pepper
- ¼ cup chopped yellow summer squash
- 2 tablespoons chopped scallion
- 2 tablespoons butter
- 5 large eggs, beaten
- ¼ teaspoon sea salt
- ⅛ teaspoon freshly ground black pepper
- 1 cup shredded Cheddar cheese, divided

Directions:

1. In a 7-inch cake pan, combine the bell pepper, summer squash, and scallion. Add the butter.
2. Set or preheat the air fryer to 350°F. Set the cake pan in the air fryer basket. Cook the vegetables for 3 to 4 minutes or until they are crisp-tender. Remove the pan from the air fryer.
3. In a medium bowl, beat the eggs with the salt and pepper. Stir in half of the Cheddar. Pour into the pan with the vegetables.
4. Return the pan to the air fryer and cook for 10 to 15 minutes, then top the frittata with the remaining cheese. Cook for another 4 to 5 minutes or until the cheese is melted and the frittata is set. Cut into wedges to serve.

Nutrition:

Calories: 260 | Total fat: 21g | Saturated fat: 11g

Cholesterol: 277mg | Sodium: 463mg | Carbohydrates: 2g

Fiber: 0g | Protein: 15g

---

15. Spicy Hash Brown Potatoes

Preparation Time: 15 minutes | Cooking Time: 20 minutes

Servings: 4

Ingredients:

- 2 tablespoons chili powder
- 2 teaspoons ground cumin
- 2 teaspoons smoked paprika
- 1 teaspoon garlic powder
- 1 teaspoon cayenne pepper
- 1 teaspoon freshly ground black pepper
- 2 large russet potatoes, peeled
- 2 tablespoons olive oil
- ⅓ cup chopped onion
- 3 garlic cloves, minced
- ½ teaspoon sea salt

Directions:

1. For the spice mix: In a small bowl, combine the chili powder, cumin, smoked paprika, garlic powder, cayenne, and black pepper. Transfer to a screw-top glass jar and store in a cool, dry place. (Some of the spice mix is used in this recipe; save the rest for other uses.)
2. Grate the potatoes in a food processor or on the large holes of a box grater. Put the potatoes in a bowl filled with ice water, and let stand for 10 minutes.
3. When the potatoes have soaked, drain them, then dry them well with a kitchen towel.
4. Put the olive oil, onion, and garlic in a 7-inch cake pan.
5. Set or preheat the air fryer to 400°F. Put the onion mixture in the air fryer and cook for 3 minutes, then remove.
6. Put the grated potatoes in a medium bowl and sprinkle with 2 teaspoons of spice mixture and toss. Add to the cake pan with the onion mixture.

7. Cook in the air fryer for 10 minutes, then stir the potatoes gently but thoroughly. Cook for 8 to 12 minutes more or until the potatoes are crisp and light golden brown. Season with salt.

Nutrition:

Calories: 235 | Total fat: 8g | Saturated fat: 1g

Cholesterol: 0mg | Sodium: 419mg

Carbohydrates: 39g | Fiber: 5g | Protein: 5g

16. Sage and Pear Sausage Patties

Preparation Time: 15 minutes | Cooking Time: 20 minutes

Servings: 6

Ingredients:

- 1 pound ground pork
- ¼ cup diced fresh pear
- 1 tablespoon minced fresh sage leaves
- 1 garlic clove, minced
- ½ teaspoon sea salt
- ⅛ teaspoon freshly ground black pepper

Directions:

1. In a medium bowl, combine the pork, pear, sage, garlic, salt, and pepper, and mix gently but thoroughly with your hands.
2. Form the mixture into 8 equal patties about ½ inch thick.
3. Set or preheat the air fryer to 375°F. Arrange the patties in the air fryer basket in a single layer. You may have to cook the patties in batches.
4. Cook the sausages for 15 to 20 minutes, flipping them halfway through the cooking time, until a meat thermometer registers 160°F. Remove from the air fryer, drain on paper towels for a few minutes, and then serve.

Nutrition:

Calories: 204 | Total fat: 16g | Saturated fat: 6g

Cholesterol: 54mg | Sodium: 236mg | Carbohydrates: 1g

Fiber: 0g | Protein: 13g

17. Bacon Bombs

Preparation Time: 10 minutes | Cooking Time: 16 minutes

Servings: 4

Ingredients:

- 3 center-cut bacon slices
- 3 large eggs, lightly beaten
- 1 oz 1/3-less-fat cream cheese, softened
- 1 tbsp chopped fresh chives
- 4 oz fresh whole wheat pizza dough
- Cooking spray

Directions:

1. Sear the bacon slices in a skillet until brown and crispy then chop into fine crumbles.
2. Add eggs to the same pan and cook for 1 minute then stir in cream cheese, chives and bacon. Mix well, then allow this egg filling to cool down. Spread the pizza dough and slice into four -5inches circles.
3. Divide the egg filling on top of each circle and seal its edge to make dumplings. Place the bacon bombs in the Air Fryer basket and spray them with cooking oil.
4. Set the Air Fryer basket inside the Air Fryer toaster oven and close the lid. Select the Air Fry mode at 350 degrees F temperature for 6 minutes. Serve warm.

Nutrition:

Calories: 278 | Protein: 7.9g | Carbs: 23g | Fat: 3.9g

18. Morning Potatoes

Preparation Time: 10 minutes | Cooking Time: 23 minutes

Servings: 4

Ingredients:

- 2 russet potatoes, washed & diced
- ½ tsp salt
- 1 tbsp. olive oil
- ¼ tsp garlic powder
- Chopped parsley, for garnish

Directions:

1. Soak the potatoes in cold water for 45 minutes, then drain and dry them.
2. Toss potato cubes with garlic powder, salt, and olive oil in the Air Fryer basket.
3. Set the Air Fryer basket inside the Air Fryer toaster oven and close the lid. Select the Air Fry mode at 400 degrees F temperature for 23 minutes.
4. Toss them well when cooked halfway through then continue cooking. Garnish with chopped parsley to serve.

Nutrition:

Calories: 146 | Protein: 6.2g | Carbs: 41.2g | Fat: 5g

19. Breakfast Pockets

Preparation Time: 10 minutes | Cooking Time: 10 minutes

Servings: 6

Ingredients:

- 1 box puff pastry sheet
- 5 eggs
- ½ cup loose sausage, cooked
- ½ cup bacon, cooked
- ½ cup cheddar cheese, shredded

Directions:

1. Stir cook egg in a skillet for 1 minute then mix with sausages, cheddar cheese, and bacon.

2. Spread the pastry sheet and cut it into four rectangles of equal size.
3. Divide the egg mixture over each rectangle. Fold the edges around the filling and seal them.
4. Place the pockets in the Air Fryer basket.
5. Set the Air Fryer basket inside the Air Fryer toaster oven and close the lid. Select the Air Fry mode at 370 degrees F temperature for 10 minutes. Serve warm.

Nutrition:
Calories: 387 | Protein: 14.6g | Carbs: 37.4g | Fat: 6g

20. Avocado Flautas

Preparation Time: 10 minutes
Cooking Time: 24 minutes
Servings: 8

Ingredients:
- 1 tbsp butter
- 8 eggs, beaten
- ½ tsp salt
- ¼ tsp pepper
- 1 ½ tsp cumin
- 1 tsp chili powder
- 8 fajita-size tortillas
- 4 oz cream cheese, softened
- 8 slices cooked bacon
- Avocado Crème:
- 2 small avocados
- ½ cup sour cream
- 1 lime, juiced
- ½ tsp salt
- ¼ tsp pepper

Directions:
1. In a skillet, melt butter and stir in eggs, salt, cumin, pepper, and chili powder, then stir cook for 4 minutes. Spread all the tortillas and top them with cream cheese and bacon. Then divide the egg scramble on top and finally add cheese.
2. Roll the tortillas to seal the filling inside. Place 4 rolls in the Air Fryer basket. Set the Air Fryer basket inside the Air Fryer toaster oven and close the lid. Select the Air Fry mode at 400 degrees F temperature for 12 minutes.
3. Cook the remaining tortilla rolls in the same manner. Meanwhile, blend avocado crème ingredients in a blender then serves with warm flautas.

Nutrition:
Calories: 212 | Protein: 17.3g | Carbs: 14.6g | Fat: 11.8g

21. Cheese Sandwiches

Preparation Time: 10 minutes
Cooking Time: 10 minutes
Servings: 2

Ingredients:
- 1 egg
- 3 tbsp half and half cream
- ¼ tsp vanilla extract
- 2 slices sourdough, white or multigrain bread
- 2½ oz sliced Swiss cheese
- 2 oz sliced deli ham
- 2 oz sliced deli turkey
- 1 tsp butter, melted
- Powdered sugar
- Raspberry jam, for serving

Directions:
1. Beat egg with half and half cream and vanilla extract in a bowl.
2. Place one bread slice on the working surface and top it with ham and turkey slice and swiss cheese.
3. Place the other bread slice on top, then dip the sandwich in the egg mixture, then place it in a suitable baking tray lined with butter.
4. Set the baking tray inside the Air Fryer toaster oven and close the lid. Select the Air Fry mode at 350 degrees F temperature for 10 minutes.
5. Flip the sandwich and continue cooking for 8 minutes.
6. Slice and serve.

Nutrition:
Calories: 412 | Protein: 18.9g | Carbs: 43.8g | Fat: 24.8g

22. Sausage Cheese Wraps

Preparation Time: 10 minutes
Cooking Time: 3 minutes
Servings: 8

Ingredients:
- 8 sausages
- 2 pieces American cheese, shredded
- 8-count refrigerated crescent roll dough

Directions:
1. Roll out each crescent roll and top it with cheese and 1 sausage.
2. Fold both the top and bottom edges of the crescent sheet to cover the sausage and roll it around the sausage.
3. Place 4 rolls in the Air Fryer basket and spray them with cooking oil. Set the Air Fryer basket inside the Air Fryer toaster oven and close the lid.

4. Select the Air Fry mode at 380 degrees F temperature for 3 minutes. Cook the remaining rolls in the same manner. Serve fresh.

Nutrition:

Calories: 296 | Protein: 34.2g | Carbs: 17g | Fat: 22.1g

23. Bacon, Mushroom & Tomato Frittata

Preparation Time: 15 minutes

Cooking Time: 16 minutes

Servings: 2

Ingredients:

- 1 cooked bacon slice, chopped
- 6 cherry tomatoes, halved
- 6 fresh mushrooms, sliced
- Salt and ground black pepper, as required
- 3 eggs
- 1 tablespoon fresh parsley, chopped
- ¼ cup Parmesan cheese, grated

Directions:

1. In a baking pan, add the bacon, tomatoes, mushrooms, salt, and black pepper and mix well.
2. Press "Power Button" of Air Fry Oven and turn the dial to select the "Air Fry" mode.
3. Press the Time button and again turn the dial to set the cooking time to 16 minutes.
4. Now push the Temp button and rotate the dial to set the temperature at 320 degrees F.
5. Press "Start/Pause" button to start.
6. When the unit beeps to show that it is preheated, open the lid.
7. Arrange pan over the "Wire Rack" and insert in the oven.
8. Meanwhile, in a bowl, add the eggs and beat well.
9. Add the parsley and cheese and mix well.
10. After 6 minutes of cooking, top the bacon mixture with egg mixture evenly.
11. Cut into equal-sized wedges and serve.

Nutrition:

Calories 228 | Total Fat 15.5 g | Saturated Fat 5.3 g

Cholesterol 270 mg | Sodium 608 mg | Total Carbs 3.5 g

Fiber 0.9 g | Sugar 2.1 g | Protein 19.8 g

24. Sausage, Spinach & Broccoli Frittata

Preparation Time: 15 minutes

Cooking Time: 30 minutes

Servings: 4

Ingredients:

- 1 teaspoon butter
- 6 turkey sausage links, cut into small pieces
- 1 cup broccoli florets, cut into small pieces
- ½ cup fresh spinach, chopped up
- 6 eggs
- 1/8 teaspoon hot sauce
- 2 tablespoons half-and-half
- 1/8 teaspoon garlic salt
- Salt and ground black pepper, as required
- ¾ cup Cheddar cheese, shredded

Directions:

1. In a skillet, melt the butter over medium heat and cook the sausage for about 7-8 minutes or until browned.
2. Add the broccoli and cook for about 3-4 minutes.
3. Add the spinach and cook for about 2-3 minutes.
4. Remove from the heat and set aside to cool slightly.
5. Meanwhile, in a bowl, add the eggs, half-and-half, hot sauce, garlic salt, salt and black pepper and beat until well combined.
6. Add the cheese and stir to combine.
7. In the bottom of a lightly greased pan, place the broccoli mixture and to with the egg mixture.
8. Press "Power Button" of Air Fry Oven and turn the dial to select the "Air Bake" mode.
9. Press the Time button and again turn the dial to set the cooking time to 15 minutes.
10. Now push the Temp button and rotate the dial to set the temperature at 400 degrees F.
11. Press "Start/Pause" button to start.
12. When the unit beeps to show that it is preheated, open the lid.
13. Arrange pan over the "Wire Rack" and insert in the oven.
14. Cut into equal-sized wedges and serve hot.

Nutrition:

Calories 339 | Total Fat 27.4g | Saturated Fat 11.6 g

Cholesterol 229 mg | Sodium 596 mg | Total Carbs 3.7 g

Fiber 0.7 g | Sugar 1.5 g | Protein 19.6 g

25. Sausage & Scallion Frittata

Preparation Time: 15 minutes

Cooking Time: 20 minutes

Servings: 2

Ingredients:

- ¼ lb. cooked breakfast sausage, crumbled
- ½ cup Cheddar cheese, shredded
- 4 eggs, beaten lightly
- 2 scallions, chopped
- Pinch of cayenne pepper

Directions:

1. In a bowl, add the sausage, cheese, eggs, scallion and cayenne and mix until well combined.
2. Place the mixture into a greased baking pan.
3. Press "Power Button" of Air Fry Oven and turn the dial to select the "Air Fry" mode.
4. Press the Time button and again turn the dial to set the cooking time to 20 minutes.
5. Now push the Temp button and rotate the dial to set the temperature at 360 degrees F.
6. Press "Start/Pause" button to start.
7. When the unit beeps to show that it is preheated, open the lid.
8. Arrange pan over the "Wire Rack" and insert in the oven.
9. Cut into equal-sized wedges and serve hot.

Nutrition:

Calories 437 | Total Fat 32.4 g | Saturated Fat 13.9 g

Cholesterol 405 mg | Sodium 726 mg | Total Carbs 2.2 g

Fiber 0.4 g | Sugar 1.2 g | Protein 29.4 g

26. Trout Frittata

Preparation Time: 15 minutes

Cooking Time: 25 minutes

Servings: 4

Ingredients:
- 1 tablespoon olive oil
- 1 onion, sliced
- 6 eggs
- ½ tablespoon horseradish sauce
- 2 tablespoons crème fraiche
- 2 hot-smoked trout fillets, chopped
- ¼ cup fresh dill, chopped

Directions:

1. In a skillet, heat the oil over medium heat and cook the onion for about 4-5 minutes.
2. Remove from the heat and set aside.
3. Meanwhile, in a bowl, add the eggs, horseradish sauce, and crème fraiche and mix well.
4. In the bottom of a baking pan, place the cooked onion and top with the egg mixture, followed by trout.
5. Press "Power Button" of Air Fry Oven and turn the dial to select the "Air Fry" mode.
6. Press the Time button and again turn the dial to set the cooking time to 20 minutes.
7. Now push the Temp button and rotate the dial to set the temperature at 320 degrees F.
8. Press "Start/Pause" button to start.
9. When the unit beeps to show that it is preheated, open the lid.
10. Arrange pan over the "Wire Rack" and insert in the oven.
11. Cut into equal-sized wedges and serve with the garnishing of dill.

Nutrition:

Calories 258 | Total Fat 15.7 g | Saturated Fat 3.9g

Cholesterol 288 mg | Sodium 141 mg | Total Carbs 5.1 g

Fiber 1 g | Sugar 1.8 g | Protein 24.4 g

27. Tasty Cinnamon Toast

Preparation time: 10 minutes

Cooking time: 5 minutes

Servings: 6

Ingredients:
- 1 stick butter, soft
- 12 bread slices
- ½ cup sugar
- 1 and ½ teaspoon vanilla extract
- 1 and ½ teaspoon cinnamon powder

Directions:

1. In a bowl, mix soft butter with sugar, vanilla and cinnamon and whisk well.
2. Spread this on bread slices, place them in your air fryer and cook at 400 degrees F for 5 minutes,
3. Divide among plates and serve for breakfast. Enjoy!

Nutrition:

Calories 221 | Fat 4g | Fiber 7g | Carbs 12g | Protein 8g

28. Delicious Potato Hash

Preparation time: 10 minutes

Cooking time: 25 minutes

Servings: 4

Ingredients:
- 1 and ½ potatoes, cubed
- 1 yellow onion, chopped
- 2 teaspoons olive oil
- 1 green bell pepper, chopped
- Salt and black pepper to the taste
- ½ teaspoon thyme, dried
- 2 eggs

Directions:

1. Heat up your air fryer at 350 degrees F, add oil, heat it up, add onion, bell pepper, salt and pepper, stir and cook for 5 minutes.
2. Add potatoes, thyme and eggs, stir, cover and cook at 360 degrees F for 20 minutes.
3. Divide among plates and serve for breakfast. Enjoy!

Nutrition:

Calories 241 | Fat 4g | Fiber 7g | Carbs 12g | Protein 7g

29. Turkey Burrito

Preparation time: 10 minutes

Cooking time: 10 minutes

Servings: 2

Ingredients:
- 4 slices turkey breast already cooked
- ½ red bell pepper, sliced
- 2 eggs
- 1 small avocado, peeled, pitted and sliced
- 2 tablespoons salsa
- Salt and black pepper to the taste
- 1/8 cup mozzarella cheese, grated
- Tortillas for serving

Directions:
1. In a bowl, whisk eggs with salt and pepper to the taste, pour them in a pan and place it in the air fryer's basket.
2. Cook at 400 degrees F for 5 minutes, take pan out of the fryer and transfer eggs to a plate.
3. Arrange tortillas on a working surface, divide eggs on them, also divide turkey meat, bell pepper, cheese, salsa and avocado.
4. Roll your burritos and place them in your air fryer after you've lined it with some tin foil.
5. Heat up the burritos at 300 degrees F for 3 minutes, divide them on plates and serve. Enjoy!

Nutrition:

Calories 349 | Fat 23g | Fiber 11g | Carbs 20g | Protein 21g

30. Biscuits Casserole

Preparation time: 10 minutes

Cooking time: 15 minutes

Servings: 8

Ingredients:
- 12 ounces biscuits, quartered
- 3 tablespoons flour
- ½ pound sausage, chopped
- A pinch of salt and black pepper
- 2 and ½ cups milk
- Cooking spray

Directions:
1. Grease your air fryer with cooking spray and heat it over 350 degrees F.
2. Add biscuits on the bottom and mix with sausage.
3. Add flour, milk, salt and pepper, toss a bit and cook for 15 minutes.
4. Divide among plates and serve for breakfast. Enjoy!

Nutrition:

Calories 321 | Fat 4g | Fiber 7g | Carbs 12g | Protein 5g

31. Cheese Air Fried Bake

Preparation time: 10 minutes

Cooking time: 20 minutes

Servings: 4

Ingredients:
- 4 bacon slices, cooked and crumbled
- 2 cups milk
- 2 and ½ cups cheddar cheese, shredded
- 1-pound breakfast sausage, casings removed and chopped
- 2 eggs
- ½ teaspoon onion powder
- Salt and black pepper to the taste
- 3 tablespoons parsley, chopped
- Cooking spray

Directions:
1. In a bowl, mix eggs with milk, cheese, onion powder, salt, pepper and parsley and whisk well.
2. Grease your air fryer with cooking spray, heat it up at 320 degrees F and add bacon and sausage.
3. Add eggs mix, spread and cook for 20 minutes.
4. Divide among plates and serve. Enjoy!

Nutrition:

Calories 214 | Fat 5g | Fiber 8g | Carbs 12g | Protein 12g

32. Oatmeal Casserole

Preparation time: 10 minutes

Cooking time: 20 minutes

Servings: 8

Ingredients:
- 2 cups rolled oats
- 1 teaspoon baking powder
- 1/3 cup brown sugar
- 1 teaspoon cinnamon powder
- ½ cup chocolate chips
- 2/3 cup blueberries
- 1 banana, peeled and mashed
- 2 cups milk
- 1 egg
- 2 tablespoons butter
- 1 teaspoon vanilla extract
- Cooking spray

Directions:
1. In a bowl, mix sugar with baking powder, cinnamon, chocolate chips, blueberries and banana and stir.

2. In a separate bowl, mix eggs with vanilla extract and butter and stir.
3. Heat up your air fryer at 320 degrees F, grease with cooking spray and add oats on the bottom.
4. Add cinnamon mix and eggs mix, toss and cook for 20 minutes.
5. Stir one more time, divide into bowls and serve for breakfast. Enjoy!

Nutrition:

Calories 300 | Fat 4g | Fiber 7g | Carbs 12g | Protein 10g

---

33. Chicken Omelet

Preparation Time: 10 minutes

Cooking Time: 18 minutes

Servings: 4

Ingredients:

- 4 eggs
- ½ cup chicken breast, cooked and diced
- 2 tbsp. shredded cheese, divided
- ½ tsp salt, divided
- ¼ tsp pepper, divided
- ¼ tsp granulated garlic, divided
- ¼ tsp onion powder, divided

Directions:

Spray 2 ramekins with cooking oil and keep them aside.

Crack two large eggs into each ramekin then add cheese and seasoning.

Whisk well, then add ¼ cup chicken. Place the ramekins in a baking tray.

Set the baking tray inside the Air Fryer toaster oven and close the lid. Select the Bake mode at 330 degrees F temperature for 18 minutes. Serve warm.

Nutrition:

Calories: 322 | Protein: 17.3g | Carbs: 4.6g | Fat: 21.8g

---

34. Sausage Burritos

Preparation Time: 10 minutes

Cooking Time: 10 minutes

Servings: 6

Ingredients:

- 6 medium flour tortillas
- 6 scrambled eggs
- ½ lb. ground sausage, browned
- ½ bell pepper, minced
- 1/3 cup bacon bits
- ½ cup shredded cheese
- Oil, for spraying

Directions:

1. Mix eggs with cheese, bell pepper, bacon, and sausage in a bowl.
2. Spread each tortilla on the working surface and top it with ½ cup egg filling.
3. Roll the tortilla like a burrito then place 3 burritos in the Air Fryer basket.
4. Spray them with cooking oil. Set the Air Fryer basket inside the Air Fryer toaster oven and close the lid. Select the Air Fry mode at 330 degrees F temperature for 5 minutes.
5. Cook the remaining burritos in the same manner. Serve fresh.

Nutrition:

Calories: 197 | Protein: 7.9g | Carbs: 58.5g | Fat: 15.4g

---

35. Sausage Patties

Preparation Time: 10 minutes

Cooking Time: 20 minutes

Servings: 4

Ingredients:

- 1.5 lbs. ground sausage
- 1 tsp chili flakes
- 1 tsp dried thyme
- 1 tsp onion powder
- ½ tsp each paprika and cayenne
- Sea salt and black pepper, to taste
- 2 tsp brown sugar
- 3 tsp minced garlic
- 2 tsp Tabasco
- Herbs for garnish

Directions:

1. Toss sausage ground with all the spices, herbs, sugar, garlic and tabasco sauce in a bowl.
2. Make 1.5-inch-thick and 3-inch round patties out of this mixture.
3. Place the sausage patties in the Air Fryer basket.
4. Set the Air Fryer basket inside the Air Fryer toaster oven and close the lid. Select the Air Fry mode at 370 degrees F temperature for 20 minutes.
5. Flip the patties when cooked halfway through then continue cooking.

Nutrition:

Calories: 208 | Protein: 24.3g | Carbs: 9.5g | Fat: 10.7g

---

36. Spicy Sweet Potato Hash

Preparation Time: 10 minutes

Cooking Time: 16 minutes

Servings: 4

Ingredients:

- 2 large sweet potato, diced
- 2 slices bacon, cooked and diced
- 2 tbsp olive oil
- 1 tbsp smoked paprika
- 1 tsp of sea salt
- 1 tsp ground black pepper
- 1 tsp dried dill weed

Directions:
1. Toss sweet potato with all the spices and olive oil in the Air Fry basket.
2. Set the Air Fryer basket inside the Air Fryer toaster oven and close the lid.
3. Select the Air Fry mode at 400 degrees F temperature for 16 minutes.
4. Toss the potatoes after every 5 minutes. Once done, toss in bacon and serve warm.

Nutrition:
Calories: 134 | Protein: 6.6g | Carbs: 36.5g | Fat: 6g

37. Cinnamon Cream Doughnuts

Preparation Time: 10 minutes
Cooking Time: 8 minutes
Servings: 4

Ingredients:
- 1/2 cup Sugar
- 2 1/2 tbsp butter
- 2 large egg yolks
- 2 1/4 cups all-purpose flour
- 1 1/2 tsp baking powder
- 1 tsp salt
- 1/2 cup sour cream
- To garnish
- 1/3 cup white Sugar
- 1 tsp cinnamon
- 2 tbsp butter, melted

Directions:
1. Beat egg with sugar and butter in a mixer until creamy, then whisk in flour, salt, baking powder, and sour cream.
2. Mix well until smooth then refrigerate the dough for 1 hour.
3. Spread this dough into ½ inch thick circle then cut 9 large circles out of it.
4. Make the hole at the center of each circle. Place the doughnuts in the Air Fryer basket.
5. Set the Air Fryer basket inside the Air Fryer toaster oven and close the lid. Select the Air Fry mode at 350 degrees F temperature for 8 minutes.
6. Cook the doughnuts in two batches to avoid overcrowding.
7. Mix sugar, cinnamon, and butter and glaze the doughnuts with this mixture. Serve.

Nutrition:
Calories: 387 | Protein: 10.6g | Carbs: 26.4g | Fat: 13g

38. Sausage Frittata

Preparation Time: 15 minutes
Cooking Time: 20 minutes
Servings: 4

Ingredients:
- 1/4-pound sausage, cooked and crumbled
- 4 eggs, beaten
- 1/2 cup shredded Cheddar cheese blend
- 2 tbsp. red bell pepper, diced
- 1 green onion, chopped
- 1 pinch cayenne pepper
- cooking spray

Directions:
1. Beat eggs with cheese, sausage, cayenne, onion, and bell pepper in a bowl.
2. Spread the egg mixture in a 6x2 inch baking tray, greased with cooking spray.
3. Set the baking tray inside the Air Fryer toaster oven and close the lid.
4. Select the Bake mode at 360 degrees F temperature for 20 minutes.
5. Slice and serve.

Nutrition:
Calories: 212 | Protein: 17.3 g | Carbs: 14.6g | Fat: 11.8g

39. Potato Jalapeno Hash

Preparation Time: 15 minutes
Cooking Time: 24 minutes
Servings: 4

Ingredients:
- 1 1/2 lbs. potatoes, peeled and diced
- 1 tbsp. olive oil
- 1 red bell pepper, seeded and diced
- 1 small onion, chopped
- 1 jalapeno, seeded and diced
- 1/2 tsp olive oil
- 1/2 tsp taco seasoning mix
- 1/2 tsp ground cumin
- Salt and black pepper to taste

Directions:
1. Soak the potato in cold water for 20 minutes then drain them.
2. Toss the potatoes with 1 tbsp olive oil. Spread them in the Air Fryer basket. Set the Air Fryer basket inside the Air Fryer

toaster oven and close the lid. Select the Air Fry mode at 370 degrees F temperature for 18 minutes.
3. And Meanwhile, toss onion, pepper, olive oil, taco seasoning, and all other ingredients in a salad bowl.
4. Add this vegetable mixture to the Air Fryer basket, and it return it to the oven. Continue cooking at 356 degrees F for 6 minutes. Serve warm

Nutrition:

Calories: 242 | Protein: 8.9g | Carbs: 36.8g | Fat: 14.4g

---

40. Bread Rolls

Preparation Time: 10 minutes

Cooking Time: 39 minutes

Servings: 8

Ingredients:

- 8 Bread Slices
- 2 Potatoes boiled and mashed
- 1 tsp Ginger grated
- 1 tbsp. Coriander powder
- 1 tsp Cumin powder
- 1/2 tsp Chili powder
- 1/2 tsp Garam Masala
- 1/2 tsp Dry Mango powder
- 1&1/2 tsp Salt
- 1 Large Bowl of Water
- Cooking Oil

Directions:

1. Mix mashed potatoes with ginger and all the spices.
2. Divide this mixture into 16 balls and keep them aside. Slice the bread slices into half to get 16 rectangles. Dip each in water for 1 second, then place one potato ball at the center and wrap the slice around it.
3. Place half of these wrapped balls in the Air Fryer basket and spray them with cooking oil. Set the Air Fryer basket inside the Air Fryer toaster oven and close the lid.
4. Select the Air Fry mode at 390 degrees F temperature for 18 minutes. Flip the balls after 10 minutes of cooking then continue cooking.
5. Cook the remaining balls in the same manner. Serve fresh.

Nutrition:

Calories: 331 | Protein: 14.8g | Carbs: 46g | Fat: 2.5g

---

41. Spinach Egg Breakfast

Preparation Time: 10 minutes

Cooking Time: 20 minutes

Servings: 4

Ingredients:

- 3 eggs
- 1/4 cup coconut milk
- 1/4 cup parmesan cheese, grated
- 4 oz spinach, chopped
- 3 oz cottage cheese

Directions:

1. Preheat the air fryer to 350 F.
2. Add eggs, milk, half parmesan cheese, and cottage cheese in a bowl and whisk well. Add spinach and stir well.
3. Pour mixture into the air fryer baking dish.
4. Sprinkle remaining half parmesan cheese on top.
5. Place dish in the air fryer and cook for 20 minutes.
6. Serve and enjoy.

Nutrition:

Calories 144 | Fat 8.5 g | Carbohydrates 2.5 g | Sugar 1.1 g

Protein 14 g | Cholesterol 135 mg

---

42. Vegetable Quiche

Preparation Time: 10 minutes

Cooking Time: 24 minutes

Servings: 6

Ingredients:

- 8 eggs
- 1 cup coconut milk
- 1 cup tomatoes, chopped
- 1 cup zucchini, chopped
- 1 tbsp butter
- 1 onion, chopped
- 1 cup Parmesan cheese, grated
- 1/2 tsp pepper
- 1 tsp salt

Directions:

1. Preheat the air fryer to 370 F.
2. Melt butter in a pan over medium heat then add onion and sauté until onion lightly brown.
3. Add tomatoes and zucchini to the pan and sauté for 4-5 minutes.
4. Transfer cooked vegetables into the air fryer baking dish.
5. Beat eggs with cheese, milk, pepper, and salt in a bowl.
6. Pour egg mixture over vegetables in a baking dish.
7. Place dish in the air fryer and cook for 24 minutes or until eggs are set.
8. Slice and serve.

Nutrition:

Calories 255 | Fat 16 g | Carbohydrates 8 g

Sugar 4.2 g | Protein 21 g | Cholesterol 257 mg

43. Breakfast Egg Tomato

Preparation Time: 10 minutes
Cooking Time: 24 minutes
Servings: 2

Ingredients:
- 2 eggs
- 2 large fresh tomatoes
- 1 tsp fresh parsley
- Pepper
- Salt

Directions:
1. Preheat the air fryer to 325 F.
2. Cut off the top of a tomato and spoon out the tomato innards.
3. Break the egg in each tomato and place in air fryer basket and cook for 24 minutes.
4. Season with parsley, pepper, and salt.
5. Serve and enjoy.

Nutrition:
Calories 95 | Fat 5 g | Carbohydrates 7.5 g
Sugar 5.1 g | Protein 7 g | Cholesterol 164 mg

44. Mushroom Leek Frittata

Preparation Time: 10 minutes
Cooking Time: 32 minutes
Servings: 4

Ingredients:
- 6 eggs
- 6 oz mushrooms, sliced
- 1 cup leeks, sliced
- Salt

Directions:
1. Preheat the air fryer to 325 F.
2. Spray air fryer baking dish with cooking spray and set aside.
3. Heat another pan over medium heat. Spray pan with cooking spray.
4. Add mushrooms, leeks, and salt in a pan sauté for 6 minutes.
5. Break eggs in a bowl and whisk well.
6. Transfer sautéed mushroom and leek mixture into the prepared baking dish.
7. Pour egg over mushroom mixture.
8. Place dish in the air fryer and cook for 32 minutes.
9. Serve and enjoy.

Nutrition:
Calories 116 | Fat 7 g | Carbohydrates 5.1 g
Sugar 2.1 g | Protein 10 g | Cholesterol 245 mg

45. Perfect Breakfast Frittata

Preparation Time: 10 minutes
Cooking Time: 32 minutes
Servings: 2

Ingredients:
- 3 eggs
- 2 tbsp parmesan cheese, grated
- 2 tbsp sour cream
- 1/2 cup bell pepper, chopped
- 1/4 cup onion, chopped
- 1/2 tsp pepper
- 1/2 tsp salt

Directions:
1. Add eggs in a mixing bowl and whisk with remaining ingredients.
2. Spray air fryer baking dish with cooking spray.
3. Pour egg mixture into the prepared dish and place in the air fryer and cook at 350 F for 5 minutes.
4. Serve and enjoy.

Nutrition:
Calories 227 | Fat 15.2 g | Carbohydrates 6 g
Sugar 2.6 g | Protein 18.2 g | Cholesterol 271 mg

46. Indian Cauliflower

Preparation Time: 10 minutes
Cooking Time: 20 minutes
Servings: 2

Ingredients:
- 3 cups cauliflower florets
- 2 tbsp water
- 2 tsp fresh lemon juice
- ½ tbsp ginger paste
- 1 tsp chili powder
- ¼ tsp turmeric
- ½ cup vegetable stock
- Pepper
- Salt

Directions:
1. Add all ingredients into the air fryer baking dish and mix well.
2. Place dish in the air fryer and cook at 400 F for 10 minutes.
3. Stir well and cook at 360 F for 10 minutes more.
4. Stir well and serve.

Nutrition:
Calories 49 | Fat 0.5 g | Carbohydrates 9 g
Sugar 3 g | Protein 3 g | Cholesterol 0 mg

47. Banana Oats

Preparation time: 5 minutes

Cooking time: 20 minutes

Servings: 4

Ingredients:

- 2 cups old fashioned oats
- 1/3 cup sugar
- 1 teaspoon vanilla extract
- 1 cup banana, peeled and mashed
- 2 cups almond milk
- 2 eggs, whisked
- Cooking spray

Directions:

1. In a bowl, combine the oats with the sugar and the other Ingredients except the cooking spray and whisk well.
2. Heat up your air fryer at 340 degrees F, grease with cooking spray, add oats mix, toss, cover and cook for 20 minutes.
3. Divide into bowls and serve for breakfast.

Nutrition:

Calories 260 | Fat 4 g | Fiber 7 g

Carbs 9 g | Protein 10 g

48. Zucchini Salad

Preparation Time: 10 minutes

Cooking Time: 25 minutes

Servings: 4

Ingredients:

- 1 lb zucchini, cut into slices
- 2 tbsp tomato paste
- ½ tbsp tarragon, chopped
- 1 yellow squash, diced
- ½ lb carrots, peeled and diced
- 1 tbsp olive oil
- Pepper
- Salt

Directions:

1. In air fryer baking dish mix together zucchini, tomato paste, tarragon, squash, carrots, pepper, and salt. Drizzle with olive oil.
2. Place in the air fryer and cook at 400 F for 25 minutes. Stir halfway through.
3. Serve and enjoy.

Nutrition:

Calories 79 | Fat 3 g | Carbohydrates 11 g

Sugar 5 g | Protein 2 g | Cholesterol 0 mg

49. Cinnamon Buns

Preparation Time: 10 minutes

Cooking Time: 10 minutes

Servings: 2

Ingredients:

- 8 oz. container crescent rolls, refrigerated
- 1 tbsp. ground cinnamon
- 2 oz. raisins
- 1/3 cup butter
- 2 tbsp. sugar, granulated
- 1/3 cup pecans, chopped
- Cooking spray (olive oil)
- 2 tbsp. maple syrup
- 1/3 cup brown sugar

Directions:

1. In a saucepan, dissolve the butter completely. Transfer to a dish and blend the maple syrup and brown sugar.
2. Layer one 8-inch pan with the olive oil spray.
3. Distribute the sugar into the pan and empty the raisins and pecans inside, stirring to incorporate.
4. In a glass dish, whisk the sugar and ground cinnamon.
5. Open the can of crescent rolls and place on a cutting board.
6. Slice the entire log of dough into eight individual pieces.
7. Cover the top and bottom of the dough pieces in cinnamon and sugar, and transfer the pan to the air fryer.
8. Adjust the settings to air crisp at 345° F for 5 minutes.
9. Turn over the individual buns and steam for another 5 minutes.
10. Take the pan out and move the buns to a serving plate.
11. Drizzle the remaining sugar liquid on the buns and serve immediately.

Nutrition:

Calories 79 | Fat 3 g | Carbohydrates 11 g | Sugar 5 g | Protein 2 g | Cholesterol 0 mg

50. Egg Cheddar Muffins

Preparation Time: 10 minutes

Cooking Time: 15 minutes

Servings: 4

Ingredients:

- 8 large eggs
- 2 medium carrots, peeled and shredded
- 1 small orange bell pepper, deseeded and diced
- ½ cup frozen corn
- ½ cup frozen peas
- Salt and black pepper to taste
- ¼ cup grated cheddar cheese

Direction:

1. Insert the drip pan at the bottom rack of the device and pre-heat the air fryer at Bake mode at 350 F for 3 to 4 minutes.
2. Crack the eggs into a medium bowl and whisk in the carrots, bell pepper, corn, peas, salt, black pepper, and half of the cheddar cheese.
3. Lightly grease 6 muffin cups with some olive oil and fill in the egg mixture, two-thirds way up. Top with the remaining cheddar cheese.
4. Open the oven and fit in the cooking tray on the middle rack. Place 3 muffin cups on the tray and close the oven. Set the timer for 15 minutes and cook until the timer reads to the end.
5. Open the lid and check for doneness using a toothpick. If undone, cook further for 5 minutes.
6. Remove the muffins cups and cook the second batch.
7. Serve the egg muffins warm.

Nutrition:

Calories 159 | Total Fat 9.36g | Total Carbs 31g

Fiber 2.3g | Protein 7.32g | Sugar 2.79g | Sodium 99mg

---

51. Go-to Easy Cornbread

Preparation Time: 15 minutes

Cooking Time: 25 minutes

Servings: 8

Ingredients:

- ¼ teaspoon salt
- 6 tablespoons unsalted butter, melted
- 1 cup cornmeal
- 2 large eggs, lightly beaten
- 1½ cups buttermilk
- 1½ teaspoons baking powder
- ½ teaspoon baking soda
- ¾ cup all-purpose flour
- 1 tablespoon sugar

Directions:

1. In a bowl, combine the cornmeal, flour, sugar, baking soda, baking powder and salt.
2. Mix the buttermilk, butter and eggs well in a second bowl.
3. Next, add the flour mixture and mix until just combined.
4. Adjust the temperature of the hot air fryer to 360 degrees F. Lightly grease an 8-inch baking dish.
5. Add the flour mixture to the prepared baking dish evenly.
6. Put the dish in the basket of the hot air fryer.
7. Fry for approximately 25 minutes, or just until a toothpick inserted in the centre emerges clean, inverting the dish once halfway through.
8. Take out of the deep fryer and put the tin on a wire rack for about 10-15 minutes.
9. Remove the bread carefully from the tin and put it on a wire rack until it is completely cool before slicing.
10. Slice the bread into slices of the desired size and serve.

Nutrition:

Calories: 217 | Carbohydrate: 24.9g | Protein: 5.6g

Fat: 10.9g | Sugar: 3.9g | Sodium: 286mg

---

52. Exotic Cornbread

Preparation Time: 10 minutes

Cooking Time: 15 minutes

Servings: 5

Ingredients:

- 1 egg
- 1 (8½-ounces) package Jiffy corn muffin
- 1/3 cup canned pineapple juice
- 7 ounces canned crushed pineapple

Directions:

1. Combine all the ingredients in a bowl.
2. Adjust the temperature of the hot air fryer to 330 degrees F. Grease a round cake tin. (6 "x 3")
3. Add the mixture evenly to the pre-prepared tin.
4. Set the cake tin in the basket of the hot air fryer.
5. Fry the cake for approximately 15 minutes or as long as a toothpick inserted in the centre comes out clean.
6. Take it out of the deep fryer and put the pan on a wire rack for around 10-15 minutes.
7. Gently remove the bread from the pan and place on a wire rack until it is completely cool before slicing.
8. Slice the bread into slices of the desired size and serve.

Nutrition:

Calories: 220 | Carbohydrate: 40g | Protein: 3.8g

Fat: 6.4g | Sugar: 14.1g | Sodium: 423mg

---

53. Mozzarella Bread & Eggs

Preparation time: 10 minutes

Cooking time: 30 minutes

Servings: 4

Ingredients:

- 8 eggs, whisked
- 1 cup mozzarella, shredded
- 1 cup whole wheat bread, cubed
- Salt and black pepper to the taste
- 1 cup tomato sauce
- 1 red onion, chopped
- 2 tablespoons olive oil

Directions:
1. Pour the oil into your hot air fryer, heat to 340 degrees F
2. Add the onion, bread and remaining ingredients, stir, cook for 20 minutes, shaking halfway through.
3. Spread on plates and serve for breakfast.

Nutrition:

Calories 211 | Fat 8 | Fiber 7 | Carbs 14 | Protein 3

54. Vanilla Flavoured Strawberry Porridge

Preparation time: 4 minutes

Cooking time: 15 minutes

Servings: 4

Ingredients:
- ¼ teaspoon vanilla extract
- 2 eggs, whisked
- 1 cup old fashioned oats
- 2 cups almond milk
- ½ cup strawberries, chopped

Directions:
1. In a bowl, mix the oatmeal with the milk and the remaining ingredients and whisk well.
2. Heat your deep fryer to 350 degrees F, then add the berry mixture and cook for 15 minutes.
3. Separate into bowls and then serve for breakfast.

Nutrition:

Calories 180 | Fat 5g | Fiber 7g | Carbs 12g | Protein 5g

55. Creamy Mushroom Porridge

Preparation time: 5 minutes

Cooking time: 20 minutes

Servings: 4

Ingredients:
- 8 eggs, whisked
- 1 tablespoon dill, chopped
- 1 cup white mushrooms, sliced
- Salt and black pepper to the taste
- ½ cup heavy cream
- 1 tablespoon avocado oil
- 1 red onion, chopped
- 1 cup old fashioned oats

Directions:
1. Combine the eggs with the oatmeal, cream and the other ingredients - except the oil and mushrooms - in a bowl and whisk.
2. Heat the air fryer with the oil to 330 degrees F, include the mushrooms and fry for 5 minutes.
3. Next, add the remaining ingredients, toss and cook for a further 15 minutes.
4. Separate into bowls and serve for breakfast.

Nutrition:

Calories: 192 | Fat: 6 | Fiber: 6 | Carbs: 14 | Protein: 7

56. Scrambled Eggs with Pesto & Cheese

Preparation time: 3 minutes

Cooking time: 15 minutes

Servings: 4

Ingredients:
- Salt and black pepper to the taste
- 8 eggs, whisked
- 1 cup mozzarella cheese, grated
- 1 tablespoon butter, melted
- ½ teaspoon sweet paprika
- 1 red onion, chopped
- 1 tablespoon basil pesto

Directions:
1. Heat the deep fryer at 350 degrees F with the butter, put in the onion, eggs and the other ingredients
2. Whisk and cook for 15 minutes, half shaking the deep fryer.
3. Spread the scrambled eggs on plates and serve.

Nutrition:

Calories 187 | Fat 6g | Fiber 6g | Carbs 13g | Protein 5g

57. Mango and Lime Bowl

Preparation Time: 5 minutes

Cooking Time: 10 minutes

Servings: 4

Ingredients:
- Juice of 1 lime
- 2 teaspoons vanilla extract
- 2 tablespoons sugar
- 1 cup mango, peeled and cubed
- 1 cup heavy cream

Directions:
1. In the pan of the air fryer, mix the mango with the cream and the other ingredients, cook at 370 degrees F for 10 minutes.
2. Separate into bowls and serve for breakfast

Nutrition:

Calories 170 | Fat 6 | Fiber 5 | Carbs 11 | Protein 2

58. Carrot Small Cakes

Preparation Time: 5 minutes

Cooking Time: 20 minutes

Servings: 4

Ingredients:
- 1 cup heavy cream
- 1 tablespoon baking powder
- Cooking spray
- 1 cup carrots, peeled and grated
- 1 tablespoon butter, melted
- 3 eggs, whisked
- 1 cup almond milk
- ½ cup almond flour

Directions:
1. Combine the eggs with the butter, carrots and the other ingredients except the cooking spray in a bowl and whisk well.
2. Lubricate a muffin tray that will fit in your hot air fryer with the cooking spray, spread the carrot mixture inside, place the tray in the hot air fryer and cook at 392 degrees F for 20 minutes.
3. Serve your carrot small cakes for breakfast.

Nutrition:
Calories 190 | Fat 12 | Fiber 2 | Carbs 11 | Protein 5

---

59. Creamy Scrambled Eggs

Preparation Time: 10 minutes
Cooking Time: 9 minutes
Servings: 2

Ingredients:
- 8 grape tomatoes, halved
- 4 eggs
- Salt and black pepper, to taste
- ¾ cup milk
- 1 tablespoon butter
- ½ cup Parmesan cheese, grated

Directions:
1. Heat the hot air fryer to 360 o F and grease a hot air fryer pan with butter.
2. In a bowl, whisk the eggs with the milk, salt and black pepper.
3. Pour the egg mixture into the prepared pan and put it in the air fryer.
4. Cook for approximately 6 minutes and stir in the grape tomatoes and cheese.
5. Cook for around 3 minutes and serve warm.

Nutrition:
Calories: 312 | Fat: 15g | Saturated Fat: 4g | Trans Fat: 0g
Cholesterol: 14g | Fiber: 2g | Sodium: 403mg | Protein: 25g

---

60. Rosti with Salmon

Preparation Time: 10 minutes
Cooking Time: 15 minutes
Servings: 2

Ingredients:
- ounces smoked salmon, cut into slices
- 1 tablespoon chives, chopped finely
- 2 tablespoons sour cream
- ½ pound russet potatoes, peeled and grated roughly
- Salt and black pepper, to taste
- 1 tablespoon olive oil
- 1/8 cup cheddar cheese
- 2 tablespoons shallots, minced

Directions:
1. Heat the hot air fryer to 365 o F and lubricate a pizza pan with the olive oil.
2. Combine the potatoes, shallots, chives, cheese, salt and black pepper in a large bowl until well mixed.
3. Add the potato mixture to the pre-prepared pizza pan and put it in the basket of the deep fryer.
4. Cook for around 15 minutes and arrange on a platter.
5. Slice the potato rösti into wedges and cover with slices of smoked salmon and sour cream to serve.

Nutrition:
Calories: 327 | Fat: 15g | Saturated Fat: 4g | Trans Fat: 0g
Cholesterol: 14g | Fiber: 2g | Sodium: 403mg | Protein: 25g

---

61. Vegetarian tofu Omelet

Preparation Time: 10 minutes
Cooking Time: 29 minutes
Servings: 2

Ingredients:
- 1 tablespoon chives, chopped
- Salt and black pepper, to taste
- 3 eggs, beaten
- ¼ of onion, chopped
- 12-ounce silken tofu, pressed and sliced
- 2 teaspoons olive oil
- 1 garlic clove, minced

Directions:
1. Heat the hot air fryer to 355 o F and grease a hot air fryer pan with olive oil.
2. Place the onion and garlic in the greased pan and fry for approximately 4 minutes.
3. Place the tofu, mushrooms and chives in and season with salt and black pepper.
4. Whisk the eggs and add to the tofu mixture.
5. Cook for about 25 minutes, piercing the eggs twice in between.
6. Arrange on plates and serve warm

Nutrition:

Calories: 248 | Fat: 29g | Saturated Fat: 3g | Trans Fat: 0g
Cholesterol: 31g | Fiber: 4g | Sodium: 374mg | Protein: 47g

---

62. Banana Bread with Walnuts

Preparation Time: 15 minutes

Cooking Time: 40 minutes

Servings: 6

Ingredients:

- ¾ cup walnuts, roughly chopped
- 1¼ teaspoons baking powder
- 2 tablespoons sour cream, 1 teaspoon vanilla extract
- ¼ teaspoon salt, 1/3 cup granulated Sugar
- ¼ cup canola oil, 2 tablespoons creamy peanut butter
- 1 cup plus 1 tablespoon all-purpose flour
- 2 medium ripe bananas, peeled and mashed
- 1 large egg

Directions:

1. Heat the hot air fryer to 330 o F and grease a non-stick baking dish.
2. Combine the flour, baking powder and salt in a bowl.
3. Beat the egg with the sugar, canola oil, sour cream, peanut butter and vanilla extract in a bowl.
4. Add in the bananas and mix until well combined.
5. Now pour in the flour mixture and gently fold in the walnuts.
6. Combine until everything is well mixed and pour the mixture evenly into the prepared baking dish.
7. Place the casserole dish in the basket of the hot air fryer and cook for around 40 minutes.
8. Take out of the deep fryer and leave to cool on a wire rack.
9. Slice the bread into slices of the desired size and serve.

Nutrition:

Calories: 510 | Fat: 29g | Saturated Fat: 3g | Trans Fat: 0g
Cholesterol: 31g | Fiber: 4g | Sodium: 374mg | Protein: 47g

---

63. Cinnamon Donuts

Preparation Time: 10 minutes

Cooking Time: 15 minutes plus 1 hour to cool

Servings: 15

Ingredients:

- 3 tablespoons pure maple syrup
- ½ teaspoon vanilla extract
- Pinch salt
- 2½ cups powdered sugar
- ½ teaspoon ground cinnamon
- 2 tablespoons butter, melted
- 1 frozen puff pastry sheet (15 by 10 inches), thawed
- 2 teaspoons all-purpose flour
- 2 tablespoons 2% milk

Directions:

1. Place the puff pastry on a work surface dusted with the flour. Slice the puff pastry into 15 squares by cutting it crosswise into five 5 cm wide strips and then divide each strip into thirds.
2. Preheat or set the air fryer to 325°F. Place a round of parchment paper in the bottom of the basket and put in as many dough squares as will fit inside without touching or overlapping.
3. Bake for 14 to 19 minutes or until the donuts are browned and no longer doughy inside. Let cool on a wire rack. Repeat the process with the remaining batter.
4. Combine the icing sugar, maple syrup, milk, melted butter, vanilla, cinnamon and salt in a small bowl and whisk until well combined.
5. Allow the donuts to cool for about 1 hour and then dip the top half of each donut into the glaze.
6. Then turn the donut over, glazed side up, and place it on a wire rack.
7. Leave them until they are firm and then serve.

Nutrition:

Calories: 109 | Total fat: 3g | Saturated fat: 1g
Cholesterol: 4mg | Sodium: 32mg | Carbohydrates: 21g
Fiber: 0g | Protein: 0g

---

64. Coffee Favoured Muffins

Preparation Time: 20 minutes

Cooking Time: 15 minutes

Servings: 6

Ingredients:

- ⅓ cup granulated sugar
- 5 tablespoons butter, melted, divided
- ¼ cup 2% milk
- ¼ cup packed light brown sugar
- Nonstick baking spray (containing flour)
- 1 teaspoon baking powder
- 1⅓ cups all-purpose flour, divided
- ½ teaspoon ground cinnamon
- Pinch salt
- 1 teaspoon vanilla extract
- 1 large egg

Directions:

1. Together in a small bowl, combine ⅓ cup flour, 2½ tablespoons butter, the brown sugar and cinnamon and mix until crumbly. Put the crumble topping aside.
2. Mix the remaining 2½ tablespoons butter, granulated sugar, milk, egg and vanilla in a medium bowl and blend well.

3. Include the remaining 1 cup of flour, the baking powder and the salt and mix until well combined.
4. Mist 6 silicone muffin tins with baking spray.
5. Place half of the batter into the prepared muffin tins. Place about 1 teaspoon of the crumble on top of each muffin and then the remaining batter.
6. Dust each muffin with the remaining sprinkles and gently press them into the batter.
7. Adjust or heat the hot air fryer to 330°F. Put the muffin tins in the basket of the air fryer. Cook the muffins for 14 to 18 minutes, or until a toothpick inserted into the centre of a muffin comes out clean.
8. Leave the muffins to cool on a wire rack for 10 minutes and then take them out of the silicone moulds. Serve them warm or cold.

Nutrition:

Calories: 285 | Total fat: 11g | Saturated fat: 7g

Cholesterol: 57mg | Sodium: 122mg | Carbohydrates: 42g

Fiber: 1g | Protein: 4g

---

65. Fruity Bacon Slices+Yogurt Dip

Preparation Time: 15 minutes

Cooking Time: 20 minutes

Servings: 4

Ingredients:

- 2 cups plain Greek yogurt
- 3 bacon slices
- 1 Bosc pear, peeled and cubed
- 1 Granny Smith apple, peeled and cubed
- ½ teaspoon ground cinnamon
- 1 cup canned cubed pineapple
- 2 tablespoons sugar

Directions:

1. Place a baking rack in a 7-inch cake tin. Fold the bacon slices in half crosswise and place them on the grate.
2. Adjust the air fryer to 350°F or preheat it. Put the cake tin in the basket of the air fryer. Fry the bacon for 7 minutes and then test to see if it is cooked. Cook it for another 2 to 3 minutes, if necessary, until it is crispy.
3. Take the bacon out of the rack and put it on paper towels to drain. Take off the rack and scoop out all but 2 teaspoons of the bacon fat from the pan.
4. Adjust or preheat the deep fryer to 380°F. Put the apple, pear and pineapple into the fat in the pan. Dust them with sugar and cinnamon and toss.
5. Fry for 10 to 15 minutes, stirring the mixture every 5 minutes, until the fruit is soft and browned around the edges.
6. Break up the bacon and add to the fruit; serve over the yoghurt

Nutrition:

Calories: 211 | Total fat: 7g | Saturated fat: 4g

Cholesterol: 24mg | Sodium: 203mg | Carbohydrates: 30g

Fiber: 3g | Protein: 8g

---

66. Vanilla & Berries French toast

Preparation Time: 15 minutes

Cooking Time: 8 minutes

Servings: 4

Ingredients:

- ⅓ cup 2% milk
- 3 tablespoons sour cream
- ⅓ cup fresh raspberries
- 2 egg yolks
- 4 (1-inch-thick) slices French bread
- 2 tablespoons raspberry jam
- ½ teaspoon vanilla extract
- 1 tablespoon sugar

Directions:

1. Slice a pocket in the side of each slice of bread, being careful not to cut through to the other side.
2. Combine the raspberry jam with the raspberries in a small bowl and mash the raspberries into the jam with a fork.
3. Whisk the egg yolks with the milk, sugar and vanilla in a shallow bowl until combined.
4. Distribute some of the sour cream in the pocket you have cut in the bread slices and then pour the raspberry mixture on top. Gently press the edges of the bread together to close the opening.
5. Immerse the bread in the egg mixture and leave it in the egg for 3 minutes. Turn the bread over and leave it on the other side for 3 minutes.
6. Adjust or heat the air fryer to 375°F. Place the stuffed bread in a single layer in the basket of the air fryer.
7. Fry for 5 minutes, then carefully turn the bread slices over and fry for a further 3 to 6 minutes until the French toast is golden brown.

Nutrition:

Calories: 278 | Total fat: 6g | Saturated fat: 3g

Cholesterol: 99mg | Sodium: 406mg | Carbohydrates: 46g

Fiber: 2g | Protein: 9g

---

67. Healthy Angel Cake

Preparation Time: 5 minutes

Cooking Time: 30 minutes

Servings: 12

Ingredients:

- 1 teaspoon strawberry extract
- 12 egg whites
- 1 cup powdered erythritol
- 2 teaspoons cream of tartar
- 1/4 cup butter, melted

Directions:

1. Heat the oven of the air fryer for 5 minutes.
2. Mix the cream of tartar and the egg whites.
3. Using a hand mixer, beat until white and fluffy.
4. Add the remaining ingredients apart from the butter and beat for a further minute.
5. Transfer to a baking dish.
6. Put in the basket of the hot air fryer and bake at 400°F for 30 minutes, or until a toothpick inserted in the centre comes out clean.
7. When cool, drizzle the cake with melted butter.

Nutrition:

Calories – 65 Protein – 3.1 g. Fat – 5 g. Carbs – 6.2

68. Cheesy Cinnamon Pancake

Preparation Time: 7 minutes

Cooking Time: 20 minutes

Servings: 4

Ingredients:

- 1 pack Stevia
- 2 eggs
- 1/2 tsp. cinnamon
- 2 cups reduced-fat cream cheese

Directions:

1. Set the hot air fryer to 330F.
2. Mix the cream cheese, cinnamon, eggs and stevia in a blender.
3. In the basket of the deep fryer, pour a quarter of the mixture.
4. Cook for 2 minutes on all sides. Do the same with the rest of the mixture. Serve.

Nutrition:

Calories: 140 kcal Carbs: 5.4g Fat: 10.6g Protein: 22.7g

69. Delicious Cinnamon Pancake

Preparation Time: 15 minutes

Cooking Time: 20 minutes

Servings: 4

Ingredients:

- 1 pack Stevia
- 1/2 tsp. cinnamon
- 2 cups low-fat cream cheese
- 2 eggs

Directions:

1. Set the temperature to 330F.
2. In a blender, combine the cream cheese, cinnamon, eggs and stevia.
3. Put a quarter of the mixture into the basket of the hot air fryer.
4. Cook for 2 minutes on both sides.
5. 5. Repeat the process with the rest of the mixture. Serve.

Nutrition:

Calories: 106 | kcal Carbs: 10g | Fat: 3.2g | Protein: 9g

70. Cinnamon French Toast

Preparation Time: 5 Minutes

Cooking Time: 10

Minutes Servings: 2

Ingredients:

- 4 slices whole meal bread
- 1 teaspoon cinnamon or nutmeg
- 2 eggs
- 1/4 cup whole milk
- 1/4 cup brown sugar

Directions:

1. Slice each piece of bread vertically into 4 equal strips.
2. Whisk the eggs in a large bowl, then combine all the other ingredients in the same bowl.
3. Immerse each bread strip in the bowl and allow the excess batter to drip off.
4. Heat the air fryer to 360 degrees and put all the strips in the basket. Fry for 10 minutes, turning halfway through.

Nutrition

Calories: 348 | Sodium: 79 mg | Dietary Fiber: 6g

Fat: 6.9g | Carbs: 56.4g | Protein: 15g.

APPETIZER

71. Sweet Cinnamon Peaches

Preparation time: 5 minutes
Cooking time: 10 minutes
Servings: 4

Ingredients:

- 2 tablespoons sugar
- ¼ teaspoon ground cinnamon
- 4 peaches, cut into wedges
- Cooking spray

Directions:

1. Grease your air fryer basket using a cooking spray.
2. In a large bowl, stir the sugar and cinnamon. Add the peaches to the bowl and toss to coat evenly.
3. Spread the coated peaches in a single layer on the basket.
4. Select Air Fry, set the temperature to 350°F (180°C), and set time to 10 minutes.
5. After 5 minutes, remove and flip the peaches over. Lightly mist them with cooking spray. Return until done.
6. Let rest for 5 minutes before serving.

Nutrition:

Calories: 80 | Carbs: 20g | Fat: 0g | Protein: 0g

72. Roasted Grapes with Yogurt

Preparation time: 5 minutes
Cooking time: 10 minutes
Servings: 6

Ingredients:

- 2 cups seedless red grapes, rinsed and patted dry
- 1 tablespoon apple cider vinegar
- 1 tablespoon honey
- 1 cup low-fat Greek yogurt
- 2 tablespoons 2 percent milk
- 2 tablespoons minced fresh basil

Directions:

1. Spread the red grapes in the baking pan and drizzle with the cider vinegar and honey. Lightly toss to coat.
2. Select Roast, set temperature to 380°F (193°C), and set time to 10 minutes.
3. Whisk the yogurt and milk in a medium bowl. Gently fold in the grapes and basil.
4. Serve immediately.

Nutrition:

Calories: 100 | Carbs: 0g | Fat: 2g | Protein: 8g

73. Garlic Edamame

Preparation time: 5 minutes
Cooking time: 9 minutes
Servings: 4

Ingredients:

- 1 bag frozen edamame in pods
- 2 tablespoon olive oil, divided
- ½ teaspoon garlic salt
- ½ teaspoon salt
- ¼ teaspoon freshly ground black pepper
- ½ teaspoon red pepper flakes (optional)

Directions:

1. Put the edamame in a medium bowl, then drizzle with 1 tablespoon of olive oil. Toss to coat well.
2. Stir the garlic salt, salt, pepper, and red pepper flakes (if desired) in a small bowl. Pour the mixture into the bowl of edamame and toss until the edamame is fully coated.
3. Grease your air fryer basket with the rest of the 1 tablespoon of olive oil.
4. Place the edamame in the greased basket.
5. Select Air Fry, set temperature to 375°F (190°C), and set time to 9 minutes.
6. Stir the edamame once halfway through the cooking time. Serve warm.

Nutrition:

Calories: 240 | Carbs: 26g | Fat: 7g | Protein: 21g

74. Baked Sardines with Sauce

Preparation time: 10 minutes
Cooking time: 20 minutes
Servings: 4

Ingredients:
- 2 pounds (907 g) fresh sardines
- 3 tablespoons olive oil, divided
- 4 Roma tomatoes, peeled and chopped
- 1 small onion, sliced thinly
- Zest of 1 orange
- Sea salt
- ground pepper
- 2 tablespoons whole-wheat bread crumbs
- ½ cup white wine

Directions:
1. Grease your baking pan using a little olive oil. Set aside.
2. Rinse the sardines under running water. Slit the belly, remove the spine, and butterfly the fish. Set aside.
3. Heat the remaining olive oil in a large skillet. Add the tomatoes, onion, orange zest, salt, and pepper to the skillet and simmer for 20 minutes, or until the mixture thickens and softens.
4. Put half of the sauce inside the greased pan. Arrange the sardines on top and spread the remaining half the sauce over the fish. Sprinkle with the bread crumbs and drizzle with the white wine.
5. Choose Convection Bake, set temperature to 425°F (220°C), and set time to 20 minutes.
6. Remove the pan from the oven, then serve immediately.

Nutrition:
Calories: 160 | Carbs: 2g | Fat: 9g | Protein: 17g

75. Cheesy Baked Potatoes

Preparation time: 5 minutes
Cooking time: 20 minutes
Servings: 6

Ingredients:
- 12 small red potatoes
- 1 teaspoon kosher salt, divided
- 1 tablespoon extra-virgin olive oil
- ¼ cup grated sharp Cheddar cheese
- ¼ cup sour cream
- 2 tablespoons chopped chives
- 2 tablespoons grated Parmesan cheese

Directions:
1. Add the potatoes to a large bowl. Sprinkle with the ½ teaspoon of the salt and drizzle with the olive oil. Toss to coat. Place the potatoes in the baking pan.
2. Slide the baking pan into Rack Position 2, select Roast, set temperature to 375°F (190°C), and set time to 15 minutes.
3. Remove, then let the potatoes rest for 5 minutes. Halve the potatoes lengthwise. Scoop the potato flesh using a spoon into a bowl, leaving a thin shell of skin. Arrange the potato halves in the pan.
4. Mash the potato flesh until smooth. Mix in the remaining ½ teaspoon of the salt, Cheddar cheese, sour cream, and chives.
5. Transfer the filling into a pastry bag with one corner snipped off. Pipe the filling into the potato shells, mounding up slightly. Sprinkle with the Parmesan cheese.
6. Select Roast, temperature to 375°F (190°C), and set time to 5 minutes.
7. Let the potatoes cool slightly before serving.

Nutrition:
Calories: 135 | Carbs: 22g | Fat: 4g | Protein: 4g

76. Sausage and Onion Rolls

Preparation time: 15 minutes
Cooking time: 15 minutes
Servings: 12

Ingredients:
- 1-pound (454 g) bulk breakfast sausage
- ½ cup finely chopped onion
- ½ cup fresh bread crumbs
- ½ teaspoon dried mustard
- ½ teaspoon dried sage
- ¼ teaspoon cayenne pepper
- 1 large egg, beaten
- 1 garlic clove, minced
- 2 sheets frozen puff pastry, thawed
- All-purpose flour, for dusting

Directions:
1. In a medium bowl, break up the sausage. Stir in the onion, bread crumbs, mustard, sage, cayenne pepper, egg, and garlic.
2. Divide the sausage mixture in half and tightly wrap each half in plastic wrap. Refrigerate for 5 to 10 minutes.
3. Lay the pastry sheets on a lightly floured work surface. Lightly roll out the pastry to smooth out the dough.
4. Take out one of the sausage packages and form the sausage into a long roll. Remove the plastic wrap and place the sausage on top of the puff pastry about 1 inch from one of the long edges.

5. Roll the pastry around the sausage and pinch the edges of the dough together to seal. Repeat with the other pastry sheet and sausage.
6. Slice the logs into lengths about 1½ inches long. Place the sausage rolls in the baking pan, cut-side down.
7. Choose 'Roast', temperature to 350°F (180°C), and set time to 15 minutes.
8. Let cool for 5 minutes before serving.

Nutrition:

Calories: 94 | Carbs: 10g | Fat: 4g | Protein: 3g

77. Green Chiles Nachos

Preparation time: 15 minutes
Cooking time: 10 minutes
Servings: 6

Ingredients:

- 8 ounces (227 g) tortilla chips
- 3 cups shredded Monterey Jack cheese, divided
- 2 (7-ounce / 198-g) cans chopped green chilies, drained
- 1 (8-ounce / 227-g) can tomato sauce
- ¼ teaspoon dried oregano
- ¼ teaspoon granulated garlic
- ¼ teaspoon freshly ground black pepper
- Pinch cinnamon
- Pinch cayenne pepper

Directions:

1. Arrange the tortilla chips close together in a single layer in the baking pan. Sprinkle 1½ cups of the cheese over the chips.
2. Arrange the green chilies over the cheese as evenly as possible. Top with the remaining 1½ cups of the cheese.
3. Select "Roast," temperature to 375°F (190°C), and set time to 10 minutes.
4. Meanwhile, stir the remaining ingredients in a bowl for the sauce.
5. Remove from when done, then drizzle the sauce over the nachos and serve warm.

Nutrition:

Calories: 5 | Carbs: 1g | Fat: 0g | Protein: 0g

78. Parmesan Cauliflower

Preparation time: 15 minutes
Cooking time: 15 minutes
Servings: 5

Ingredients:

- 8 cups small cauliflower florets (about 1¼ pounds / 567 g)
- 3 tablespoons olive oil
- 1 teaspoon garlic powder
- ½ teaspoon salt
- ½ teaspoon turmeric
- ¼ cup shredded Parmesan cheese

Directions:

1. In a bowl, combine the cauliflower florets, olive oil, garlic powder, salt, turmeric, and toss to coat. Transfer to the air fryer basket.
2. Select "Air Fry" temperature to 390°F (199°C), and set time to 15 minutes.
3. After 5 minutes, remove, then stir the cauliflower florets. Return to the oven and continue cooking.
4. After 6 minutes, remove and stir the cauliflower again. Return and cook again for 4 minutes. The cauliflower florets should be crisp-tender.
5. Sprinkle with the shredded Parmesan cheese and toss well. Serve warm.

Nutrition:

Calories: 58 | Carbs: 6g | Fat: 3g | Protein: 3g

79. Cheesy Jalapeño Poppers

Preparation time: 15 minutes
Cooking time: 15 minutes
Servings: 8

Ingredients:

- 6 ounces (170 g) cream cheese, at room temperature
- 4 ounces (113 g) shredded Cheddar cheese
- 1 teaspoon chili powder
- 12 large jalapeño peppers, deseeded and sliced in half lengthwise
- 2 slices cooked bacon, chopped
- ¼ cup panko bread crumbs
- 1 tablespoon butter, melted

Directions:

1. Mix the cream cheese, Cheddar cheese, and chili powder in a medium bowl. Spoon the cheese mixture into the jalapeño halves and arrange them in the baking pan.
2. In a small bowl, stir the bacon, bread crumbs, and butter. Sprinkle the mixture over the jalapeño halves.
3. Roast, then temperature to 375°F (190°C) and set time to 15 minutes.
4. Remove, then let the poppers cool for 5 minutes before serving.

Nutrition:

Calories: 280 | Carbs: 24g | Fat: 19g | Protein: 4g

80. Salty Baked Almonds

Preparation time: 5 minutes
Cooking time: 25 minutes

Servings: 4

Ingredients:

- 1 cup of raw almonds
- 1 egg white, beaten
- ½ teaspoon coarse sea salt

Directions:

1. Spread the almonds in the baking pan in an even layer.
2. Choose the "Convection Bake" set temperature to 350°F (180°C) and set time to 20 minutes.
3. Remove, then coat the almonds with the egg white and sprinkle with the salt. Return the pan to the oven within 5 minutes.
4. Cool completely before serving.

Nutrition:

Calories: 180 | Carbs: 5g | Fat: 16g | Protein: 6g

81. Lemon-Pepper Wings

Preparation time: 5 minutes

Cooking time: 24 minutes

Servings: 10

Ingredients:

- 2 pounds (907 g) chicken wings
- 4½ teaspoons salt-free lemon pepper seasoning
- 1½ teaspoons baking powder
- 1½ teaspoons kosher salt

Directions:

1. Toss all the fixings until well coated in a large bowl. Put the wings in the air fryer basket, making sure they don't crowd each other too much.
2. Select "Air Fry" set temperature to 375°F (190°C) and set time to 24 minutes.
3. After 12 minutes, remove and turn the wings over. Return to the oven to continue cooking until done. Let rest for 5 minutes before serving.

Nutrition:

Calories: 110 | Carbs: 0g | Fat: 9g | Protein: 8g

82. Spicy and Sweet Roasted Nuts

Preparation time: 5 minutes

Cooking time: 15 minutes

Servings: 4

Ingredients:

- 1-pound (454 g) walnut halves and pieces
- ½ cup granulated sugar
- 3 tablespoons vegetable oil
- 1 teaspoon cayenne pepper
- ½ teaspoon fine salt

Directions:

1. Soak the walnuts in a large bowl with boiling water for a minute or two. Drain the walnuts.
2. Stir in the sugar, oil, and cayenne pepper to coat well. Spread the walnuts in a single layer in the baking pan.
3. Select "Roast" set temperature to 325°F (163°C) and set time to 15 minutes.
4. After 7 or 8 minutes, remove, and stir the nuts. Return, and check frequently.
5. When done, the walnuts should be dark golden brown. Sprinkle the nuts with the salt and let cool. Serve warm.

Nutrition:

Calories: 205 | Carbs: 5g | Fat: 20g | Protein: 4g

83. Paprika Deviled Eggs

Preparation time: 20 minutes

Cooking time: 16 minutes

Servings: 12

Ingredients:

- 3 cups ice
- 12 large eggs
- ½ cup mayonnaise
- 10 hamburger dill pickle chips, diced
- ¼ cup diced onion
- 2 teaspoons salt
- 2 teaspoons yellow mustard
- 1 teaspoon freshly ground black pepper
- ½ teaspoon paprika

Directions:

1. Put the ice in a large bowl, then set aside. Carefully place the eggs in the baking pan.
2. Set "Convection Bake," set the temperature to 250°F (121°C), and set time to 16 minutes.
3. After that, transfer the eggs to the large bowl of ice to cool.
4. Peel the eggs, then slice it in half lengthwise, then take out yolks into a small bowl.
5. Stir in the mayonnaise, pickles, onion, salt, mustard, and pepper. Mash the mixture with a fork until well combined.
6. Fill each egg white half with 1 to 2 teaspoons of the egg yolk mixture.
7. Put the paprika on top and serve immediately.

Nutrition:

Calories: 150 | Carbs: 0g | Fat: 4g | Protein: 6g

84. Sausage Balls with Cheese

Preparation time: 10 minutes

Cooking time: 10 minutes

Servings: 8

Ingredients:

- 12 ounces (340 g) mild ground sausage
- 1½ cups baking mix
- 1 cup shredded mild Cheddar cheese
- 3 ounces cream cheese
- 1 to 2 tablespoons olive oil

Directions:
1. Line with parchment paper the air fryer basket. Set aside.
2. Mix the ground sausage, baking mix, Cheddar cheese, and cream cheese in a large bowl and stir to incorporate.
3. Divide the sausage mixture into 16 equal portions and roll them into 1-inch balls with your hands.
4. Arrange the sausage balls on the parchment, leaving space between each ball. Brush the sausage balls with olive oil.
5. Choose "Air Fry," set temperature to 325°F (163°C), and set time to 10 minutes.
6. Flip the balls halfway through the cooking time. Remove, and serve warm.

Nutrition:
Calories: 95 | Carbs: 4g | Fat: 7g | Protein: 5g

85. Mozzarella Pepperoni Pizza Bites

Preparation time: 5 minutes
Cooking time: 12 minutes
Servings: 8

Ingredients:
- 1 cup finely shredded Mozzarella cheese
- ½ cup chopped pepperoni
- ¼ cup Marinara sauce
- 1 (8-ounce / 227-g) can crescent roll dough
- All-purpose flour, for dusting

Directions:
1. In a small bowl, stir the cheese, pepperoni, and marinara sauce.
2. Lay the dough on a lightly floured work surface. Separate it into 4 rectangles. Firmly pinch the perforations together and pat the dough pieces flat.
3. Divide the cheese mixture evenly between the rectangles and spread it out over the dough, leaving a ¼-inch border.
4. Roll a rectangle up tightly, beginning with the short end. Pinch the edge down to seal the roll. Repeat with the remaining rolls.
5. Slice the rolls into 4 or 5, even slices. Place the slices in the baking pan, leaving a few inches between each slice.
6. Choose the "Roast" function, set the temperature to 350°F (180°C), and set time to 12 minutes. Serve.

Nutrition:
Calories: 190 | Carbs: 27g | Fat: 6g | Protein: 7g

86. Air Fry Bacon

Preparation Time: 5 minutes
Cooking Time: 10 minutes
Servings: 11

Ingredients:
- 11 bacon, slices

Directions:
1. Put half of the bacon slices in the air fryer basket. Cook at 400 F for 10 minutes.
2. Cook the rest of the half bacon slices using the same steps. Serve and enjoy.

Nutrition:
Calories 103 | Fat 7.9 g | Carbohydrates 0.3 g
Sugar 0 g | Protein 7 g | Cholesterol 21 mg

87. Crunchy Bacon Bites

Preparation Time: 5 minutes
Cooking Time: 10 minutes
Servings: 12

Ingredients:
- 4 bacon strips
- 1/2 cup pork rinds, crushed
- 1/4 cup hot sauce

Directions:
1. Put the bacon pieces in a bowl, then put the hot sauce and toss well.
2. Put the crushed pork rinds and toss until bacon pieces are well coated.
3. Transfer bacon pieces in the air fryer basket and cook at 350 F for 10 minutes.
4. Serve and enjoy.

Nutrition:
Calories 112 | Fat 9.7 g | Carbohydrates 0.3 g
Sugar 0.2 g | Protein 5.2 g | Cholesterol 3 mg

88. Easy Jalapeno Poppers

Preparation Time: 10 minutes
Cooking Time: 13 minutes
Servings: 5

Ingredients:
- 5 jalapeno peppers, slice in half and deseeded
- 2 tbsp salsa
- 4 oz goat cheese, crumbled
- 1/4 tsp chili powder
- 1/2 tsp garlic, minced
- Pepper

- Salt

Directions:
1. In a small bowl, mix cheese, salsa, chili powder, garlic, pepper, and salt.
2. Spoon cheese mixture into each jalapeno halves and place in the air fryer basket.
3. Cook jalapeno poppers at 350 F for 13 minutes.
4. Serve and enjoy.

Nutrition:
Calories 111 | Fat 8.3 g | Carbohydrates 2.1 g
Sugar 1.2 g | Protein 7.3 g | Cholesterol 24 mg

89. Perfect Crab Dip

Preparation Time: 5 minutes
Cooking Time: 7 minutes
Servings: 4

Ingredients:
- 1 cup crabmeat
- 2 tbsp parsley, chopped
- 2 tbsp fresh lemon juice
- 2 tbsp hot sauce
- 1/2 cup green onion, sliced
- 2 cups cheese, grated
- 1/4 cup mayonnaise
- 1/4 tsp pepper
- 1/2 tsp salt

Directions:
1. In a 6-inch dish, mix crabmeat, hot sauce, cheese, mayo, pepper, and salt.
2. Put the dish in the air fryer basket, then cook dip at 400 F for 7 minutes.
3. Remove dish from air fryer.
4. Drizzle dip with lemon juice and garnish with parsley. Serve and enjoy.

Nutrition:
Calories 313 | Fat 23.9 g | Carbohydrates 8.8 g
Sugar 3.1 g | Protein 16.2 g | Cholesterol 67 mg

90. Spinach Dip

Preparation Time: 10 minutes
Cooking Time: 40 minutes
Servings: 8

Ingredients:
- 8 oz cream cheese, softened
- 1/4 teaspoon garlic powder
- 1/2 cup onion, minced
- 1/3 cup water chestnuts, chopped
- 1 cup mayonnaise
- 1 cup parmesan cheese, grated
- 1 cup frozen spinach, thawed and squeeze
- 1/2 teaspoon pepper

Directions:
1. Spray the air fryer baking dish using a cooking spray.
2. Put all the fixings into the bowl and mix.
3. Put the batter into the prepared baking dish and put it in the air fryer basket.
4. Cook at 300 F for 35-40 minutes. After 20 minutes of cooking, stir dip.
5. Serve and enjoy.

Nutrition:
Calories 220 | Fat 20.5 g | Carbohydrates 9.3 g
Sugar 2.3 g | Protein 3.8 g | Cholesterol 41 mg

91. Sweet Potato Tots

Preparation Time: 10 minutes
Cooking Time: 31 minutes
Servings: 24

Ingredients:
- 2 sweet potatoes, peeled
- 1/2 teaspoon Cajun seasoning
- Salt

Directions:
1. Put the water in pot and boil, then put the sweet potatoes. Boil for 15 minutes, then drains well.
2. Grate the boil sweet potatoes into a bowl.
3. Put the Cajun seasoning plus salt in grated sweet potatoes and mix until well combined.
4. Lightly spray your air fryer basket using a cooking spray.
5. Form a small tot of the mixture and put it in an air fryer basket.
6. Cook at 400 F within 8 minutes. Turn the sweet potato tots to another side and cook for 8 minutes more. Serve and enjoy.

Nutrition:
Calories 15 | Fat 0 g | Carbohydrates 3.5 g
Sugar 0.1 g | Protein 0.2 g | Cholesterol 0 mg

92. Herb Zucchini Slices

Preparation Time: 10 minutes
Cooking Time: 15 minutes
Servings: 4

Ingredients:
- 2 zucchinis, sliced in half lengthwise
- 1 tbsp olive oil
- 4 tbsp parmesan cheese, grated

- 2 tbsp almond flour
- 1 tbsp parsley, chopped
- Pepper
- Salt

Directions:

1. Preheat the air fryer to 350 F.
2. In a bowl, mix cheese, parsley, oil, almond flour, pepper plus salt.
3. Top with cheese mixture the zucchini pieces and put in the air fryer basket.
4. Cook within 15 minutes at 350 F. Serve and enjoy.

Nutrition:

Calories 157 | Fat 11.4 g | Carbohydrates 5.1 g

Sugar 1.7 g | Protein 11 g | Cholesterol 20 mg

93. Ranch Kale Chips

Preparation Time: 5 minutes

Cooking Time: 5 minutes

Servings: 4

Ingredients:

- 4 cups kale, stemmed
- 1 tbsp nutritional yeast flakes
- 2 tsp ranch seasoning
- 2 tbsp olive oil
- 1/4 tsp salt

Directions:

1. Mix all fixing into the large mixing bowl.
2. Lightly oiled your air fryer basket with cooking spray.
3. Add kale in air fryer basket and cook for 4-5 minutes at 370 F. Shake halfway, then serve and enjoy.

Nutrition:

Calories 102 | Fat 7 g | Carbohydrates 8 g

Sugar 0 g | Protein 3 g | Cholesterol 0 mg

94. Curried Sweet Potato Fries

Preparation Time: 10 minutes

Cooking Time: 20 minutes

Servings: 3

Ingredients:

- 2 small sweet potatoes, peel and cut into fries' shape
- 1/4 tsp coriander
- 1/2 tsp curry powder
- 2 tbsp olive oil
- 1/4 tsp sea salt

Directions:

1. Put all ingredients into the large mixing bowl and toss well.
2. Spray air fryer basket with cooking spray.
3. Transfer sweet potato fries in the air fryer basket.
4. Cook for 20 minutes at 370 F. Shake halfway through.
5. Serve and enjoy.

Nutrition:

Calories 118 | Fat 9 g | Carbohydrates 9 g

Sugar 2 g | Protein 1 g | Cholesterol 0 mg

95. Roasted Almonds

Preparation Time: 5 minutes

Cooking Time: 8 minutes

Servings: 8

Ingredients:

- 2 cups almonds
- 1/4 teaspoon pepper
- 1 teaspoon paprika
- 1 tablespoon garlic powder
- 1 tablespoon soy sauce

Directions:

1. Mix the pepper, paprika, garlic powder, and soy sauce in a bowl.
2. Add almonds and stir to coat.
3. Grease air fryer basket using a cooking spray.
4. Put the almonds into the air fryer basket and cook for 6-8 minutes at 320 F. Shake basket after every 2 minutes. Serve and enjoy.

Nutrition:

Calories 143 | Fat 11.9 g | Carbohydrates 6.2 g

Sugar 1.3 g | Protein 5.4 g | Cholesterol 0 mg

96. Pepperoni Chips

Preparation Time: 2 minutes

Cooking Time: 8 minutes

Servings: 6

Ingredients:

- 6 oz pepperoni slices

Directions:

1. Place one batch of pepperoni slices in the air fryer basket. Cook for 8 minutes at 360 F.
2. Cook remaining pepperoni slices using the same steps. Serve and enjoy.

Nutrition:

Calories 51 | Fat 1 g | Carbohydrates 2 g

Sugar 1.3 g | Protein 0 g | Cholesterol 0 mg

97. Crispy Eggplant

Preparation Time: 5 minutes

Cooking Time: 20 minutes

Servings: 4

Ingredients:

- 1 eggplant, cut into 1-inch pieces
- 1/2 tsp Italian seasoning
- 1 tsp paprika
- 1/2 tsp red pepper
- 1 tsp garlic powder
- 2 tbsp olive oil

Directions:

1. Toss all ingredients into the large mixing bowl. Transfer eggplant mixture into the air fryer basket.
2. Cook at 375 F for 20 minutes. Shake your air fryer basket halfway through. Serve and enjoy.

Nutrition:

Calories 99 | Fat 7.5 g | Carbohydrates 8.7 g

Sugar 4.5 g | Protein 1.5 g | Cholesterol 0 mg

98. Steak Nuggets

Preparation Time: 10 minutes

Cooking Time: 15 minutes

Servings: 4

Ingredients:

- 1 lb. beef steak, cut into chunks
- 1 large egg, lightly beaten
- 1/2 cup pork rind, crushed
- 1/2 cup parmesan cheese, grated
- 1/2 tsp salt

Directions:

1. Add egg in a small bowl.
2. In a shallow bowl, mix pork rind, cheese, plus salt.
3. Soak each steak chunk in egg, then coat with pork rind mixture and place on a plate. Place in the refrigerator for 30 minutes.
4. Lightly grease the air fryer basket using cooking spray. Preheat your air fryer at 400 F.
5. Put the steak nuggets in the air fryer basket, then cook for 15-18 minutes or until cooked. Shake after every 4 minutes. Serve and enjoy.

Nutrition:

Calories 609 | Fat 38 g | Carbohydrates 2 g

Sugar 0.4 g | Protein 63 g | Cholesterol 195 mg

99. Cabbage Chips

Preparation Time: 10 minutes

Cooking Time: 30 minutes

Servings: 6

Ingredients:

- 1 large cabbage head, tear cabbage leaves into pieces
- 2 tbsp olive oil
- 1/4 cup parmesan cheese, grated
- Pepper
- Salt

Directions:

1. Preheat the air fryer to 250 F.
2. Add all the items into the large mixing bowl and toss well.
3. Grease your air fryer basket with cooking spray.
4. Divide cabbage in batches.
5. Add one cabbage chips batch in the air fryer basket and cook for 25-30 minutes at 250 F or until chips are crispy and lightly golden brown. Serve and enjoy.

Nutrition:

Calories 96 | Fat 5.1 g | Carbohydrates 12.1 g

Sugar 6.7 g | Protein 3 g | Cholesterol 1 mg

100. Healthy Broccoli Tots

Preparation Time: 10 minutes

Cooking Time: 25 minutes

Servings: 4

Ingredients:

- 1 lb. broccoli, chopped
- 1/2 cup almond flour
- 1/4 cup ground flaxseed
- 1/2 teaspoon garlic powder
- 1 teaspoon salt

Directions:

1. Microwave the broccoli for 3 minutes, then transfer steamed broccoli into the food processor, then process.
2. Transfer it to a mixing bowl, then put the rest of the ingredients into the bowl and mix until well combined.
3. Spritz your air fryer basket using a cooking spray.
4. Form small broccoli tots and put it into the air fryer basket.
5. Cook the broccoli tots within 12 minutes at 375 F.
6. Serve and enjoy.

Nutrition:

Calories 161 | Fat 9.2 g | Carbohydrates 12.8 g

Sugar 2.1 g | Protein 7.5 g | Cholesterol 0 mg

101. Classic French Fries

Preparation time: 35 minutes

Cooking time: 30 minutes

Servings: 6

Ingredients:

- 3 large russet potatoes
- 1 tablespoon canola oil
- 1 tablespoon extra-virgin olive oil
- Salt
- Pepper

Directions:

1. Peel the potatoes and cut lengthwise to create French fries.
2. Place the potatoes in a large bowl of cold water. Allow the potatoes to soak in the water for at least 30 minutes, preferably an hour.
3. Spread the fries onto a baking sheet and coat them with the canola oil, olive oil, and salt and pepper to taste.
4. Transfer half of the fries to the air fryer basket. Cook for 10 minutes.
5. Shake the basket—Cook for an additional 5 minutes.
6. When the first half finished, remove the cooked fries, repeat steps 4 and 5 for the remaining fries.
7. Cool before serving.

Nutrition:

Calories: 168 | Fat: 5g | Cholesterol: 0mg | Sodium: 38mg Carbohydrates: 29g | Fiber: 4g | Protein: 3g

102. Olive Oil Sweet Potato Chips

Preparation time: 40 minutes

Cooking time: 20 minutes

Servings: 5

Ingredients:

- 3 sweet potatoes
- 2 teaspoons extra-virgin olive oil
- 1 teaspoon cinnamon (optional)
- Salt
- Pepper

Directions:

1. Cut the sweet potatoes crosswise into thin slices.
2. Put the sweet potatoes in a bowl of cold water for 30 minutes.
3. Drain the sweet potatoes. Dry the slices thoroughly with paper towels or napkins.
4. Place the sweet potatoes in another large bowl. Drizzle with the olive oil and sprinkle with the cinnamon, if using, and salt and pepper to taste. Toss to coat thoroughly.
5. Place the sweet potato slices in the air fryer. You may need to cook the chips in two batches—Cook the potatoes for 10 minutes.
6. Open and shake the basket. Cook the chips for an additional 10 minutes.
7. Cool before serving.

Nutrition:

Calories: 94 | Fat: 2g | Cholesterol: 0mg | Sodium: 58mg

Carbohydrates: 20g | Fiber: 2g | Protein: 1g

103. Low-Carb Cheese-Stuffed Jalapeño Poppers

Preparation time: 15 minutes

Cooking time: 5 minutes

Servings: 5

Ingredients:

- 10 jalapeño peppers
- 6 ounces cream cheese
- ¼ cup shredded Cheddar cheese
- 2 tablespoons panko bread crumbs
- Cooking oil

Directions:

1. Halve the jalapeños lengthwise. Remove the seeds and the white membrane.
2. Microwave the cream cheese within 15 seconds to soften.
3. Remove the bowl from the microwave, then put the Cheddar cheese. Mix well.
4. Stuff each of the jalapeño halves with the cheese mixture, then sprinkle the panko bread crumbs on top of each popper.
5. Place the poppers in the air fryer, spray cooking oil—Cook for 5 minutes.
6. Cool before serving.

Nutrition:

Calories: 156 | Fat: 14g | Cholesterol: 43mg

Sodium: 874mg | Carbohydrates: 3g | Fiber: 1g|Protein: 4g

104. Vidalia Onion Blossom

Preparation time: 55 minutes

Cooking time: 25 minutes

Servings: 4

Ingredients:

- 1 large Vidalia onion
- 1½ cups all-purpose flour
- 1 teaspoon garlic powder
- 1 teaspoon paprika
- Salt
- Pepper

- 2 eggs
- 1 cup milk
- Cooking oil

Directions:

1. Cut off the pointy stem end of the onion. Leave the root end intact. Peel the onion and place it cut-side down.
2. Starts with ½ inch from the root end, then cut down to make 4 spaced cuts. In each part, make 3 additional cuts. You should make 16 cuts in the onion.
3. Flip the onion over and fluff out the "petals."
4. Place the flour in a large bowl and season it with the garlic powder, paprika, and salt and pepper to taste.
5. In another large bowl, whisk the eggs. Add the milk and stir. It will form a batter.
6. Put the onion with the flour mixture in the bowl. Use a large spoon to cover the onion petals in flour.
7. Transfer the onion to the batter. Use a spoon or basting brush to cover the onion altogether.
8. Return the onion to the flour mixture. Cover completely.
9. Wrap the battered onion in foil and place in the freezer for 45 minutes.
10. Spatter the air fryer basket using cooking oil. Unwrap the foil covering and place the onion in the air fryer basket—Cook for 10 minutes.
11. Open and spray the onion with cooking oil. If areas of the onion are still white from the flour, focus the spray on these areas.
12. Cook again within 10 to 15 minutes, or until crisp.

Nutrition:

Calories: 253 | Fat: 4g | Cholesterol: 87mg| Sodium: 101mg Carbohydrates: 43g | Fiber: 2g | Protein: 10g

105. Spiced Nuts

Preparation time: 5 minutes
Cooking time: 15 minutes
Servings: 4

Ingredients:

- ½ teaspoon cinnamon
- ½ teaspoon stevia
- Pepper
- 1 cup nuts (walnuts, pecans, and almonds work well)
- 1 egg white
- Cooking oil

Directions:

1. In a small bowl, combine the cinnamon, stevia, and pepper to taste.
2. Place the nuts in another bowl with the egg white. Add the spices to the nuts.
3. Spray the basket using cooking oil.
4. Place the nuts in the air fryer, then spray it using cooking oil—Cook for 10 minutes.
5. Shake the basket, then cook for an additional 3 to 4 minutes.
6. Serve warm.

Nutrition:

Calories: 210 | Fat: 18g | Cholesterol: 0mg | Sodium: 237mg Carbohydrates: 9g | Fiber: 3g | Protein: 7g

106. Pigs in a Blanket

Preparation time: 15 minutes
Cooking time: 20 minutes
Servings: 1

Ingredients:

- 1 (8-ounce) can of crescent rolls or croissant biscuit rolls
- 16 cocktail franks or mini smoked hot dogs
- Cooking oil

Directions:

1. Divide the crescent roll dough into 8 triangles and place them on a flat work surface. Cut each triangle in half to make 16 triangles.
2. Dry the franks with a paper towel. Place 1 frank on the bottom of a triangle. It should be the widest part of the dough. Roll up the dough. Repeat for the remaining franks and triangles.
3. Spray your air fryer basket using cooking oil.
4. Place 8 pigs in a blanket in the air fryer. It is okay to stack them, but do not overcrowd the basket. Spray with cooking oil—Cook for 8 minutes.
5. Remove the cooked pigs in a blanket from the air fryer, then repeat step 4 for the remaining 8 pigs in a blanket. Cool before serving.

Nutrition:

Calories: 75 | Fat: 5g | Cholesterol: 5mg | Sodium: 170mg Carbohydrates: 6g | Fiber: 0g | Protein: 2g

107. Crunchy Pork Egg Rolls

Preparation time: 15 minutes
Cooking time: 15 minutes
Servings: 1

Ingredients:

- Cooking oil
- 2 garlic cloves, minced
- 1 teaspoon sesame oil
- ¼ cup of soy sauce
- 2 teaspoons grated fresh ginger
- 12 ounces ground pork

- ½ cabbage, shredded (2 cups)
- 4 scallions, green parts (white parts optional), chopped
- 24 egg roll wrappers

Directions:

1. Spray a skillet using cooking oil, then place over medium-high heat. Add the garlic. Cook for 1 minute, until fragrant.
2. Add the ground pork to the skillet. Using a spoon, break the pork into smaller chunks.
3. Mix the sesame oil, soy sauce, and ginger in a small bowl.
4. Add the sauce to the skillet. Stir to combine. Continue cooking for 5 minutes, until the pork is browned.
5. When the pork has browned, add the cabbage and scallions. Mix well.
6. Transfer the pork mixture to a large bowl.
7. Lay the egg roll wrappers on a flat surface. Dip a basting brush in water and glaze each of the egg roll wrappers along the edges with the wet brush.
8. Stack 2 egg roll wrappers. Scoop 1 to 2 tablespoons of the pork mixture onto the center.
9. Roll one long side of the wrappers up over the filling. Press firmly on the area with the filling, tucking it in lightly to secure it in place. Fold in the left and right sides.
10. Continue rolling to close. Use the basting brush to wet the seam and seal the egg roll.
11. Place the egg rolls in the basket of the air fryer. It is okay to stack them. Then, spray cooking oil—Cook for 8 minutes.
12. Flip the egg rolls. Cook for an additional 4 minutes. Cool before serving.

Nutrition:

Calories: 244 | Fat: 4g | Cholesterol: 27mg
Sodium: 683mg | Carbohydrates: 39g
Fiber: 2g | Protein: 12g

108. Spinach and Artichoke Dip Wontons

Preparation time: 15 minutes
Cooking time: 40 minutes
Servings: 10

Ingredients:

- 6 ounces cream cheese
- ¼ cup sour cream
- ¼ cup shredded Parmesan cheese
- ¼ cup shredded mozzarella cheese
- 5 ounces frozen chopped spinach
- 6 ounces marinated artichoke hearts, drained
- 2 garlic cloves, chopped
- Salt
- Pepper
- 20 wonton wrappers
- Cooking oil

Directions:

1. Microwave the cream cheese within 20 seconds to soften.
2. Mix the cream cheese, sour cream, Parmesan, mozzarella, spinach, artichoke hearts, garlic, salt, and pepper to taste in a medium bowl. Stir to mix well.
3. Arrange the wonton wrappers on your cutting board.
4. Scoop 1½ teaspoons of the artichoke mixture onto each wrapper. Be careful not to overfill.
5. Fold each wrapper diagonally to form a triangle. Bring the two bottom corners up toward each other. Do not close the wrapper yet. Bring up the two open sides and push out any air. Squeeze the open edges together to seal.
6. Place the wontons in the air fryer basket and cook in batches or stack. Spray the wontons with cooking oil—Cook for 10 minutes.
7. Remove the basket and flip the wontons. Return it and cook for an additional 5 to 8 minutes, until the wontons have reached your desired level of golden-brown crispiness.
8. Cool before serving.

Nutrition:

Calories: 166 | Fat: 7g | Cholesterol: 14mg |Sodium: 345mg
Carbohydrates: 21g | Fiber: 1g | Protein: 5g

109. Loaded Disco Fries

Preparation time: 15 minutes
Cooking time: 25 minutes
Servings: 5

Ingredients:

- 1 (28-ounce) bag frozen steak fries
- Cooking oil
- Salt
- Pepper
- ½ cup beef gravy
- 1 cup shredded mozzarella cheese
- 2 scallions, green parts only, chopped

Directions:

1. Place the frozen steak fries in the air fryer. Cook for 10 minutes.
2. Open and shake, then spray the fries with cooking oil. Sprinkle with salt and pepper to taste—Cook for an additional 8 minutes.
3. Pour the beef gravy into a medium, microwave-safe bowl—microwave for 30 seconds, or until the gravy is warm.
4. Sprinkle the fries with the cheese—Cook for an additional 2 minutes until the cheese is melted.
5. Transfer the fries to a serving dish. Drizzle the fries with gravy and sprinkle the scallions on top for a green garnish. Serve.

Nutrition:

Calories: 291 | Fat: 11g | Cholesterol: 18mg

Sodium: 774mg | Carbohydrates: 39g

Fiber: 3g | Protein: 1g

---

110. Fried Olives

Preparation time: 15 minutes

Cooking time: 10 minutes

Servings: 4

Ingredients:

- 1 (5½-ounce) jar pitted green olives
- ½ cup all-purpose flour
- Salt
- Pepper
- ½ cup bread crumbs
- 1 egg
- Cooking oil

Directions:

1. Pat dry using a paper cloth the olives from the jar.
2. Mix the flour with salt and pepper to taste in a small bowl. Place the bread crumbs in another small bowl. In a third small bowl, beat the egg.
3. Grease the basket using cooking oil.
4. Dip the olives in the flour, then the egg, and then the bread crumbs.
5. Place the breaded olives in the air fryer. It is okay to stack them. Spray the olives with cooking oil—Cook for 6 minutes.
6. Flip the olives. Cook again within 2 minutes, or until brown and crisp.
7. Cool before serving.

Nutrition:

Calories: 165 | Fat: 5g | Cholesterol: 41mg |Sodium: 828mg

Carbohydrates: 24g | Fiber: 4g | Protein: 5g

LUNCH

111. Garlic Duck Breasts

Preparation Time: 1 day
Cooking Time: 20 minutes
Servings: 2

Ingredients:

- garlic cloves, minced
- Salt and black pepper to the taste
- ¼ cup soy sauce
- 1 tablespoon butter
- tarragon springs
- duck breasts
- ¼ cup sherry wine
- 1 cup white wine

Directions:

1. Combine the duck breasts with white wine, soy sauce, garlic, tarragon, salt and pepper in a bowl, mix well and store in the refrigerator for 1 day.
2. Place the duck breasts in the preheated hot air fryer (350 degrees) and fry for 10 minutes, turning halfway through.
3. In the meantime, transfer the marinade to a pan, heat over medium heat, adding the butter and sherry, stir, bring to a simmer, and cook for 5 minutes, then remove from heat.
4. Arrange the duck breasts on plates, pour the sauce over them and serve. Enjoy your meal!

Nutrition:

Calories 475 | Fat 12 | Carbs 10 | Protein 48

112. Healthy Chicken Thighs

Preparation Time: 10 minutes
Cooking Time: 30 minutes
Servings: 4

Ingredients:

- 1 cup chicken stock
- Salt and black pepper to the taste
- 1 tablespoon olive oil
- 1 tablespoon chives, chopped
- 2 radishes, halved
- 1 teaspoon sugar
- 3 carrots cut into thin sticks
- 4 chicken things, bone-in

Directions:

1. Heat a saucepan that will fit in your deep fryer over medium heat, add stock, carrots, sugar and radishes
2. Carefully mix, lower the heat to medium, partially cover and allow to simmer for 20 minutes
3. Coat the chicken with olive oil, season with salt and pepper, place in your deep fryer and cook at 350 degrees F for 4 minutes.
4. Place the chicken in the radish mixture, stir through, place everything in the deep fryer, cook for a further 4 minutes, place on plates and serve. Enjoy your meal!

Nutrition:

Calories 237 | Fat 10 | Carbs 19 | Protein 29

113. Chili Sauce Chicken

Preparation Time: 10 minutes
Cooking Time: 20 minutes
Servings: 6

Ingredients:

- 1 teaspoon chili powder
- 1 teaspoon sweet paprika
- ¼ cup honey
- 6 chicken breasts, skinless and boneless
- 1 teaspoon garlic powder
- chili sauce to taste
- Salt and black pepper to the taste

- ½ teaspoon liquid smoke
- ketchup (optional)
- 1 teaspoon mustard powder
- 1 cup pear jelly

Directions:

1. Salt and pepper chicken breasts, place in preheated hot air fryer and cook at 350 degrees F for 10 minutes.
2. In the meantime, warm a pan with the chilli sauce over medium heat, add the ketchup, pear jelly, honey, liquid smoke, chilli powder, mustard powder, sweet paprika powder, salt, pepper and the garlic powder, mix, heat to a simmer and let cook for 10 minutes.
3. Put in the roasted chicken breasts, toss well, spread on plates and serve. Enjoy your meal!

Nutrition:

Calories 473 | Fat 13 | Carbs 39 | Protein 33

114. Exotic Duck Breasts

Preparation Time: 1 hour
Cooking Time: 20 minutes
Servings: 4

Ingredients:

- 2 garlic cloves, minced
- Salt and black pepper to taste
- 2 tablespoons olive oil
- 2 tablespoons lemon juice
- 1 and ½ tablespoons lemongrass, chopped
- 4 duck breasts
  For the mango mix:
- 1 and ½ tablespoon lemon juice
- 1 teaspoon ginger, grated
- 1 mango, peeled and chopped
- 1 red onion, chopped
- ¾ teaspoon sugar
- 1 tablespoon sweet chili sauce
- 1 tablespoon coriander, chopped

Directions:

1. Combine duck breasts with salt, pepper, lemongrass, 3 tablespoons lemon juice, olive oil and garlic in a bowl, mix well, refrigerate for 1 hour
2. Place in deep fryer and cook at 360 degrees F for 10 minutes, turning once.
3. In the meantime, combine mango with coriander, onion, chilli sauce, lemon juice, ginger and sugar in a bowl and stir well.
4. Place the duck on plates, arrange the mango mixture on the side and serve. Enjoy!

Nutrition:

Calories 465 | Fat 11 | Carbs 29 | Protein 38

115. Peachy Chicken

Preparation Time: 10 minutes
Cooking Time: 30 minutes
Servings: 6

Ingredients:

- Salt and black pepper to the taste
- peaches, halved
- 1/3 cup honey
- ¼ cup olive oil
- 1 whole chicken, cut into medium pieces
- ¾ cup water

Directions:

1. Place water in a saucepan, heat to a simmer over medium heat, add honey, whisk well and set aside.
2. Coat chicken pieces with oil, salt and pepper, place in the basket of the deep fryer and cook at 350 degrees F for 10 minutes.
3. Coat chicken with a little honey mixture, cook for another 6 minutes, turn over, brush again with honey mixture and cook for a further 7 minutes. Place chicken pieces on plates and leave to keep warm.
4. Brush the peaches with the rest of the honey marinade, put them in the fryer and cook for 3 minutes alongside the chicken pieces on plates and serve. Enjoy your meal!

Nutrition:

Calories 430 | Fat 14 | Carbs 15 | Protein 20

116. Tea Flavoured Chicken

Preparation Time: 10 minutes
Cooking Time: 30 minutes
Servings: 6

Ingredients:

- black tea bags
- 1 tablespoon olive oil
- chicken legs
- 1 onion, chopped
- 1 cup hot water
- ½ cup apricot preserves
- Salt and black pepper to the taste
- ½ cup pineapple preserves
- 1 tablespoon soy sauce
- ¼ teaspoon red pepper flakes

Directions:

1. Pour hot water into a bowl, adding tea bags, cover and leave to brew for 10 minutes, discarding the bags at the end and transferring the tea to another bowl.
2. Pour in soy sauce, red pepper flakes, apricot and pineapple jam, stir well and remove from heat.

3. Add salt and pepper to chicken, rub with oil, place in hot air fryer and cook at 350 degrees F for 5 minutes.
4. Place onion in the bottom of a baking dish that fits in the hot air fryer, add chicken pieces, pour the tea glaze over, place in the hot air fryer and cook at 320 degrees F for 25 minutes. Enjoy your meal!

Nutrition:

Calories 298l Fat 14 I Carbs 14 I Protein 30

117. Healthy Ratatouille

Preparation Time: 10 minutes

Cooking Time: 20 minutes

Servings: 4

Ingredients:

- 1 red bell pepper, chopped
- 1 teaspoon olive oil
- 1 baby eggplant, peeled and chopped
- garlic cloves, sliced
- 1 small onion, chopped
- Roma tomatoes, seeded and chopped
- 1 yellow bell pepper, chopped
- 1 teaspoon Italian seasoning

Directions:

1. Mix carefully the tomatoes, garlic, aubergine, red and yellow peppers, onion, Italian spices and olive oil in a medium metal bowl.
2. Put the bowl in the hot air fryer. Fry the vegetables for 12 to 16 minutes, mixing once, until they are tender. Serve warm or cold.

Nutrition:

Calories 69 I Fat 2g I Protein 2g I Carbs 11g

118. Veggy Egg Rolls

Preparation Time: 15 minutes

Cooking Time: 10 minutes

Servings: 4

Ingredients:

- scallions, white and green parts, chopped
- egg roll wrappers (see Tip)
- ½ cup chopped red bell pepper
- 1 tablespoon cornstarch
- ½ cup chopped yellow summer squash
- 1 egg, beaten
- ⅓ cup grated carrot
- 1 teaspoon low-sodium soy sauce

Directions:

1. Combine the yellow pumpkin, carrot, red pepper, spring onions and soy sauce in a medium bowl.
2. Place the spring roll wrappers on a work surface. Put about 3 tablespoons of the vegetable mixture on each.
3. Whisk the cornflour and egg thoroughly in a small bowl. Coat the edges of each wrap with a little of the egg mixture.
4. Open the wraps and fold the sides over to contain the filling. Coat the outside of each spring roll with the egg mixture.
5. Air fry them for 7 to 10 minutes until they are golden brown and crispy and serve immediately.

Nutrition:

Calories 130 I Fat 2g I Protein 6g I Carbs 23g

119. Red Lentils English Muffins

Preparation Time: 15 minutes

Cooking Time: 10 minutes

Servings: 4

Ingredients:

- ⅓ cup chopped mushrooms
- scallions, white and green parts, sliced
- 1 cup shredded carrot
- slices low-sodium low-fat Swiss cheese, halved
- low-sodium whole-wheat English muffins split
- ⅓ cup nonfat Greek yogurt
- tablespoons low-sodium stone-ground mustard
- 1 (6-ounce) red lentils

Directions:

1. Lay the English muffin halves in the basket of the hot air fryer. Fry them for 3 to 4 minutes or until they are crispy. Take them out of the basket and set aside.
2. In a medium-sized bowl, combine the red lentils, carrots, mushrooms, spring onions, yoghurt and mustard thoroughly.
3. Cover each half of the muffins with a quarter of the tuna mixture and half a slice of Swiss cheese.
4. Fry the muffins in the air fryer for 4 to 7 minutes or the tuna mixture is hot and the cheese melts and starts to turn brown. Serve immediately.

Nutrition:

Calories 191 I Fat 4g I Protein 23g I Carbs 16g

120. Italian Flag English Muffin

Preparation Time: 10 minutes

Cooking Time: 5 minutes

Servings: 4

Ingredients:

- 1 ripe tomato, cut into 4 slices
- fresh basil leaves

- ½ ripe avocados, peeled, pitted, and sliced lengthwise (see Tip)
- 2 fresh baby spinach leaves
- 1 tablespoon crumbled fat-free low-sodium feta cheese, divided (you can opt for a vegan cheese)
- 2 low-sodium whole-wheat English muffins split
- 1½ tablespoons nonfat Greek yogurt

Directions:
1. Place the English muffin halves in the hot air fryer. Allow them to toast for 2 minutes or until lightly golden brown. Remove them to a work surface.
2. Brush each muffin half with 1½ teaspoons of yoghurt.
3. Top for each muffin half with 2 spinach leaves, 1 tomato slice, a quarter of the avocado and 2 basil leaves.
4. Spread each with 1 tablespoon of feta cheese. Top with the feta cheese.
5. Place the sandwiches in the hot air fryer and toast for 3 to 4 minutes, or until the cheese is soft and the sandwich is hot. Serve immediately.

Nutrition:
Calories 110 | Fat 3g | Protein 8g | Carbs 13g

121. Veggy Pita

Preparation Time: 10 minutes
Cooking Time: 20 minutes
Servings: 4

Ingredients:
- 1 teaspoon olive oil
- low-sodium whole-wheat pita breads, halved crosswise
- ½ cup diced red onion
- 1 baby eggplant peeled and chopped (see Tip)
- ½ cup shredded carrot
- ½ teaspoon dried tarragon
- 1 red bell pepper, sliced
- ⅓ cup low-fat Greek yogurt

Directions:
1. Mix together the aubergine, red pepper, red onion, carrot and olive oil in a 6 x 2-inch pan. Put the vegetable mixture in the basket of the air fryer and fry for 7 to 9 minutes, stirring once, until the vegetables are tender. Pat dry if necessary.
2. Combine the yoghurt and tarragon thoroughly in a small bowl until well mixed.
3. Mix the yoghurt mixture into the vegetables. Pour a quarter of this mixture into each pita pocket.
4. Put the sandwiches in the hot air fryer and fry for 2 to 3 minutes or until the bread is toasted. Serve immediately.

Nutrition:
Calories 176 | Fat 4g | Protein 7g | Carbs 27g

122. Vegan Falafel

Preparation Time: 10 minutes
Cooking Time: 20 minutes
Servings: 4

Ingredients:
- 2 garlic cloves, minced
- 1 tablespoon olive oil
- ⅓ cup minced red onion
- ¼ teaspoon cayenne pepper
- ⅓ cup whole-wheat pastry flour
- tablespoons minced fresh cilantro
- ½ teaspoon ground cumin
- 1 (16-ounce) can no-salt-added chickpeas rinsed and Dry outed

Directions:
1. Mash the chickpeas in a medium bowl with a potato masher until they are mostly smooth.
2. Mix in the pastry flour, red onion, garlic, cilantro, olive oil, cumin and cayenne pepper until everything is well combined.
3. Shape the chickpea mixture into 12 balls. Air fry the falafel balls in batches for 11 to 13 minutes until the falafel are firm and lightly golden brown. Serve.

Nutrition:
Calories 172 | Fat 5g | Protein 7g | Carbs 25g

123. Stuffed Tomatoes

Preparation Time: 5 minutes
Cooking Time: 20 minutes
Servings: 4

Ingredients:
- 1 garlic clove, minced
- 1 cups fresh baby spinach
- ½ cup grated carrot
- 4 medium beefsteak tomatoes, rinsed and patted dry
- ½ teaspoon dried basil
- ¼ cup crumbled low-sodium feta cheese
- 1 medium onion, chopped
- teaspoons olive oil

Directions:
1. Slice off about 1.5 cm of the top of each tomato. Hollow them out carefully (see tip), leaving a wall about 1.5 cm thick. Allow the tomatoes to dry, top side down, on paper towels while you prepare the filling.
2. Mix the onion, carrot, garlic and olive oil in a 6 x 2-inch pan. Fry for 4 to 6 minutes, or until the vegetables are crisp-tender.
3. Add the spinach, feta cheese and basil.

4. Stuff each tomato with a quarter of the vegetable mixture. Fry the tomatoes in the deep fryer basket for 12 to 14 minutes or until hot and tender.
5. Serve immediately.

Nutrition:

Calories 79 | Fat 3g | Protein 3g | Carbs 9g

124. Tasty Small Potatoes

Preparation Time: 5 minutes

Cooking Time: 25 minutes

Servings: 2

Ingredients:

- ½ teaspoon dried basil
- 1 tablespoon low-sodium stone-ground mustard (see Tip)
- 2 tablespoons chopped fresh chives
- 2 scallions, white and green parts, chopped
- 1 teaspoon olive oil
- ½ cup low-fat Greek yogurt
- 24 small new potatoes, or creamer potatoes, rinsed, scrubbed, and patted dry
- Roma tomatoes, seeded and chopped (as needed to top up)

Directions:

1. Swirl the potatoes in a large bowl with the olive oil. Take them over to the basket of the deep fryer.
2. Fry the potatoes for 20 to 25 minutes, turning the basket once, until the potatoes are crispy on the outside and soft on the inside. In the meantime, mix the yoghurt, mustard and basil in a small bowl.
3. Put the potatoes on a serving plate and carefully mash each one with the bottom of a drinking glass. Top the potatoes with the yoghurt mixture.
4. Top them with the tomatoes, spring onions and chives. Serve immediately.

Nutrition:

Calories 100 | Fat 2g | Protein 5g | Carbs 19g

125. Vegetables Quiche

Preparation Time: 5 minutes

Cooking Time: 20 minutes

Servings: 3

Ingredients:

- ½ cup chopped mushrooms
- 1 egg
- ⅓ cup minced red onion
- 1 tablespoon low-sodium mustard
- 1 red bell pepper, chopped
- Nonstick cooking spray with flour, for greasing the pan
- 1 slice low-sodium low-fat Swiss cheese, torn into small pieces
- 1 cup frozen chopped spinach, thawed and Dry outed
- egg whites

Directions:

1. Whisk the egg whites and egg in a medium bowl until blended.
2. Add the spinach, red pepper, mushrooms, onion and mustard.
3. Stir in the Swiss cheese.
4. Mist a 6 x 2-inch pan with nonstick cooking spray.
5. Add the egg mixture to the prepared pan.
6. Cook for 18 to 22 minutes or until the egg mixture is puffed, lightly golden brown and set. Leave to cool for 5 minutes before serving.

Nutrition:

Calories 76 | Fat 3g | Protein 8g | Carbs 4g

125. Healthy Beans Pizza

Preparation Time: 10 minutes

Cooking Time: 20 minutes

Servings: 4

Ingredients:

- 1 cup chopped kale
- ½ teaspoon dried thyme
- 2 cups chopped fresh baby spinach
- 1 tablespoon olive oil, divided
- 1 piece low-sodium string cheese, torn into pieces
- 1 cup canned no-salt-added cannellini beans, rinsed and Dry outed (see Tip)
- ¾ cup whole-wheat pastry flour
- ½ teaspoon low-sodium baking powder

Directions:

1. Combine the baking flour and baking powder in a small bowl until well mixed.
2. Pour in ¼ cup of water and 2 teaspoons of olive oil. Blend until a dough forms.
3. Punch down or roll the dough into a 7-inch round on a floured surface. Put the dough aside while you prepare the greens: Combine the kale, spinach and remaining teaspoon of olive oil in a 6 x 2-inch skillet. Air roast for 3 to 5 minutes until the greens have wilted. Drain well.
4. Place the pizza dough in the basket of the air fryer. Cover with the greens, cannellini beans, thyme and cheese spread. Fry for 11 to 14 minutes or until the crust is golden brown and the cheese is melted. To serve, cut into quarters.

Nutrition:

Calories 175 | Fat 5g | Protein 9g | Carbs 24g

127. Pork Bites with Yogurt Sauce

Preparation Time: 10 minutes

Cooking Time: 30 minutes

Servings: 4

Ingredients:

- 1 teaspoon turmeric powder
- 3 tablespoons avocado oil
- 2 pounds pork chops
- Salt and black pepper to the taste
- 1 cup yogurt
- 1 tablespoon oregano, chopped
- 2 garlic cloves, minced

Directions:

1. Combine the pork chops in the pan of the air fryer with the yoghurt and the other ingredients, toss and cook at 400 degrees F for 30 minutes.
2. Spread the mixture on plates and serve.

Nutrition:

Calories 301 | Fat 7 | Carbs 19 | Protein 22

128. Baby Spinach Nutty Lamb

Preparation Time: 10 minutes

Cooking Time: 20 minutes

Servings: 4

Ingredients:

- ½ cup beef stock
- 3 tablespoons macadamia nuts, peeled
- 2 garlic cloves, minced
- 1 cup baby spinach
- 1 tablespoon oregano, chopped
- Salt and black pepper to the taste
- 2 pounds lamb stew meat, cubed

Directions:

1. Combine the lamb with the nuts and the other ingredients in the pan of the air fryer,
2. Fry at 380 degrees F for 20 minutes,
3. Spread on plates and serve.

Nutrition:

Calories 280 | Fat 12 | Carbs 20 | Protein 19

129. Creamy Beef Strips

Preparation Time: 10 minutes

Cooking Time: 20 minutes

Servings: 4

Ingredients:

- 1 cup heavy cream
- 2 tablespoons olive oil
- 2 cucumbers, sliced
- Salt and black pepper to the taste
- 1 pound beef stew meat, cut into strips
- 2 eggplants, cubed
- 2 garlic cloves, minced

Directions:

1. In a casserole dish that will fit in your deep fryer, combine the beef with the aubergines and other ingredients,.
2. Stir through, insert the pan into the deep fryer and cook at 400 degrees F for 20 minutes.
3. Spread everything into bowls and serve.

Nutrition:

Calories 283 | Fat 11 | Carbs 22 | Protein 14

130. Mustard Lamb Bites

Preparation Time: 15 minutes

Cooking Time: 30 minutes

Servings: 4

Ingredients:

- ½ teaspoon olive oil
- 1 teaspoon dried tarragon
- 1 tablespoon fresh lemon juice
- Salt and black pepper, to taste
- 4-ounceslamb loin chops
- 3 tablespoons Dijon mustard

Directions:

1. Heat the hot air fryer to 390 degrees F and lubricate a hot air fryer basket.
2. Combine the mustard, lemon juice, oil, tarragon, salt and black pepper in a large bowl.
3. Brush the chops generously with the mustard mixture and place them in the basket of the deep fryer.
4. Fry for approximately 15 minutes, turning once in between, and serve hot.

Nutrition:

Calories 433, | Fat 17.6g, | Carbs 0.6g, | Protein 64.1g,

131. Aromatic Lamb Bites

Preparation Time: 10 minutes

Cooking Time: 10 minutes

Servings: 2

Ingredients:

- 1 teaspoon dried rosemary
- 1 teaspoon dried thyme
- 1 teaspoon dried oregano
- 1 tablespoon olive oil

- ½ teaspoon ground cumin
- ½ teaspoon ground coriander
- Salt and black pepper, to taste
- 4: 4-ounceslamb chops
- 1 tablespoon fresh lemon juice

Directions:
1. Heat the hot air fryer to 390 degrees F and grease a hot air fryer basket.
2. Combine the lemon juice, oil, herbs and spices in a large bowl.
3. Brush the chops generously with the herb mixture and place in the fridge for approximately 1 hour to marinate.
4. Place the chops in the basket of the deep fryer and cook for around 7 minutes, turning once in between.
5. Arrange the lamb chops on a platter and serve hot.

Nutrition:

Calories 491 | Fat 24g | Carbs 1.6g | Protein 64g

132. Za'atar Lamb Loin Bites

Preparation Time: 10 minutes
Cooking Time: 30 minutes
Servings: 4

Ingredients:
- 2 garlic cloves, crushed
- 1 teaspoon olive oil
- 1 tablespoon Za'ataro
- 1 tablespoon fresh lemon juice
- Salt and black pepper, to taste
- 8: 3½-ounces bone-in lamb loin chops, trimmed

Directions:
1. Heat the hot air fryer to 400 degrees F and grease a hot air fryer basket.
2. Combine the garlic, lemon juice, oil, za'atar, salt and black pepper in a large bowl.
3. Generously coat the chops with the herb mixture and place the chops in the fryer basket.
4. Fry for approx. 15 minutes, turning twice in between, and arrange the lamb chops to serve hot.

Nutrition:

Calories 433 | Fat 17.6g | Carbs 0.6g | Protein 64.1g

133. Honey Minty Lamb

Preparation Time: 15 minutes
Cooking Time: 15 minutes
Servings: 4

Ingredients:
- 1 garlic clove
- ½ tablespoon honey
- 1 ½ poundsrack of lamb
- Salt and black pepper, to taste
- ¼ cup extra-virgin olive oil
- ½ bunch fresh mint

Directions:
1. Heat the hot air fryer to 200 degrees and oil a hot air fryer basket.
2. Add the mint, garlic, oil, honey, salt and black pepper to a blender and pulse until the pesto is smooth.
3. Spread this pesto on both sides of the rack of lamb and place it in the frying basket.
4. Fry the rack of lamb for around 15 minutes and cut into individual chops to serve.

Nutrition:

Calories 406 | Fat 27.7g | Carbs 2.9g | Protein 34.9g

134. Lamb & Brussels Sprout

Preparation Time: 20 minutes
Cooking Time: 1 hour 30 minutes
Servings: 4

Ingredients:
- 1½ pounds Brussels sprouts, trimmed
- 1 garlic clove, minced
- 1 tablespoon fresh lemon thyme
- 2 tablespoons honey
- 2¼ pounds leg of lamb
- 2 tablespoons olive oil, divided
- Salt and ground black pepper, as required
- 1 tablespoon fresh rosemary, minced

Directions:
1. Heat the hot air fryer to 300 degrees F and grease a hot air fryer basket.
2. Use a sharp knife to make slits in the leg of lamb.
3. Combine 2 tablespoons of oil, herbs, garlic, salt and black pepper in a bowl.
4. Brush the leg of lamb generously over the oil mixture and place in the Airfryer basket.
5. Fry for about 75 minutes and set the airfryer to 390 degrees F.
6. Brush the Brussels sprouts evenly with the remaining oil and honey and place in the airfryer basket with the leg of lamb.
7. Fry for around 15 minutes and serve warm.

Nutrition:

Calories 449 | Fats 19.9g | Carbs 16.6g | Protein 51.7g

135. Garlic Cheesy Meatballs

Preparation Time: 15 minutes

Cooking Time: 15 minutes

Servings: 8

Ingredients:

- 5 tablespoons cheddar cheese, grated
- 2 teaspoons honey
- 2 teaspoons mustard
- 3 tablespoons fresh basil, chopped
- 2 teaspoons garlic paste
- Salt and black pepper, to taste
- 2 onions, chopped
- 1 pound ground beef

Directions:

1. Heat the hot air fryer to 3850 F and oil a hot air fryer basket.
2. Combine all the ingredients in a bowl until well mixed.
3. Carefully shape the mixture into equal sized balls and place the meatballs in the fryer basket.
4. Fry for around 15 minutes and serve warm.

Nutrition:

Calories 134 | Fat 4.4g | Carbs 4.6g | Protein 18.2g

136. Chili Beef

Preparation Time: 10 minutes

Cooking Time: 30 minutes

Servings: 4

Ingredients:

- 2 tablespoons chives, chopped
- Salt and black pepper to the taste
- ½ teaspoon chili powder
- ¼ cup beef stock
- 2 pounds beef stew meat, cubed
- 1 teaspoon nutmeg, ground
- 2 tablespoons avocado oil

Directions:

1. Mix the beef with the nutmeg and the other ingredients in a pan that will fit in your deep fryer, swirl the pan into the deep fryer and cook at 400 degrees F for 30 minutes.
2. Distribute the mixture into bowls and serve.

Nutrition:

Calories 280 | Fat 12 | Carbs 17 | Protein 14

137. Sage Daikon

Preparation Time: 10 minutes

Cooking Time: 10 minutes

Servings: 5

Ingredients:

- 1 tablespoon olive oil
- 1 teaspoon dried oregano
- 1 teaspoon salt
- 1-pound daikon
- ½ teaspoon sage

Directions:

1. Remove the skin from the daikon and dice it.
2. Dust the daikon cubes with sage, salt and dried oregano.
3. Blend well
4. Heat the hot air fryer to 360F.
5. Put the daikon cubes in the rack of the air fryer and sprinkle them with olive oil.
6. Fry the daikon for 6 minutes
7. Flip the daikon and continue cooking for another 4 minutes or until soft and golden brown.

Nutrition:

Calories 43 | Fat 2.8 | Carbs 3.9 | Protein 1.9

138. Parmesan Spinach

Preparation Time: 10 minutes

Cooking Time: 12 minutes

Servings: 4

Ingredients:

- 1 cup heavy cream
- 1 teaspoon paprika
- 1 cup chicken stock
- ½ teaspoon minced garlic
- 1 teaspoon ground black pepper
- ½ oz chive stems
- 1 teaspoon salt
- 1 oz. Parmesan, shredded
- 1 cup spinach
- ½ teaspoon chili flakes

Directions:

1. Heat the hot air fryer to 390F.
2. Roughly chop the spinach.
3. Put the spinach into the bowl of the deep fryer basket.
4. Then add the chicken stock and the cream.
5. Put in the salt, paprika, chilli flakes and ground black pepper.
6. Include the chives and chopped garlic.
7. Stir gently and cook for 10 minutes.
8. Puree with a hand blender. You should get the creamy consistency of a soup.
9. Dust the soup with the grated cheese and let it cook at 400 F for 2 minutes.
10. Serve hot.

Nutrition:

Calories 187 | Fat 16 | Carbs 4.4 | Protein 8.4

139. Parmesan Sticks

Preparation Time: 10 minutes
Cooking Time: 10 minutes
Servings: 3

Ingredients:

- 2 tablespoons almond flour
- ¼ teaspoon ground black pepper
- ½ cup heavy cream
- 1 oz. Parmesan
- 1 egg

Directions:

1. Break the egg into a bowl and whisk.
2. Include the heavy cream and the almond flour.
3. Dust the mixture with ground black pepper.
4. Carefully whisk or use a hand mixer.
5. Slice the cheese into thick, short sticks.
6. Drop the sticks into the heavy cream mixture.
7. Put the cheese sticks in freezer bags and freeze them.
8. Heat the deep fryer to 400F.
9. Put the cheese sticks in the grate of the deep fryer.
10. Fry for 8 minutes

Nutrition:

Calories 389 | Fat 29.5 | Carbs 5.5 | Protein 28.6

140. Buttery Snow Peas

Preparation Time: 10 minutes
Cooking Time: 5 minutes
Servings: 5

Ingredients:

- 1 teaspoon paprika
- ¼ teaspoon nutmeg
- 1-pound snow peas
- 1 teaspoon salt
- ½ cup heavy cream
- 1 teaspoon butter

Directions:

1. Heat the air fryer to 400F.
2. Carefully wash the sugar snap peas and place them in the basket of the air fryer.
3. Then dust the sugar snap peas with the butter, salt, paprika, nutmeg and cream.
4. Fry the sugar snap peas for 5 minutes.
5. Once the time is up: gently shake the sugar snap peas and transfer them to the serving plates.
6. Enjoy!

Nutrition:

Calories 98 | Fat 5.9 | Carbs 6.9 | Protein 3.5

141. Sesame Seed Okra

Preparation Time: 10 minutes
Cooking Time: 4 minutes
Servings: 4

Ingredients:

- ½ teaspoon salt
- 1 egg
- 2 oz. okra
- 1 tablespoon sesame oil
- 1 teaspoon sesame seed

Directions:

1. Rinse the okra and coarsely chop it.
2. Break the egg into a bowl and mix it.
3. Put the chopped okra into the beaten egg.
4. Dust with sesame seeds and salt.
5. Heat the hot air fryer to 400F.
6. Thoroughly mix the okra mixture.
7. Put the mixture in the basket of the deep fryer.
8. Sprinkle with olive oil.
9. Fry the okra for 4 minutes.
10. Give them a stir and serve.

Nutrition:

Calories 81 | Fat 5 | Carbs 6.1 | Protein 3

142. Chili Fennel Wedges

Preparation Time: 15 minutes
Cooking Time: 6 minutes
Servings: 4

Ingredients:

- 1 teaspoon olive oil
- 1 teaspoon dried oregano
- ½ teaspoon salt
- ½ teaspoon chili flakes
- 1 teaspoon stevia extract
- 1 teaspoon butter
- ½ teaspoon fresh thyme
- 14 oz. fennel

Directions:

1. Cut the fennel into wedges. Heat the butter until it melts. In a bowl, combine the butter, olive oil, dried oregano and chilli flakes.
2. Blend well.
3. Pour in the salt, fresh thyme and stevia extract. Whisk gently.

4. Coat the fennel wedges with the mixture. Heat the hot air fryer to 370F.
5. Put the fennel wedges on the rack of the deep fryer.
6. Fry the fennel wedges for 3 minutes on each side.

Nutrition:

Calories 41 | Fat 1.9 | Carbs 6.1 | Protein 1

---

143. Chili Bamboo Shoots

Preparation Time: 10 minutes

Cooking Time: 4 minutes

Servings: 2

Ingredients:

- ½ teaspoon chili flakes
- 2 tablespoons fish stock
- 2 oz. bamboo shoots
- 2 garlic cloves, sliced
- tablespoon chives
- ½ teaspoon salt
- 1 tablespoon olive oil

Directions:

1. Heat the air fryer to 400F. Slice the bamboo shoots into strips.
2. In the basket insert of the air fryer, combine the sliced garlic cloves, olive oil, chilli flakes, salt and fish stock. Cook for 1 minute.
3. Carefully stir the mixture. Pour in the bamboo strips and the chives.
4. Carefully stir the dish and cook for a further 3 minutes.
5. Before serving, stir again.

Nutrition:

Calories 100 | Fat 7.6 | Carbs 7 | Protein 3.7

---

144. Buttery Rosmary Mushrooms

Preparation Time: 10 minutes

Cooking Time: 10 minutes

Servings: 2

Ingredients:

- 1 teaspoon olive oil
- ¼ teaspoon ground nutmeg
- 1/3 teaspoon salt
- 1 cup white mushrooms
- ½ oz chive stems
- 1 teaspoon dried rosemary
- 1 tablespoon butter

Directions:

1. Heat the air fryer to 400F.
2. Add the olive oil and butter to the basket insert of the deep fryer.
3. Pour in the dried rosemary, salt and ground nutmeg.
4. Gently stir.
5. Chop the chives into cubes.
6. Put the diced chives into the deep fryer basket.
7. Fry for 5 minutes.
8. In the meantime, cut the white mushrooms.
9. Put the mushrooms in the frying basket.
10. Mix and cook for another 5 minutes at the same temperature.
11. Give it a stir and serve.

Nutrition:

Calories 104 | Fat 8.4 | Carbs 6.8 | Protein 1.8

---

145. Spinach Quiche

Preparation Time: 15 minutes

Cooking Time: 10 minutes

Servings: 5

Ingredients:

- 1 tablespoon butter
- 1 teaspoon salt
- ¼ cup heavy cream
- ½ cup almond flour
- 1 teaspoon ground black pepper
- 1 teaspoon olive oil
- 1 oz. fennel, chopped
- 1 cup spinach
- 5 eggs

Directions:

1. In a large bowl, chop the spinach and combine with the chopped fennel.
2. Break the eggs into a separate bowl and whisk.
3. Mix the beaten eggs with the almond flour, butter, salt, heavy cream and ground black pepper.
4. Whisk to combine.
5. Heat the deep fryer to 360F.
6. Lubricate the basket insert of the deep fryer with the olive oil.
7. Add both mixtures.
8. Bake the quiche for 18 minutes.
9. Leave the quiche to cool.
10. Take it out of the deep fryer and cut it into portions.

Nutrition:

Calories 209 | Fat 16.1 | Carbs 7.4 | Protein 8.3

---

146. Aromatic Baby Potatoes

Preparation Time: 10 minutes

Cooking Time: 25 minutes

Servings: 6

Ingredients:

- Salt and black pepper to the taste
- 2 garlic cloves, minced
- 2 tablespoons lemon juice
- 2 tablespoons oregano, chopped
- 2 pounds baby potatoes
- 3 tablespoons olive oil
- 1 springs rosemary, chopped
- 2 tablespoons parsley, chopped
- 1 tablespoon lemon rind, grated

Directions:

1. Combine baby potatoes with oil, rosemary, parsley, oregano, salt, pepper, lemon zest, garlic and lemon juice in a bowl, toss.
2. Place potatoes in the basket of your deep fryer and cook at 356 degrees F for 25 minutes.
3. Place potatoes on plates and serve on the side.
4. Enjoy your meal!

Nutrition:

Calories 204 | Fat 4 | Carbs 17 | Protein 6

DINNER

147. Tumeric Indian Wrap

Preparation Time: 20 minutes

Cooking Time: 8 minutes

Servings: 4

Ingredients:

- ½ teaspoon sea salt
- ½ teaspoon turmeric
- 1 cup cooked garbanzo beans (canned are fine), rinsed and Dry out
- 2 large garlic cloves, minced or pressed
- 4 large flour tortillas, preferably whole grain or sprouted
- Cooking oil spray (sunflower, safflower, or refined coconut)
- 1½ tablespoons fresh lime juice
- 1½ teaspoons cumin powder
- ¼ cup minced red onion or scallion
- 1 teaspoon onion granules
- Cilantro Chutney
- ½ cup finely chopped cabbage
- 1 teaspoon coriander powder
- 2¾ cups diced potato, cooked until tender
- 2 teaspoons oil (coconut, sunflower, or safflower)
- ¼ teaspoon cayenne powder

Directions:

1. Prepare the coriander chutney and set aside.
2. In a large bowl, mash the potatoes well with a potato masher or large fork. Put in the oil, garlic, lime, cumin, onion, coriander, salt, turmeric and cayenne. Mix very well until everything is well blended. Put to one side.
3. Place the tortillas flat on the work surface. Divide the potato filling evenly in the centre of each tortilla. Add some of the chickpeas, cabbage and red onion to each tortilla, on top of the potatoes.
4. Drizzle the frying basket with oil and set aside. Gently fold the Indian wraps by folding the bottom of the tortillas up and over the filling, then folding in the sides and finally rolling the bottom up to essentially form a closed burrito.
5. Put the wraps seam side down in the frying basket. They can touch a little, but if they are too close together, you will need to cook them in batches. Deep-fry for 5 minutes. Drizzle with oil again, flip them over and cook for another 2 to 3 minutes until they are nicely browned and crispy. Serve garnished with the coriander chutney.

Nutrition:

Calories 288 | Fat 7g | Carbs 50g | Protein 9g

148. Lemony Lentils

Preparation Time: 10 minutes

Cooking Time: 30 minutes

Servings: 4

Ingredients:

- ½ cup kale, stems removed, thinly sliced
- 3 teaspoons nutritional yeast
- ¾ teaspoons freshly ground black pepper
- Cooking oil spray (coconut, sunflower, or safflower)
- 2 tablespoons fresh lemon juice
- 1 teaspoon lemon zest (see Ingredient Tip)
- 1 medium-size onion, peeled and cut into ¼-inch-thick rings
- Sea salt
- 1 teaspoon sea salt
- 1 cup red lentils
- 2 cups water
- 2 large garlic cloves, pressed or minced

Directions:

1. Bring the lentils and water to the boil in a medium saucepan over medium-high heat.
2. Lower the heat to low and let the lentils simmer, covered, for approximately 30 minutes (or until they have completely dissolved). Be sure to stir every 5 minutes or so while they are cooking (so the lentils don't stick to the bottom of the pot).
3. At the same time as the lentils are cooking, get the rest of the dish ready.

4. Sprinkle the basket of the deep fryer with oil and place the onion rings inside, keeping them as far apart as possible. Sprinkle them with the oil and sprinkle with a little salt. Deep-fry for 5 minutes.
5. Take out the frying basket, shake or stir, spray with oil again and fry for another 5 minutes.
6. (Note: You want all the onion slices to be crispy and well browned, so if some of the pieces start to do this, remove them from the frying basket onto a plate).
7. Take out the frying basket, spray the onions with oil again and fry for another 5 minutes or until all the pieces are crispy and browned.
8. In order to finish the lentils: Put the kale to the hot lentils and stir well, as the heat from the lentils will steam the thinly sliced greens.
9. Mix in the garlic, lemon juice, nutritional yeast, salt, zest and pepper.
10. Mix very well and then divide evenly into bowls. Garnish with the crispy onion rings and serve.

Nutrition:

Calories 220 | Fat 1g | Carbs 39g | Protein 15g

149. Delicious Daily Bean

Preparation Time: 5 minutes

Cooking Time: 10 minutes

Servings: 4

Ingredients:

- ½ teaspoon dried oregano
- ½ teaspoon cumin
- 2 tablespoons nutritional yeast
- 1 (15-ounce) can pinto beans, Dry out
- ¼ teaspoon sea salt
- Cooking oil spray (sunflower, safflower, or coconut)
- ⅛ Teaspoon freshly ground black pepper
- 2 large garlic cloves, pressed or minced
- ¼ cup tomato sauce

Directions:

1. Mix the beans, tomato sauce, nutritional yeast, garlic, oregano, cumin, salt and pepper together in a medium bowl until well blended.
2. Drizzle the round, 2 inch deep baking dish with oil and pour in the bean mixture. Cook them for 4 minutes. Remove them, stir well and bake for another 4 minutes or until the blend is thickened and heated through.
3. A small crust will probably form on the top and be lightly browned in some places. To serve hot. Cooled in an airtight container, this mixture will keep for up to a week.

Nutrition:

Calories 284 | Fat 4g | Carbs 47g | Protein 20g

150. Taco Salad

Preparation Time: 10 minutes

Cooking Time: 10 minutes

Servings: 4

Ingredients:

For The Sauce

- 2 large garlic cloves, peeled
- 1 teaspoon sea salt
- Zest of 1 large lime (1 teaspoon)
- ½ teaspoon ground chipotle powder
- 1½ tablespoons coconut sugar
- 1 (12.3-ounce) package of silken-firm tofu
- ¼ cup plus 1 tablespoon fresh lime juice

For The Salad

- 3 medium tomatoes, chopped
- ½ cup chopped cilantro
- 1 cup chopped red cabbage
- ¼ cup minced scallions
- Double batch of garlic lime tortilla chips
- 1 large head romaine lettuce, chopped
- 1 (15-ounce) can vegan refried beans (or whole pinto or black beans if you prefer)

Directions:

1. To prepare the sauce
2. Dry the tofu (pour off all liquid) and put it in a blender.
3. Mix in the lime juice and zest, coconut sugar, garlic, salt and chipotle powder. Process until everything is smooth. Set aside.
4. To prepare the salad
5. Distribute the salad evenly into three large bowls.
6. Heat the beans in a small pan over medium heat, stirring frequently, until hot (this should take less than a minute). Put them on top of the salad.
7. Add the cabbage, tomatoes, coriander and spring onions over the beans.
8. Generously drizzle with the creamy lime sauce and serve with a double portion of air-dried chips. Enjoy immediately.

Nutrition:

Calories 422 | Fat 7g | Carbs 71g | Protein 22g

151. BBQ Lime Nachos

Preparation Time: 30 minutes

Cooking Time: 20 minutes

Servings: 4

Ingredients:

- 1 tablespoon fresh lemon juice
- 1 teaspoon onion granules

- ¼ cup water
- Double batch garlic lime tortilla chips
- ½ cup minced red onion
- 2 tablespoons tamari or shoyu
- 1 (20-ounce) can jackfruit, dry out
- 3 medium-size tomatoes, chopped
- 2½ cups prepared cheesy sauce
- ⅓ cup prepared vegan bbq sauce
- ⅛ Teaspoon liquid smoke
- ⅛ Teaspoon cayenne powder
- ¾ cup chopped cilantro
- 1 jalapeño, seeds removed and thinly sliced (optional)
- 2 large garlic cloves, pressed or minced
- ¾ cup guacamole of your choice

Directions:

1. Put the jackfruit, BBQ sauce, water, tamari, lemon juice, garlic, onion granules, cayenne and liquid smoke in a large pan over high heat. Mix well and break up the jackfruit a little with a spatula.
2. Reduce the heat to low as soon as the mixture boils. Cook for about 20 minutes, stirring frequently (and breaking up the jackfruit as you stir), until all the liquid is absorbed. Take off the heat and set aside.
3. Arrange the nachos: Divide the chips among three plates and top evenly with the jackfruit mixture, warmed Cheesy Sauce, tomatoes, guacamole, cilantro, onion and jalapeños (if using). Eat immediately, because soggy chips are tragic.

Nutrition:

Calories 661 | Fat 15g | Carbs 124g | Protein 22g

152. Aromatic Garlic Eggplants

Preparation Time: 15 minutes
Cooking Time: 15 minutes
Servings: 2

Ingredients:

- ½ teaspoon garlic powder
- ½ teaspoon dried oregano, crushed
- ½ teaspoon dried marjoram, crushed
- Olive oil cooking spray
- 1 large eggplant, cubed
- ½ teaspoon dried thyme, crushed
- Salt and ground black pepper, as required

Directions:

1. Adjust the temperature of the hot air fryer to 390 degrees F. Oil a hot air fryer basket.
2. Combine herbs, garlic powder, salt and black pepper in a small bowl.
3. Evenly spray the aubergine cubes with cooking spray and then rub them with the herb mixture.
4. Put the aubergine cubes in a single layer in the prepared frying basket.
5. Fry for about 6 minutes.
6. Turn and spray the aubergine cubes with cooking spray.
7. Fry for a further 6 minutes
8. Turn over and spray the aubergine cubes with cooking spray again.
9. Fry for a further 2-3 minutes
10. Take out of the deep fryer and place the aubergine cubes on serving plates.
11. Serve hot.

Nutrition:

Calories 62 | Carbs 14.5g | Protein 2.4g | Fat 0.5g

153. Exotic Eggplant Recipe

Preparation Time: 15 minutes
Cooking Time: 12 minutes
Servings: 4

Ingredients:

- ½ teaspoon ground turmeric
- ½ teaspoon garlic powder
- ¾ tablespoon ground coriander
- 4 baby eggplants
- teaspoons olive oil, divided
- ¾ tablespoon dry mango powder
- Salt, to taste
- ½ teaspoon ground cumin

Directions:

1. Combine a teaspoon of oil and the spices in a small bowl.
2. Make 2 slits from the bottom of each aubergine, leaving the stems intact.
3. Using a small spoon, fill each slit in the aubergines with the spice mixture.
4. Now coat the outside of each aubergine with the remaining oil.
5. Adjust the temperature of the deep fryer to 369 degrees F. Oil a deep fryer basket.
6. Lay the aubergines in a single layer in the prepared fryer basket.
7. Deep fry for about 8-12 minutes.
8. Take out of the deep fryer and transfer the aubergines to serving plates.
9. Serve hot.

Nutrition:

Calories 317 | Carbs 65g | Protein 10.9g | Fat 6.7g

154. Tomato Filled Eggplants

Preparation Time: 15 minutes

Cooking Time: 25 minutes

Servings: 2

Ingredients:

- 2 tablespoons tomato salsa
- Salt and ground black pepper, as required
- 2 teaspoons olive oil, divided
- ½ tablespoon fresh parsley
- 10 cherry tomatoes, quartered
- 1 large eggplant
- 2 teaspoons fresh lemon juice, divided

Directions:

1. Adjust the temperature of the deep fryer to 390 degrees F. Grease a deep fryer basket.
2. Put the aubergine in the prepared fryer basket.
3. Fry for about 15 minutes.
4. Take out of the deep fryer and cut the aubergine in half lengthwise.
5. Sprinkle the aubergine halves evenly with a teaspoon of oil.
6. Now turn the temperature of the deep fryer to 355 degrees F. Oil the deep fryer basket.
7. Put the aubergines in the prepared fryer basket with the cut side facing up.
8. Fry for a further 10 minutes.
9. Take the aubergine out of the deep fryer and set aside for about 5 minutes.
10. Gently lift out the flesh, leaving about ¼-inch from the edge.
11. Sprinkle the aubergine halves with a teaspoon of lemon juice.
12. Put the aubergine flesh in a bowl.
13. Include the tomatoes, salsa, parsley, salt, black pepper, remaining oil and lemon juice and mix well.
14. Fill the aubergine halves with the salsa mixture and serve.

Nutrition:

Calories 192 | Carbs 33.8g | Protein 6.9g | Fat 6.1g

155. Sesame Bok Choy

Basic Recipe

Preparation Time: 10 minutes

Cooking Time: 6 minutes

Servings: 4

Ingredients:

- 1 teaspoon sesame seeds
- 1 teaspoon garlic powder
- bunches baby bok choy, bottoms removed and leaves separated
- Olive oil cooking spray

Directions:

1. Adjust the temperature of the air fryer to 325 degrees F.
2. Put the bok choi leaves in a single layer in the basket of the air fryer.
3. Sprinkle with the cooking spray and sprinkle with garlic powder.
4. Fry for about 5-6 minutes, turning every 2 minutes.
5. Take out of the deep fryer and transfer the bok choy to serving plates.
6. Decorate with sesame seeds and serve hot.

Nutrition:

Calories 26 | Carbs 4g | Protein 2.5g | Fat 0.7g

156. Cheesy Pork Rinds

Preparation Time: 5 minutes

Cooking Time: 5 minutes

Servings: 2

Ingredients:

- ½ cup almond flour
- Salt and pepper, to taste
- ½ cup grated Parmesan cheese
- ¼ cup pork rinds, crushed
- 1 cup pickle slices
- 1 egg, beaten

Directions:

1. Put the pickles in a bowl and pour the beaten egg over them. Leave it to soak.
2. In another bowl, mix the Parmesan cheese, almond flour, pork rinds, salt and pepper.
3. Sprinkle the Parmesan cheese mixture over the cucumbers and place them on the double-layer rack.
4. Put the rack with the pickles into the deep fryer.
5. Shut the lid and cook for 5 minutes at 3900 F.

Nutrition:

Calories 664 | Carbs 17.9g | Protein 42g | Fat 49.9g

157. Salty Green Beans

Preparation Time: 5 minutes

Cooking Time: 5 minutes

Servings: 2

Ingredients:

- Salt and pepper, to taste
- 1 cup green beans, trimmed
- ½ teaspoon oil

Directions:

1. Put the green beans in a bowl and add oil, salt and pepper.

2. Pan the beans until they are coated.
3. Put the grill pan in the hot air fryer and put the green beans in in a single layer.
4. Shut the lid and cook them for 5 minutes at 3900F.

Nutrition:

Calories 54 | Fat 2.5g | Carbs 7.7g | Protein 2g

158. Salty Grilled Corn

Preparation Time: 5 minutes

Cooking Time: 10 minutes

Servings: 2

Ingredients:
- Salt and pepper, to taste
- 2 corns on the cob cut into halves widthwise
- ½ teaspoon oil

Directions:
1. Coat the corn on the cob with oil and season with salt and pepper.
2. Insert the grill pan accessory into the hot air fryer.
3. Put the corn cobs on the grill pan.
4. Shut the lid and cook them at 3900 F for 3 minutes.
5. Turn the corn on the cob over and open the hot air fryer.
6. Continue cooking for another 3 minutes at the same temperature.

Nutrition:

Calories 173 | Carbs 29g | Protein 4.5 g | Fat 4.5g

159. Mozzarella Bean Bake

Preparation Time: 5 minutes

Cooking Time: 55 minutes

Servings: 6

Ingredients:
- 1 1/3 cups dried beans
- ½ tsp. kosher salt
- 1 tbsp. extra-virgin olive oil
- 1 1/2 tsp. garlic, sliced
- 5 tbsp. tomato paste
- ½ tsp. black pepper
- 1 1/3 cups mozzarella coarsely grate

Directions:
1. Boil beans with 4 cups of water for 25 minutes on high. Fry the beans with oil.
2. Then add garlic and cook for 1 minute. Add beans, tomato paste, water, a pinch of salt and pepper.
3. Sprinkle with cheese.
4. Grill with the lid of the hot air fryer for 7 minutes. To serve with toasted bread or nacho chips.

Nutrition:

Calories 761 kcal | Fat 28 g | Carbs 54 g | Protein 45 g

160. Maple Brisket

Preparation Time: 15 minutes

Cooking Time: 1hour and 20 minutes

Servings: 4

Ingredients:
- smoked sea salt to taste
- 1 tbsp. liquid smoke
- 1 tbsp. maple sugar
- 2 lb. beef brisket
- ½ tsp. smoked paprika
- 1 tsp. black pepper
- fresh thyme sprigs
- bone broth or stock of choice
- 1 tsp. onion powder
- 1 tsp. mustard powder

Directions:
1. Sprinkle the brisket with all the spices and sugar.
2. Fry the brisket in oil for 3 minutes.
3. Add the stock, liquid smoke and thyme to the hot air fryer and cover.
4. Cook for 50 minutes at high pressure
5. Take out the brisket.
6. Simmer the sauce for 10 minutes
7. Serve sliced beef brisket with any whipped vegetables and sauce.

Nutrition:

Calories 1671 kcal | Fat 43g | Carbs 98 g | Protein 56g

161. Cheesy Beef Sandwiches

Preparation Time: 5 minutes

Cooking Time: 30 minutes

Servings: 8

Ingredients:
- 2 garlic cloves, minced
- 2 onions, julienned
- 1/2 cup pickled pepper rings
- 1 package Italian salad dressing mix
- 4 slices provolone cheese
- 3-pound beef top sirloin steak, sliced
- 2 large red peppers, julienned
- tsp. beef base
- 1/2 tsp. pepper
- 1 can condensed French onion soup, undiluted

Directions:

1. In a pressure cooker, combine the first 7 ingredients. Set the pressure and cook on high for 10 minutes. Put in the peppers and pepper rings. Pressure cook on high for 5 minutes.
2. Add beef, cheese and vegetables to the bun bottoms. Grill for 1-2 minutes and serve.

Nutrition:

Calories 4852 kcal | Fat 67g | Carbs 360 g | Protein 86g

162. Chicken Meatball Wraps

Preparation Time: 5 minutes
Cooking Time: 15 minutes
Servings: 12

Ingredients:

- tsp. curry powder
- 1-pound lean ground chicken
- 1 onion, chopped
- 1/2 cup Rice Krispies
- 1 carrot, shredded
- 1 egg, beaten
- tbsp. olive oil
- 3 Boston lettuce leaves
- 1 cup plain yogurt
- 1/4 cup golden raisins
- 1/2 cup chopped salted peanuts
- 1/4 cup minced cilantro
- 1/2 tsp. salt

Directions:

1. Combine the first 7 ingredients.
2. Form the mixture into 24 meatballs.
3. Fry the meatballs with oil on medium heat.
4. Put water in the saucepan.
5. Place meatballs on the trivet in the pressure cooker.
6. Cook for 7 minutes on the highest setting in the pressure cooker.
7. Mix yoghurt and coriander.
8. Put 2 teaspoons of sauce and 1 meatball in each lettuce leaf; garnish with remaining ingredients and serve.

Nutrition:

Calories 2525 | Fat 80g | Carbs 225g| Protein 120g

163. Paprika Whole Chicken

Intermediate Recipe
Preparation Time: 10 minutes
Cooking Time: 1hour and 10 minutes
Servings: 4

Ingredients:

- ¼ tbsp. black pepper
- 1 tbsp. chili powder
- 1 tbsp. smoked paprika
- 1 tbsp. chopped parsley
- 2/3 c. low-sodium chicken broth
- 1 tsp. chopped thyme leaves
- 1 whole small chicken
- 1 tbsp. packed brown sugar
- 1 tbsp. extra-virgin olive oil
- ¼ tbsp. kosher salt

Directions:

1. Sprinkle chicken with brown sugar, chilli powder, sugar, pepper, paprika and thyme.
2. Fry chicken in oil for 3-4 minutes.
3. Add stock to the pot.
4. Cook on high for 25 minutes
5. Decorate sliced chicken with parsley and serve.

Nutrition:

Calories 1212 | Fat 10g | Carbs 31g | Protein 15g

164. Coco Curry Rice Plate

Preparation Time: 5 minutes
Cooking Time: 40minutes
Servings: 6

Ingredients:

- oz. no salt added chickpeas
- 1 cup matchstick carrots
- oz. coconut milk
- 1 cup chopped green onion
- 1 tbsp. grated ginger
- 2/3 cup uncooked brown rice
- 1 cup sliced red bell pepper
- 1 cup chopped red cabbage
- 1 tsp. curry powder
- 1 1/2 tbsp. sugar
- 3/4 tsp. salt divided

Directions:

1. Put the rice into a large bowl.
2. And all the vegetables and the chickpeas to the rice bowl.
3. Next up, add the coconut milk, the ginger and a tablespoon of curry powder. Finish with salt.
4. Mix, mix, mix until well combined.
5. Transfer mixture to a 7-inch round metal cake pan or air fryer insert. Place pan into the air fryer basket.
   Air fry for 15 minutes, stirring halfway through cook time.

Nutrition:

Calories 1530 | Fat 110g | Carbs 250g | Protein 80g

165. Soy Sauce Egg Roll

Preparation Time: 5 minutes

Cooking Time: 20 minutes

Servings: 4

Ingredients:

- 2 cloves garlic, minced
- 1 oz. shiitake mushrooms, sliced
- 1 cup matchstick cut carrots
- 2 tbsp. sesame oil
- 1 bunch green onions, sliced
- 1/3 cup low-sodium soy sauce
- 2 bags coleslaw mix
- 1 1/2 cups chicken broth
- 1 lb. ground chicken
- 3 tbsp. sesame seeds

Directions:

1. Put the sesame oil, ground chicken, soy sauce, garlic, chicken stock and mushrooms into the airfryer.
2. Heat on high pressure for 2 minutes.
3. Pour in the coleslaw mix and carrots.
4. Leave to infuse for 5 minutes.
5. Garnish with sesame seeds and spring onions.

Nutrition:

Calories 345 | Fat 130g | Carbs 301g | Protein 150g

166. Korean Lamb Bites

Intermediate Recipe

Preparation Time: 10 minutes

Cooking Time: 50minutes

Servings: 6

Ingredients:

- 1 tbsp. garlic, minced
- 2 cups onions, diced
- 1 tbsp. curry powder
- 1/2 tbsp. soy sauce
- 2 lbs. Lamb chops
- 1/2 tsp. Red pepper powder
- 1/2 tbsp. sesame oil
- 1 tsp. black pepper
- 1 cup red wine
- 1/2 tsp. cinnamon powder
- 2 tbsp. Korean red pepper paste
- 2 tbsp. rice wine
- 1/2 tbsp. Green plum extract
- 2 tbsp. granulated sugar
- 1/3 cup Asian pear ground
- 1 tsp. ginger, minced
- bay leaves as preferred
- 2 tbsp. Corn syrup
- 1 cup carrots, diced
- 1 tsp. sesame seeds
- 1 cup celery, diced
- 1/3 cup onion powder
- 1 tbsp. ketchup

Directions:

1. Place all ingredients except coriander and spring onions in the hot air fryer.
2. Cook for 20 minutes under pressure.
3. Continue to saute until the sauce has thickened.
4. Place water and lamb on trivets in pot.
5. Grill for 5 minutes at 400°F.
6. Garnish with chopped coriander and spring onions.

Nutrition:

Calories 2728 | Fat 220g | Carbs 551g | Protein 250g

167. Air Fried Chicken Kabobs

Preparation Time: 15 minutes

Cooking Time: 15 minutes

Servings: 2

Ingredients:

- 1 teaspoon Pepper, crushed
- Cooking oil spray as required
- ⅓ Cup honey
- 4 Mushrooms cut into halves
- ⅓ Cup Soy sauce -
- 1 teaspoon Sesame seeds
- Bell peppers, in different colors
- Chicken breasts, chopped

Directions:

1. Dice the chicken breasts, wash and pat dry.
2. Coat the chicken with a little pepper and salt. Sprinkle it with a little oil. In a small bowl, mix the honey and soy sauce well.
3. Stir the sesame seeds into the mixture. Thread the chicken, peppers and mushrooms onto the skewers.
4. Adjust the air fryer to 170 degrees Celsius and preheat.
5. Sprinkle the skewers with the honey-soy sauce mixture.
6. Put all the skewered chicken kabobs in the basket of the air fryer and cook for 20 minutes.
7. Turn the skewers in between.
8. Serve hot.

Nutrition:

Calories 392 | Fat 5g | Carbs 65.4g | Protein 6.7g

168. Panko Breaded Cheesy Chicken

Preparation Time: 10 minutes

Cooking Time: 20 minutes

Servings: 4

Ingredients:

- ½ cup parmesan cheese, shredded
- ¾ cup marinara sauce
- ⅛ cup egg whites
- ½ teaspoon salt
- 1 cup panko bread crumbs
- 1 teaspoon ground pepper
- 2 teaspoons italian seasoning
- Cooking spray, as required
- ½ cup mozzarella cheese, grated
- 2 ounces chicken breasts, skinless

Directions:

1. Slice each chicken breast in half to make 4 breast pieces. Wash and pat dry.
2. Put the chicken on a cutting board and pat it flat.
3. Spray the basket of the air fryer with cooking oil.
4. Adjust the temperature of the air fryer to 200 degrees Celsius and preheat it.
5. Combine the cheese, panko breadcrumbs and seasoning ingredients in a large bowl.
6. Place the egg whites in a large bowl.
7. Dunk the battered chicken in the egg white and sprinkle with the breadcrumb mixture.
8. Now put the coated chicken in the basket of the deep fryer and spray on some cooking oil.
9. Begin to cook the chicken breasts for 7 minutes
10. Spread grated mozzarella and marinara sauce over the chicken breasts.
11. Cook for another 3 minutes and remove to serve when the cheese starts to melt.

Nutrition:

Calories 347 | Fat 15g | Carbs 7.4g | Protein 37g

MAIN COURSE

169. Vegetable Egg Rolls

Preparation Time: 15 minutes

Cooking Time: 10 minutes

Servings: 8

Ingredients:

- ½ cup chopped mushrooms
- ½ cup grated carrots
- ½ cup chopped zucchini
- 2 green onions, chopped
- 2 tablespoons low-sodium soy sauce
- 8 egg roll wrappers
- 1 tablespoon cornstarch
- 1 egg, beaten

Directions:

1. In a medium bowl, combine the mushrooms, carrots, zucchini, green onions, and soy sauce, and stir together.
2. Place the egg roll wrappers on a work surface. Top each with about 3 tablespoons of the vegetable mixture.
3. In a small bowl, combine the cornstarch and egg and mix well. Brush some of this mixture on the edges of the egg roll wrappers. Roll up the wrappers, enclosing the vegetable filling. Brush some of the egg mixture on the outside of the egg rolls to seal.
4. Air-fry for 7 to 10 minutes or until the egg rolls are brown and crunchy.

Nutrition:

Calories: 112 | Total Fat: 1g | Saturated Fat: 0g

Cholesterol: 23mg | Sodium: 417mg | Carbohydrates: 21g

Fiber: 1g | Protein: 4g

170. Veggies on Toast

Preparation Time: 12 minutes

Cooking Time: 11 minutes

Servings: 4

Ingredients:

- 1 red bell pepper, cut into ½-inch strips
- 1 cup sliced button or cremini mushrooms
- 1 small yellow squash, sliced
- 2 green onions, cut into ½-inch slices
- Extra light olive oil for misting
- 4 to 6 pieces sliced French or Italian bread
- 2 tablespoons softened butter
- ½ cup soft goat cheese

Directions:

1. Combine the red pepper, mushrooms, squash, and green onions in the air fryer and mist with oil. Roast for 7 to 9 minutes or until the vegetables are tender, shaking the basket once during cooking time.
2. Remove the vegetables from the basket and set aside.
3. Spread the bread with butter and place in the air fryer, butter-side up. Toast for 2 to 4 minutes or until golden brown.
4. Spread the goat cheese on the toasted bread and top with the vegetables; serve warm.
5. Variation tip: To add even more flavor, drizzle the finished toasts with extra-virgin olive oil and balsamic vinegar.

Nutrition:

Calories: 162 | Total Fat: 11g | Saturated Fat: 7g

Cholesterol: 30mg | Sodium: 160mg | Carbohydrates: 9g

Fiber: 2g | Protein: 7g

171. Jumbo Stuffed Mushrooms

Preparation Time: 10 minutes

Cooking Time: 20 minutes

Servings: 4

Ingredients:

- 4 jumbo portobello mushrooms
- 1 tablespoon olive oil
- ¼ cup ricotta cheese

- 5 tablespoons Parmesan cheese, divided
- 1 cup frozen chopped spinach, thawed and drained
- ⅓ cup bread crumbs
- ¼ teaspoon minced fresh rosemary

Directions:
1. Wipe the mushrooms with a damp cloth. Remove the stems and discard. Using a spoon, gently scrape out most of the gills.
2. Rub the mushrooms with the olive oil. Put in the air fryer basket, hollow side up, and bake for 3 minutes. Carefully remove the mushroom caps, because they will contain liquid. Drain the liquid out of the caps.
3. In a medium bowl, combine the ricotta, 3 tablespoons of Parmesan cheese, spinach, bread crumbs, and rosemary, and mix well.
4. Stuff this mixture into the drained mushroom caps. Sprinkle with the remaining 2 tablespoons of Parmesan cheese. Put the mushroom caps back into the basket.
5. Bake for 4 to 6 minutes or until the filling is hot and the mushroom caps are tender.

Nutrition:
Calories: 117 | Total Fat: 7g | Saturated Fat: 3g
Cholesterol: 10mg | Sodium: 180mg | Carbohydrates: 8g
Fiber: 1g | Protein: 7g

172. Mushroom Pita Pizzas

Preparation Time: 10 minutes
Cooking Time: 5 minutes
Servings: 4

Ingredients:
- 4 (3-inch) pitas
- 1 tablespoon olive oil
- ¾ cup pizza sauce
- 1 (4-ounce) jar sliced mushrooms, drained
- ½ teaspoon dried basil
- 2 green onions, minced
- 1 cup grated mozzarella or provolone cheese
- 1 cup sliced grape tomatoes

Directions:
1. Brush each piece of pita with oil and top with the pizza sauce.
2. Add the mushrooms and sprinkle with basil and green onions. Top with the grated cheese.
3. Bake for 3 to 6 minutes or until the cheese is melted and starts to brown. Top with the grape tomatoes and serve immediately.

Nutrition:
Calories: 231 | Total Fat: 9g | Saturated Fat: 4g
Cholesterol: 15mg | Sodium: 500mg | Carbohydrates: 25g
Fiber: 2g | Protein: 13g

173. Spinach Quiche

Preparation Time: 10 minutes
Cooking Time: 20 minutes
Servings: 3

Ingredients:
- 3 eggs
- 1 cup frozen chopped spinach, thawed and drained
- ⅓ cup heavy cream
- 2 tablespoons honey mustard
- ½ cup grated Swiss or Havarti cheese
- ½ teaspoon dried thyme
- Pinch salt
- 1 Freshly ground black pepper
- Nonstick baking spray with flour

Directions:
1. In a medium bowl, beat the eggs until blended. Stir in the spinach, cream, honey mustard, cheese, thyme, salt, and pepper.
2. Spray a 6-by-6-by-2-inch pan baking pan with nonstick spray. Pour the egg mixture into the pan.
3. Bake for 18 to 22 minutes or until the egg mixture is puffed, light golden brown, and set.
4. Let cool for 5 minutes, then cut into wedges to serve.

Nutrition:
Calories: 203 | Total Fat: 15g | Saturated Fat: 8g
Cholesterol: 199mg | Sodium: 211mg | Carbohydrates: 6g
Fiber: 0g | Protein: 11g

174. Yellow Squash Fritters

Preparation Time: 15 minutes
Cooking Time: 7 minutes
Servings: 4

Ingredients:
- 1 (3-ounce) package cream cheese, softened
- 1 egg, beaten
- ½ teaspoon dried oregano
- Pinch salt
- 1 Freshly ground black pepper
- 1 medium yellow summer squash, grated
- ⅓ cup grated carrot
- ⅔ cup bread crumbs
- 2 tablespoons olive oil

Directions:
1. In a medium bowl, combine the cream cheese, egg, oregano, and salt and pepper. Add the squash and carrot, and mix well. Stir in the breadcrumbs.

2. Form about 2 tablespoons of this mixture into a patty about ½ inch thick. Repeat with remaining mixture. Brush the fritters with olive oil.
3. Air-fry until crisp and golden, about 7 to 9 minutes.

Nutrition:

Calories: 234 | Total Fat: 17g | Saturated Fat: 6g

Cholesterol: 64mg | Sodium: 261mg | Carbohydrates: 16g

Fiber: 2g | Protein: 6g

175. Pesto Gnocchi

Preparation Time: 5 minutes

Cooking Time: 20 minutes

Servings: 4

Ingredients:

- 1 tablespoon olive oil
- 1 onion, finely chopped
- 3 cloves garlic, sliced
- 1 (16-ounce) package shelf-stable gnocchi
- 1 (8-ounce) jar pesto
- ⅓ cup grated Parmesan cheese

Directions:

1. Combine the oil, onion, garlic, and gnocchi in a 6-by-6-by-2-inch pan and put into the air fryer.
2. Bake for 10 minutes, then remove the pan and stir.
3. Return the pan to the air fryer and cook for 8 to 13 minutes or until the gnocchi are lightly browned and crisp.
4. Remove the pan from the air fryer. Stir in the pesto and Parmesan cheese, and serve immediately.

Nutrition:

Calories: 646 | Total Fat: 32g | Saturated Fat: 7g

Cholesterol: 103mg | Sodium: 461mg

Carbohydrates: 69g | Fiber: 2g | Protein: 22g

176. English Muffin Tuna Sandwiches

Preparation Time: 8 minutes

Cooking Time: 5 minutes

Servings: 4

Ingredients:

- 1 (6-ounce) can chunk light tuna, drained
- ¼ cup mayonnaise
- 2 tablespoons mustard
- 1 tablespoon lemon juice
- 2 green onions, minced
- 3 English muffins, split with a fork
- 3 tablespoons softened butter
- 6 thin slices provolone or Muenster cheese

Directions:

1. In a small bowl, combine the tuna, mayonnaise, mustard, lemon juice, and green onions.
2. Butter the cut side of the English muffins. Grill butter-side up in the air fryer for 2 to 4 minutes or until light golden brown. Remove the muffins from the air fryer basket.
3. Top each muffin with one slice of cheese and return to the air fryer. Grill for 2 to 4 minutes or until the cheese melts and starts to brown.
4. Remove the muffins from the air fryer, top with the tuna mixture, and serve.

Nutrition:

Calories: 389 | Total Fat: 23g | Saturated Fat: 10g

Cholesterol: 50mg | Sodium: 495mg

Carbohydrates: 25g | Fiber: 3g | Protein: 21g

177. Tuna Zucchini Melts

Preparation Time: 15 minutes

Cooking Time: 10 minutes

Servings: 4

Ingredients:

- 4 corn tortillas
- 3 tablespoons softened butter
- 1 (6-ounce) can chunk light tuna, drained
- 1 cup shredded zucchini, drained by squeezing in a kitchen towel
- ⅓ cup mayonnaise
- 2 tablespoons mustard
- 1 cup shredded Cheddar or Colby cheese

Directions:

1. Spread the tortillas with the softened butter. Place in the air fryer basket and grill for 2 to 3 minutes or until the tortillas are crisp. Remove from basket and set aside.
2. In a medium bowl, combine the tuna, zucchini, mayonnaise, and mustard, and mix well.
3. Divide the tuna mixture among the toasted tortillas. Top each with some of the shredded cheese.
4. Grill in the air fryer for 2 to 4 minutes or until the tuna mixture is hot, and the cheese melts and starts to brown. Serve.

Nutrition:

Calories: 428 | Total Fat: 30g | Saturated Fat: 13g

Cholesterol: 71mg | Sodium: 410mg | Carbohydrates: 19g

Fiber: 3g | Protein: 22g

178. Shrimp and Grilled Cheese Sandwiches

Preparation Time: 10 minutes

Cooking Time: 5 minutes

Servings: 4

Ingredients:

- 1¼ cups shredded Colby, Cheddar, or Havarti cheese
- 1 (6-ounce) can tiny shrimp, drained
- 3 tablespoons mayonnaise
- 2 tablespoons minced green onion
- 4 slices whole grain or whole-wheat bread
- 2 tablespoons softened butter

Directions:
1. In a medium bowl, combine the cheese, shrimp, mayonnaise, and green onion, and mix well.
2. Spread this mixture on two of the slices of bread. Top with the other slices of bread to make two sandwiches. Spread the sandwiches lightly with butter.
3. Grill in the air fryer for 5 to 7 minutes or until the bread is browned and crisp and the cheese is melted. Cut in half and serve warm.

Nutrition:
Calories: 276 | Total Fat: 14g | Saturated Fat: 6g
Cholesterol: 115mg | Sodium: 573mg | Carbohydrates: 16g
Fiber: 2g | Protein: 22g

179. Shrimp Croquettes

Preparation Time: 12 minutes
Cooking Time: 8 minutes
Servings: 3-4

Ingredients:
- ⅔ pound cooked shrimp, shelled and deveined
- 1½ cups bread crumbs, divided
- 1 egg, beaten
- 2 tablespoon lemon juice
- 2 green onions, finely chopped
- ½ teaspoon dried basil
- Pinch salt
- 1 Freshly ground black pepper
- 2 tablespoons olive oil

Directions:
1. Finely chop the shrimp. Take about 1 tablespoon of the finely chopped shrimp and chop it further until it's almost a paste. Set aside.
2. In a medium bowl, combine ½ cup of the bread crumbs with the egg and lemon juice. Let stand for 5 minutes.
3. Stir the shrimp, green onions, basil, salt, and pepper into the bread crumb mixture.
4. Combine the remaining 1 cup of bread crumbs with the olive oil on a shallow plate; mix well.
5. Form the shrimp mixture into 1½-inch round balls and press firmly with your hands. Roll in the bread crumb mixture to coat.
6. Air-fry the little croquettes in batches for 6 to 8 minutes or until they are brown and crisp. Serve with cocktail sauce for dipping, if desired.

Nutrition:
Calories: 330 | Total Fat: 12g | Saturated Fat: 2g
Cholesterol: 201mg | Sodium: 539mg
Carbohydrates: 31g | Fiber: 2g | Protein: 24g

180. Crispy Salt and Pepper Tofu

Preparation Time: 5 minutes
Cooking Time: 15 minutes
Servings: 4

Ingredients:
- ¼ cup chickpea flour
- ¼ cup arrowroot (or cornstarch)
- 1 teaspoon sea salt
- 1 teaspoon granulated garlic
- ½ teaspoon freshly grated black pepper
- 1 (15-ounce) package tofu, firm or extra-firm
- Cooking oil spray (sunflower, safflower, or refined coconut)
- Asian Spicy Sweet Sauce, optional

Directions:
1. In a medium bowl, combine the flour, arrowroot, salt, garlic, and pepper. Stir well to combine.
2. Cut the tofu into cubes (no need to press—if it's a bit watery, that's fine!). Place the cubes into the flour mixture. Toss well to coat. Spray the tofu with oil and toss again. (The spray will help the coating better stick to the tofu.)
3. Spray the air fryer basket with the oil. Place the tofu in a single layer in the air fryer basket (you may have to do this in 2 batches, depending on the size of your appliance) and spray the tops with oil. Fry for 8 minutes. Remove the air fryer basket and spray again with oil. Toss gently or turn the pieces over. Spray with oil again and fry for another 7 minutes, or until golden-browned and very crisp.
4. Serve immediately, either plain or with the Asian Spicy Sweet Sauce.

Nutrition:
Calories: 148 | Total fat: 5g | Saturated fat: 0g
Cholesterol: 0mg | Sodium: 473mg
Carbohydrates: 14g | Fiber: 1g | Protein: 11g

181. Crispy Indian Wrap

Preparation Time: 20 minutes
Cooking Time: 8 minutes
Servings: 4

Ingredients:
- Cilantro Chutney

- 2¾ cups diced potato, cooked until tender
- 2 teaspoons oil (coconut, sunflower, or safflower)
- 3 large garlic cloves, minced or pressed
- 1½ tablespoons fresh lime juice
- 1½ teaspoons cumin powder
- 1 teaspoon onion granules
- 1 teaspoon coriander powder
- ½ teaspoon sea salt
- ½ teaspoon turmeric
- ¼ teaspoon cayenne powder
- 4 large flour tortillas, preferably whole grain or sprouted
- 1 cup cooked garbanzo beans (canned are fine), rinsed and drained
- ½ cup finely chopped cabbage
- ¼ cup minced red onion or scallion
- Cooking oil spray (sunflower, safflower, or refined coconut)

Directions:

1. Make the Cilantro Chutney and set aside.
2. In a large bowl, mash the potatoes well, using a potato masher or large fork. Add the oil, garlic, lime, cumin, onion, coriander, salt, turmeric, and cayenne. Stir very well, until thoroughly combined. Set aside.
3. Lay the tortillas out flat on the counter. In the middle of each, evenly distribute the potato filling. Add some of the garbanzo beans, cabbage, and red onion to each, on top of the potatoes.
4. Spray the air fryer basket with oil and set aside. Enclose the Indian wraps by folding the bottom of the tortillas up and over the filling, then folding the sides in—and finally rolling the bottom up to form, essentially, an enclosed burrito.
5. Place the wraps in the air fryer basket, seam side down. They can touch each other a little bit, but if they're too crowded, you'll need to cook them in batches. Fry for 5 minutes. Spray with oil again, flip over, and cook an additional 2 or 3 minutes, until nicely browned and crisp. Serve topped with the Cilantro Chutney.

Nutrition:

Calories: 288 | Total fat: 7g | Saturated fat: 1g

Cholesterol: 0mg | Sodium: 821mg

Carbohydrates: 50g | Fiber: 5g | Protein: 9g

182. Easy Peasy Pizza

Preparation Time: 5 minutes

Cooking Time: 9 minutes

Servings: 1

Ingredients:

- Cooking oil spray (coconut, sunflower, or safflower)
- 1 flour tortilla, preferably sprouted or whole grain
- ¼ cup vegan pizza or marinara sauce
- ⅓ cup grated vegan mozzarella cheese or Cheesy Sauce
- Toppings of your choice

Directions:

1. Spray the air fryer basket with oil. Place the tortilla in the air fryer basket. If the tortilla is a little bigger than the base, no probs! Simply fold the edges up a bit to form a semblance of a "crust."
2. Pour the sauce in the center, and evenly distribute it around the tortilla "crust" (I like to use the back of a spoon for this purpose).
3. Sprinkle evenly with vegan cheese, and add your toppings. Bake for 9 minutes, or until nicely browned. Remove carefully, cut into four pieces, and enjoy.

Nutrition:

Calories: 210 | Total fat: 6g | Saturated fat: 1g

Cholesterol: 0mg | Sodium: 700mg

Carbohydrates: 33g | Fiber: 2g | Protein: 5g

183. Eggplant Parmigiana

Preparation Time: 15 minutes

Cooking Time: 40 minutes

Servings: 4

Ingredients:

- 1 medium eggplant (about 1-pound), sliced into ½-inch-thick rounds
- 2 tablespoons tamari or shoyu
- 3 tablespoons nondairy milk, plain and unsweetened
- 1 cup chickpea flour (see Substitution Tip)
- 1 tablespoon dried basil
- 1 tablespoon dried oregano
- 2 teaspoons garlic granules
- 2 teaspoons onion granules
- ½ teaspoon sea salt
- ½ teaspoon freshly ground black pepper
- Cooking oil spray (sunflower, safflower, or refined coconut)
- Vegan marinara sauce (your choice)
- Shredded vegan cheese (preferably mozzarella; see Ingredient Tip)

Directions:

1. Place the eggplant slices in a large bowl, and pour the tamari and milk over the top. Turn the pieces over to coat them as evenly as possible with the liquids. Set aside.
2. Make the coating: In a medium bowl, combine the flour, basil, oregano, garlic, onion, salt, and pepper and stir well. Set aside.
3. Spray the air fryer basket with oil and set aside.
4. Stir the eggplant slices again and transfer them to a plate (stacking is fine). Do not discard the liquid in the bowl.

5. Bread the eggplant by tossing an eggplant round in the flour mixture. Then, dip in the liquid again. Double up on the coating by placing the eggplant again in the flour mixture, making sure that all sides are nicely breaded. Place in the air fryer basket.
6. Repeat with enough eggplant rounds to make a (mostly) single layer in the air fryer basket. (You'll need to cook it in batches, so that you don't have too much overlap and it cooks perfectly.)
7. Spray the tops of the eggplant with enough oil so that you no longer see dry patches in the coating. Fry for 8 minutes. Remove the air fryer basket and spray the tops again. Turn each piece over, again taking care not to overlap the rounds too much. Spray the tops with oil, again making sure that no dry patches remain. Fry for another 8 minutes, or until nicely browned and crisp.
8. Repeat steps 5 to 7 one more time, or until all of the eggplant is crisp and browned.
9. Finally, place half of the eggplant in a 6-inch round, 2-inch deep baking pan and top with marinara sauce and a sprinkle of vegan cheese.
10. Fry for 3 minutes, or until the sauce is hot and cheese is melted (be careful not to overcook, or the eggplant edges will burn). Serve immediately, plain or over pasta.
11. Otherwise, you can store the eggplant in the fridge for several days and then make a fresh batch whenever the mood strikes by repeating this step!

Nutrition:

Calories: 217 | Total fat: 9g | Saturated fat: 1g

Cholesterol: 0mg | Sodium: 903mg | Carbohydrates: 38g

Fiber: 10g | Protein: 9g

---

184. Luscious Lazy Lasagna

Preparation Time: 15 minutes

Cooking Time: 15 minutes

Servings: 4

Ingredients:

- 8 ounces lasagna noodles, preferably bean-based, but any kind will do
- 1 tablespoon extra-virgin olive oil
- 2 cups crumbled extra-firm tofu, drained and water squeezed out
- 2 cups loosely packed fresh spinach
- 2 tablespoons Nutrition yeast
- 2 tablespoons fresh lemon juice
- 1 teaspoon onion granules
- 1 teaspoon sea salt
- ⅛ teaspoon freshly ground black pepper
- 4 large garlic cloves, minced or pressed
- 2 cups vegan pasta sauce, your choice
- ½ cup shredded vegan cheese (preferably mozzarella)

Directions:

1. Cook the noodles until a little firmer than al dente (they'll get a little softer after you air-fry them in the lasagna). Drain and set aside.
2. While the noodles are cooking, make the filling. In a large pan over medium-high heat, add the olive oil, tofu, and spinach. Stir-fry for a minute, then add the Nutrition yeast, lemon juice, onion, salt, pepper, and garlic. Stir well and cook just until the spinach is nicely wilted. Remove from heat.
3. To make half a batch (one 6-inch round, 2-inch deep baking pan) of lasagna: Spread a thin layer of pasta sauce in the baking pan. Layer 2 or 3 lasagna noodles on top of the sauce. Top with a little more sauce and some of the tofu mixture.
4. Place another 2 or 3 noodles on top, and add another layer of sauce and then another layer of tofu. Finish with a layer of noodles, and then a final layer of sauce. Sprinkle about half of the vegan cheese on top (omit if you prefer; see the Ingredient Tip from the Eggplant Parmigiana).
5. Place the pan in the air fryer and bake for 15 minutes, or until the noodles are browning around the edges and the cheese is melted. Cut and serve.
6. If making the entire recipe now, repeat steps 3 and 4 (see Cooking Tip).

Nutrition:

Calories: 317 | Total fat: 8g | Saturated fat: 1g

Cholesterol: 0mg | Sodium: 1203mg | Carbohydrates: 46g

Fiber: 4g | Protein: 20g

---

185. Pasta With Creamy Cauliflower Sauce

Preparation Time: 10 minutes

Cooking Time: 18 minutes

Servings: 4

Ingredients:

- 4 cups cauliflower florets
- Cooking oil spray (sunflower, safflower, or refined coconut)
- 1 medium onion, chopped
- 8 ounces pasta, your choice (about 4 cups cooked; use gluten-free pasta if desired)
- Fresh chives or scallion tops, for garnish
- ½ cup raw cashew pieces (see Ingredient Tip)
- 1½ cups water
- 1 tablespoon Nutrition yeast
- 2 large garlic cloves, peeled
- 2 tablespoons fresh lemon juice
- 1½ teaspoons sea salt
- ¼ teaspoon freshly ground black pepper

Directions:

1. Place the cauliflower in the air fryer basket, spritz the tops with oil spray, and roast for 8 minutes. Remove the air fryer basket, stir, and add the onion. Spritz with oil again and roast for another 10 minutes, or until the cauliflower is browned and the onions are tender.
2. While the vegetables are roasting in the air fryer, cook the pasta according to the package directions and mince the chives or scallions. Set aside.
3. In a blender jar, place the roasted cauliflower and onions along with the cashews, water, Nutrition yeast, garlic, lemon, salt, and pepper. Blend well, until very smooth and creamy. Serve a generous portion of the sauce on top of the warm pasta, and top with the minced chives or scallions. The sauce will store, refrigerated in an airtight container, for about a week.

Nutrition:

Calories: 341 | Total fat: 9g | Saturated fat: 1g

Cholesterol: 0mg | Sodium: 312mg | Carbohydrates: 51g

Fiber: 6g | Protein: 14g

186. Lemony Lentils With "Fried" Onions

Preparation Time: 10 minutes

Cooking Time: 30 minutes

Servings: 4

Ingredients:

- 1 cup red lentils
- 4 cups water
- Cooking oil spray (coconut, sunflower, or safflower)
- 1 medium-size onion, peeled and cut into ¼-inch-thick rings
- Sea salt
- ½ cup kale, stems removed, thinly sliced
- 3 large garlic cloves, pressed or minced
- 2 tablespoons fresh lemon juice
- 2 teaspoons Nutrition yeast
- 1 teaspoon sea salt
- 1 teaspoon lemon zest (see Ingredient Tip)
- ¾ teaspoon freshly ground black pepper

Directions:

1. In a medium-large pot, bring the lentils and water to a boil over medium-high heat. Reduce the heat to low and simmer, uncovered, for about 30 minutes (or until the lentils have dissolved completely), making sure to stir every 5 minutes or so as they cook (so that the lentils don't stick to the bottom of the pot).
2. While the lentils are cooking, get the rest of your dish together. Spray the air fryer basket with oil and place the onion rings inside, separating them as much as possible. Spray them with the oil and sprinkle with a little salt. Fry for 5 minutes.
3. Remove the air fryer basket, shake or stir, spray again with oil, and fry for another 5 minutes. (Note: You're aiming for all of the onion slices to be crisp and well browned, so if some of the pieces begin to do that, transfer them from the air fryer basket to a plate.)
4. Remove the air fryer basket, spray the onions again with oil, and fry for a final 5 minutes or until all the pieces are crisp and browned.
5. To finish the lentils: Add the kale to the hot lentils, and stir very well, as the heat from the lentils will steam the thinly sliced greens. Stir in the garlic, lemon juice, Nutrition yeast, salt, zest, and pepper. Stir very well and then distribute evenly in bowls.
6. Top with the crisp onion rings and serve.

Nutrition:

Calories: 220 | Total fat: 1g | Saturated fat: 0g

Cholesterol: 0mg | Sodium: 477mg | Carbohydrates: 39g

Fiber: 16g | Protein: 15g

187. Our Daily Bean

Preparation Time: 5 minutes

Cooking Time: 8 minutes

Servings: 2

Ingredients:

- 1 (15-ounce) can pinto beans, drained
- ¼ cup tomato sauce
- 2 tablespoons Nutrition yeast
- 2 large garlic cloves, pressed or minced
- ½ teaspoon dried oregano
- ½ teaspoon cumin
- ¼ teaspoon sea salt
- ⅛ teaspoon freshly ground black pepper
- Cooking oil spray (sunflower, safflower, or refined coconut)

Directions:

1. In a medium bowl, stir together the beans, tomato sauce, Nutrition yeast, garlic, oregano, cumin, salt, and pepper until well combined.
2. Spray the 6-inch round, 2-inch deep baking pan with oil and pour the bean mixture into it.
3. Bake for 4 minutes. Remove, stir well, and bake for another 4 minutes, or until the mixture has thickened and is heated through. It will most likely form a little crust on top and be lightly browned in spots.
4. Serve hot. This will keep, refrigerated in an airtight container, for up to a week.

Nutrition:

Calories: 284 | Total fat: 4g | Saturated fat: 1g

Cholesterol: 0mg | Sodium: 807mg | Carbohydrates: 47g

Fiber: 16g | Protein: 20g

188. Taco Salad with Creamy Lime Sauce

Preparation Time: 7 minutes

Cooking Time: 20 minutes

Servings: 3

Ingredients:

For the sauce

- 1 (12.3-ounce) package of silken-firm tofu
- ¼ cup plus 1 tablespoon fresh lime juice
- Zest of 1 large lime (1 teaspoon)
- 1½ tablespoons coconut sugar
- 3 large garlic cloves, peeled
- 1 teaspoon sea salt
- ½ teaspoon ground chipotle powder

For the salad

- 6 cups romaine lettuce, chopped (1 large head)
- 1 (15-ounce) can vegan refried beans (or whole pinto or black beans if you prefer)
- 1 cup chopped red cabbage
- 2 medium tomatoes, chopped
- ½ cup chopped cilantro
- ¼ cup minced scallions
- Double batch of Garlic Lime Tortilla Chips

Directions:

To make the sauce

1. Drain the tofu (pour off any liquid) and place in a blender.
2. Add the lime juice and zest, coconut sugar, garlic, salt, and chipotle powder. Blend until very smooth. Set aside.

To make the salad

3. Distribute the lettuce equally into three big bowls.
4. In a small pan over medium heat, warm the beans, stirring often, until hot (this should take less than a minute).
5. Place on top of the lettuce. Top the beans with the cabbage, tomatoes, cilantro, and scallions.
6. Drizzle generously with the Creamy Lime Sauce and serve with the double batch of air-fried chips. Enjoy immediately.

Nutrition:

Calories: 422 | Total fat: 7g | Saturated fat: 1g

Cholesterol: 0mg | Sodium: 1186mg | Carbohydrates: 71g

Fiber: 15g | Protein: 22g

189. Bbq Jackfruit Nachos

Preparation Time: 30 minutes

Cooking Time: 20 minutes

Servings: 3

Ingredients:

- 1 (20-ounce) can jackfruit, drained
- ⅓ cup prepared vegan BBQ sauce
- ¼ cup water
- 2 tablespoons tamari or shoyu
- 1 tablespoon fresh lemon juice
- 4 large garlic cloves, pressed or minced
- 1 teaspoon onion granules
- ⅛ teaspoon cayenne powder
- ⅛ teaspoon liquid smoke
- Double batch Garlic Lime Tortilla Chips
- 2½ cups prepared Cheesy Sauce
- 3 medium-size tomatoes, chopped
- ¾ cup guacamole of your choice
- ¾ cup chopped cilantro
- ½ cup minced red onion
- 1 jalapeño, seeds removed and thinly sliced (optional)

Directions:

1. In a large skillet over high heat, place the jackfruit, BBQ sauce, water, tamari, lemon juice, garlic, onion granules, cayenne, and liquid smoke. Stir well and break up the jackfruit a bit with a spatula.
2. Once the mixture boils, reduce the heat to low. Continue to cook, stirring often (and breaking up the jackfruit as you stir), for about 20 minutes, or until all of the liquid has been absorbed. Remove from the heat and set aside.
3. Assemble the nachos: Distribute the chips onto three plates, and then top evenly with the jackfruit mixture, warmed Cheesy Sauce, tomatoes, guacamole, cilantro, onion, and jalapeño (if using). Enjoy immediately, because soggy chips are tragic.

Nutrition:

Calories: 661 | Total fat: 15g | Saturated fat: 1g

Cholesterol: 0mg | Sodium: 1842mg | Carbohydrates: 124g

Fiber: 19g | Protein: 22g

190. 10-Minute Chimichanga

Preparation Time: 2 minutes

Cooking Time: 8 minutes

Servings: 1

Ingredients:

- 1 whole-grain tortilla
- ½ cup vegan refried beans
- ¼ cup grated vegan cheese (optional)
- Cooking oil spray (sunflower, safflower, or refined coconut)
- ½ cup fresh salsa (or Green Chili Sauce)
- 2 cups chopped romaine lettuce (about ½ head)
- Guacamole (optional)
- Chopped cilantro (optional)
- Cheesy Sauce (optional)

Directions:

1. Lay the tortilla on a flat surface and place the beans in the center. Top with the cheese, if using.
2. Wrap the bottom up over the filling, and then fold in the sides. Then roll it all up so as to enclose the beans inside the tortilla (you're making an enclosed burrito here).
3. Spray the air fryer basket with oil, place the tortilla wrap inside the basket, seam-side down, and spray the top of the chimichanga with oil.
4. Fry for 5 minutes. Spray the top (and sides) again with oil, flip over, and spray the other side with oil. Fry for an additional 2 or 3 minutes, until nicely browned and crisp.
5. Transfer to a plate. Top with the salsa, lettuce, guacamole, cilantro, and/or Cheesy Sauce, if using. Serve immediately.

Nutrition:

Calories: 317 | Total fat: 6g | Saturated fat: 2g

Cholesterol: 0mg | Sodium: 955mg | Carbohydrates: 55g

Fiber: 11g | Protein: 13g

191. Mexican Stuffed Potatoes

Preparation Time: 15 minutes

Cooking Time: 40 minutes

Servings: 4

Ingredients:

- 4 large potatoes, any variety (I like Yukon Gold or russets for this dish; see Cooking Tip)
- Cooking oil spray (sunflower, safflower, or refined coconut)
- 1½ cups Cheesy Sauce
- 1 cup black or pinto beans (canned beans are fine; be sure to drain and rinse)
- 2 medium tomatoes, chopped
- 1 scallion, finely chopped
- ⅓ cup finely chopped cilantro
- 1 jalapeño, finely sliced or minced (optional)
- 1 avocado, diced (optional)

Directions:

1. Scrub the potatoes, prick with a fork, and spray the outsides with oil. Place in the air fryer (leaving room in between so the air can circulate) and bake for 30 minutes.
2. While the potatoes are cooking, prepare the Cheesy Sauce and additional items. Set aside.
3. Check the potatoes at the 30-minute mark by poking a fork into them. If they're very tender, they're done. If not, continue to cook until a fork inserted proves them to be well-done. (As potato sizes vary, so will your cook time—the average cook time is usually about 40 minutes.)
4. When the potatoes are getting very close to being tender, warm the Cheesy Sauce and the beans in separate pans.
5. To assemble: Plate the potatoes and cut them across the top. Then, pry them open with a fork—just enough to get all the goodies in there. Top each potato with the Cheesy Sauce, beans, tomatoes, scallions, cilantro, and jalapeño and avocado, if using. Enjoy immediately.

Nutrition:

Calories: 420 | Total fat: 5g | Saturated fat: 0g

Cholesterol: 0mg | Sodium: 503mg | Carbohydrates: 80g

Fiber: 17g | Protein: 15g

192. Kids' Taquitos

Preparation Time: 5 minutes

Cooking Time: 7 minutes

Servings: 4

Ingredients:

- 8 corn tortillas
- Cooking oil spray (coconut, sunflower, or safflower)
- 1 (15-ounce) can vegan refried beans
- 1 cup shredded vegan cheese
- Guacamole (optional)
- Cheesy Sauce (optional)
- Vegan sour cream (optional)
- Fresh salsa (optional)

Directions:

1. Warm the tortillas (so they don't break): Run them under water for a second, and then place in an oil-sprayed air fryer basket (stacking them is fine). Fry for 1 minute.
2. Remove to a flat surface, laying them out individually. Place an equal amount of the beans in a line down the center of each tortilla. Top with the vegan cheese.
3. Roll the tortilla sides up over the filling and place seam-side down in the air fryer basket (this will help them seal so the tortillas don't fly open). Add just enough to fill the basket without them touching too much (you may need to do another batch, depending on the size of your air fryer basket).
4. Spray the tops with oil. Fry for 7 minutes, or until the tortillas are golden-brown and lightly crisp. Serve immediately with your preferred toppings.

Nutrition:

Calories: 286 | Total fat: 9g | Saturated fat: 4g

Cholesterol: 0mg | Sodium: 609mg | Carbohydrates: 44g

Fiber: 9g | Protein: 9g

193. Immune-Boosting Grilled Cheese Sandwich

Preparation Time: 3 minutes

Cooking Time: 12 minutes

Servings: 1

Ingredients:

- 2 slices sprouted whole-grain bread (or substitute a gluten-free bread)
- 1 teaspoon vegan margarine or neutral-flavored oil (sunflower, safflower, or refined coconut)
- 2 slices vegan cheese (Violife cheddar or Chao creamy original) or Cheesy Sauce
- 1 teaspoon mellow white miso
- 1 medium-large garlic clove, pressed or finely minced
- 2 tablespoons fermented vegetables, kimchi, or sauerkraut
- Romaine or green leaf lettuce

Directions:
1. Spread the outsides of the bread with the vegan margarine.
2. Place the sliced cheese inside and close the sandwich back up again (buttered sides facing out).
3. Place the sandwich in the air fryer basket and fry for 6 minutes.
4. Flip over and fry for another 6 minutes, or until nicely browned and crisp on the outside.
5. Transfer to a plate. Open the sandwich and evenly spread the miso and garlic clove over the inside of one of the bread slices.
6. Top with the fermented vegetables and lettuce, close the sandwich back up, cut in half, and serve immediately.

Nutrition:

Calories: 288 | Total fat: 13g | Saturated fat: 5g

Cholesterol: 0mg | Sodium: 1013mg | Carbohydrates: 34g

Fiber: 4g | Protein: 8g

194. Tamale Pie With Cilantro Lime Cornmeal Crust

Preparation Time: 25 minutes

Cooking Time: 20 minutes

Servings: 4

Ingredients:

For the filling
- 1 medium zucchini, diced (1¼ cups)
- 2 teaspoons neutral-flavored oil (sunflower, safflower, or refined coconut)
- 1 cup cooked pinto beans, drained
- 1 cup canned diced tomatoes (unsalted) with juice
- 3 large garlic cloves, minced or pressed
- 1 tablespoon chickpea flour
- 1 teaspoon dried oregano
- 1 teaspoon onion granules
- ½ teaspoon salt
- ½ teaspoon crushed red chili flakes
- Cooking oil spray (sunflower, safflower, or refined coconut)

For the crust
- ½ cup yellow cornmeal, finely ground
- 1½ cups water
- ½ teaspoon salt
- 1 teaspoon Nutrition yeast
- 1 teaspoon neutral-flavored oil (sunflower, safflower, or refined coconut)
- 2 tablespoons finely chopped cilantro
- ½ teaspoon lime zest (see Cooking Tip)

Directions:

To make the filling
1. In a large skillet set to medium-high heat, sauté the zucchini and oil for 3 minutes, or until the zucchini begins to brown.
2. Add the beans, tomatoes, garlic, flour, oregano, onion, salt, and chili flakes to the mixture.
3. Cook over medium heat, stirring often, for 5 minutes, or until the mixture is thickened and no liquid remains. Remove from the heat.
4. Spray a 6-inch round, 2-inch deep baking pan with oil and place the mixture in the bottom. Smooth out the top and set aside.

To make the crust
5. In a medium pot over high heat, place the cornmeal, water, and salt. Whisk constantly as you bring the mixture to a boil. Once it boils, reduce the heat to very low.
6. Add the Nutrition yeast and oil and continue to cook, stirring very often, for 10 minutes or until the mixture is very thick and hard to whisk. Remove from the heat.
7. Stir the cilantro and lime zest into the cornmeal mixture until thoroughly combined. Using a rubber spatula, gently spread it evenly onto the filling in the baking pan to form a smooth crust topping.
8. Place in the air fryer basket and bake for 20 minutes, or until the top is golden-brown. Let it cool for 5 to 10 minutes, then cut and serve.

Nutrition:

Calories: 165 | Total fat: 5g | Saturated fat: 1g

Cholesterol: 0mg | Sodium: 831mg | Carbohydrates: 26g

Fiber: 6g | Protein: 6g

195. Garlic Parmesan Chicken Wings

Preparation Time: 5 minutes

Cooking Time: 35 minutes

Servings: 5

Ingredients:
- 10 Chiken Wings
- Freshly ground black pepper
- Garlic powder
- Onion powder
- Baking powder

For the sauce:

- 6 tbsp. Butter, melted
- 2tbsp. honey
- 3. Cloves garlic, minced
- 3/4 c. Freshly grated Parmesan
- Chopped fresh parsley, for garnish

Directions:

1. Take the chicken wing parts out of the refrigerator and pat them dry.
2. Mix sea salt, black pepper, bell pepper, garlic powder, onion powder and baking powder in a small bowl.
3. Sprinkle the spice mixture on the wings and throw it to cover.
4. Place the wings on a flat layer in the air fryer.
5. Use the chicken air fryer (400 degrees) and cook for 30 minutes. To make the wings crispy quickly, you have to turn them about halfway.
6. Mix all the ingredients for the garlic parmesan sauce by stirring them in a small bowl.
7. Put the wings in the garlic-parmesan mixture and serve immediately.

Nutrition:

Calories: 176 kcal | Protein: 2.02 g | Fat: 15.19 g

Carbohydrates: 9.79 g

196. Buffalo Cauliflower Bites

Preparation Time: 5 minutes

Cooking Time: 25 minutes

Servings: 4

Ingredients:

- 1 Cauliflower
- 3 cloves garlic
- 3 tbsp. Extra-virgin olive oil
- Salt
- Pepper

  For the sauce:
- Hot sauce
- Butter
- Worcestershire sauce

Directions:

1. Cut the cauliflower into florets of equal size and place in a large bowl.
2. Cut each clove of garlic into 3 pieces and smash them with the side of your knife. Don't be afraid to smash the garlic. You want to expose as much of the garlic surface as possible so that it cooks well. Add this to the cauliflower.
3. Pour over the oil and add salt. Mix well until the cauliflower is well covered with oil and salt.
4. Turn on the air fryer at 400 F for 20 minutes and add the cauliflower. Turn it in half once.
5. To make the Sauce:
6. While the cauliflower is cooking, make the sauce. Whisk the hot sauce, butter and Worcestershire sauce in a small bowl.
7. Once the cauliflower is cooked, place it in a large bowl. Pour the hot sauce over the cauliflower and mix well.
8. Put the cauliflower back in the air fryer. Set it to 400F for 3-4 minutes so the sauce becomes a little firm.
9. Serve with blue cheese dressing.

Nutrition:

Calories: 69 kcal | Protein: 1.87 g

Fat: 6.06 g | Carbohydrates: 1.99 g

197. Spicy Dry-Rubbed Chicken Wings

Preparation Time: 5 minutes

Cooking Time: 45 minutes

Servings: 6

Ingredients:

- 12 Chicken wings
- Extra-virgin olive oil, for brushing

Marinade:

- Paprika
- Cayenne pepper
- Chili powder
- Freshly ground black pepper
- Garlic powder
- Onion powder
- Sea salt
- Oregano
- Kosher salt

Directions:

1. Marinating the wings:
2. Take the chicken out of the fridge and let it approach room temperature (30 minutes). Preheat the oven to 400 degrees.
3. Place the chicken in a freezer bag with 1/4 cup of the spicy dry massage. You can keep the rest in a mason jar.
4. Shake the bag so that the mixture covers the chicken evenly.
5. Store in the refrigerator for at least four hours, ideally overnight.
6. Put the wings in the air fryer basket, making sure they don't crowd each other too much.
7. Select "Air Fry" set temperature to 375°F (190°C) and set time to 24 minutes.
8. After 12 minutes, remove and turn the wings over.
9. Return to the oven to continue cooking until done.
10. Let rest for 5 minutes before serving.

Nutrition:

Calories: 230 kcal | Protein: 31.02 g | Fat: 11.54 g

Carbohydrates: 1.11 g

198. Air Fryer Steak Bites and Mushrooms

Preparation Time: 5 minutes

Cooking Time: 25 minutes

Servings: 4

Ingredients:

- 1 lb. Steaks cut into 1/2" cubes (ribeye, sirloin, tri-tip)
- 8 oz. mushrooms
- Extra-virgin olive oil
- 1 tsbp. Chili polder
- 1 tsp. Drie oregano
- 1/2 tsp. Garlic powder
- 1/4 tsp. Cayenne
- Kosher salt
- Freshly ground black pepper
- Coriander
- Dill
- Red pepper flakes

Directions:

1. Preheat the empty air fryer to 390 ° F with a crisp plate or basket for 4 minutes.
2. Pat the meat dry. As the air fryer heats up, throw beef cubes with olive oil and Montreal spices.
3. Halve or halve mushrooms. Pour beef cubes and mushrooms into the preheated air fryer and gently shake to combine.
4. Set the air fryer temperature to 390 ° F and the timer for 8 minutes.
5. Stop after 3 minutes and shake the basket. Repeat this process every 2 minutes until the beef cubes have reached the desired degree of cooking. Lift a large piece out and test it with a meat thermometer or cut and look in the middle to see the progress. Note that the meat will continue to cook as soon as it is removed from the air fryer and resting. Meat is medium at 145 ° F and has a warm pink center.
6. Let the meat rest for a few minutes before serving and then enjoy

Nutrition:

Calories: 583 kcal | Protein: 32.38 g

Fat: 27.25 g | Carbohydrates: 61.98 g

199. Pecan Crusted Chicken

Preparation Time: 10 minutes

Cooking Time: 25 minutes

Servings: 6

Ingredients:

- 6 chine tenders
- Kosher salt
- Freshly ground black pepper
- Paprika
- 2 tbsp. honey
- 1 tbsp. mustard
- Peacans

Directions:

1. Place the chicken tenders in a large bowl.
2. Add salt, pepper and smoked paprika and mix well until the chicken is covered with the spices.
3. Pour in honey and mustard and mix well.
4. Place the finely chopped pecans on a plate.
5. Roll the tender into the shredded pecans, one chicken tender at a time, until both sides are covered. Brush off excess material.
6. Place the offers in the air fryer basket and continue until all offers have been coated and are in the air fryer basket.
7. Set the air fryer to 350F for 12 minutes until the chicken is cooked through and the pecans are golden brown before serving.

Nutrition:

Calories: 95 kcal | Protein: 3.08 g

Fat: 8.18 g | Carbohydrates: 3.16 g

200. Chicken Tikka Kebab

Preparation Time: 10 minutes

Cooking Time: 30 minutes

Servings: 6

Ingredients:

- 6 Boneless, skinless chicken thighs
- 1 Red onion
- 2 Green & red bell pepper

For the marinade:

- 1 cup yogurt
- Ginger (optional)
- 2 Garlic cloves, crushed
- Indian spices, as preferred

Directions:

1. Mix all the ingredients for the marinade in a bowl and mix well.
2. Add chicken and spread the marinade on each side. Let it rest in the fridge for between 30 minutes and 8 hours.
3. Add oil, onions, green and red peppers to the marinade for cooking. Mix well.
4. Thread the marinated chicken, peppers and onions into the skewers in between.
5. Lightly grease the air fryer basket.
6. Arrange the chicken sticks in the Air fryer. Cook them at 180 degrees for 10 minutes.

7. Turn the chicken sticks and cook for another 7 minutes, then serve.

Nutrition:

Calories: 147 kcal | Protein: 10.25 g

Fat: 10.68 g | Carbohydrates: 1.85 g

201. Air Fryer Brussels sprouts

Preparation Time: 10 minutes

Cooking Time: 15 minutes

Servings: 2

Ingredients:

- 10 Brussel sprouts
- 1/4 c. balsamic vinegar
- 3 tbsp. extra-virgin olive oil
- Kosher salt
- Freshly ground black pepper

Directions:

1. Remove the hard ends of the Brussels sprouts and remove any damaged outer leaves. Rinse under cold water and pat dry. If your sprouts are large, cut them in half. Add oil, salt and pepper.
2. Arrange Brussels sprouts in a single layer in your air fryer and work in batches if not all fit. Cook for 8 to 12 minutes at 190 ° C and shake the pan halfway through the cooking process to brown it evenly. They are done when they are lightly browned and crispy at the edges.
3. Serve sprouts warm, optionally with balsamic reduction and parmesan.

Nutrition:

Calories: 1197 kcal | Protein: 125.58 g

Fat: 65.97 g | Carbohydrates: 16.97 g

202. Crispy Air Fried Tofu

Preparation Time: 10 minutes

Cooking Time: 50 minutes

Servings: 8

Ingredients:

- 2 16-oz block extra-firm tofu 453 g
- 2 tbsp soy sauce 30 mL
- 1 Tbsp. Toasted sesame oil
- 1 Tbsp. Olive oil
- 1 clove garlic minced

Directions:

1. Squeeze the tofu for at least 15 minutes by placing either a heavy pan or a pan on top and letting the moisture drain. When you're done, cut the tofu into bite-sized blocks and put it in a bowl.
2. Mix all remaining ingredients in a small bowl. Drizzle over the tofu and toss to cover. Let the tofu marinate for another 15 minutes.
3. Preheat your air fryer to 190 ° C. Add tofu blocks to your air fryer basket in a single layer. Let cook for 10 to 15 minutes and shake the pan occasionally to promote even cooking.

Nutrition:

Calories: 247 kcal | Protein: 3.83 g

Fat: 18.05 g | Carbohydrates: 21.99 g

203. Buttermilk Fried Mushrooms

Preparation Time: 5 minutes

Cooking Time: 30 minutes

Servings: 2

Ingredients:

- 2 heaping cups oyster mushrooms
- 1 cup buttermilk
- 1 1/2 cups all-purposes flour 200 g
- 1 tsp. Salt
- 1 tsp. Pepper
- 1 tsp. smoked paprika
- 1 tsp. garlic powder
- 1 tsp. onion powder
- 1 tsp. Cumin
- 1 tbsp oil

Directions:

1. Preheat the air fryer to 190 ° C. Clean the mushrooms and place in a large bowl with buttermilk. Let marinate for 15 minutes.
2. Mix the flour and spices in a large bowl. Put the mushrooms out of the buttermilk (keep the buttermilk). Dip each mushroom in the flour mixture, shake off excess flour, dip again in the buttermilk and then again in the flour (short: wet> dry> wet> dry).
3. Grease the bottom of your air pan well and place the mushrooms in a layer, leaving space between the mushrooms. Let it cook for 5 minutes, then roughly coat all sides with a little oil to promote browning.
4. Cook for another 5 to 10 minutes until golden brown and crispy.

Nutrition:

Calories: 380 kcal | Protein: 49.65 g

Fat: 18.15 g | Carbohydrates: 6.86 g

204. Crispy Baked Avocado Tacos

Preparation Time: 10 minutes

Cooking Time: 20 minutes

Servings: 5

Ingredients:

Salsa:
- 1 cup finely shopped pineapple
- 1 Roma tomato, finely chopped
- 1/2 red bell pepper, finely chopped
- 1/2 of a medium red onion
- 1 clove garlic minced
- 1/2 jalapeno finely chopped
- Pinch each cumin and salt

Avocado tacos:
- 1 avocado
- 1/4 cup all-purpose flour 35 g
- 1 large egg whisked
- 1/2 cup panko crumbs 65 g
- Pinch each salt and pepper
- 4 flour tortillas click for recipes

Adobo Sauce:
- 1/4 cup plain yogurt 60 g
- 2 tbsp. Mayonnaise 30 g
- 1/4 tsp lime juice
- 1 tbsp. Adobo sauce from a jar of chipotle peppers
- Polte peppers

Directions:
1. Combine all the salsa ingredients and put them in the fridge.
2. Prepare avocado: Halve the length of the avocado and remove the pit. Lay the avocado skin face down and cut each half into 4 equal pieces. Then gently peel off the skin.
3. Preheat the oven to 230 ° C or the air fryer to 190 ° C. Arrange your work area so that you have a bowl of flour, a bowl of whisk, a bowl of Panko with S&P, and a baking sheet lined with parchment at the end.
4. Dip each avocado slice first in the flour, then in the egg and then in the panko. Place on the prepared baking sheet and bake for 10 minutes or fry in the air. Lightly brown after half of the cooking process.
5. While cooking avocados, combine all the sauce ingredients.
6. Put salsa on a tortilla, top with 2 pieces of avocado and drizzle with sauce. Serve immediately and enjoy!

Nutrition:

Calories: 193 kcal | Protein: 13.7 g
Fat: 13.25 g | Carbohydrates: 4.69 g

205. Buttery Cod

Preparation Time: 5 minutes
Cooking Time: 15 minutes
Servings: 4

Ingredients:
- 1 tbsp. Parsley, chopped
- 3 tbsp. Butter, melted
- 8 Cherry tomatoes, halved
- 0.25 cup Tomato sauce
- 2 Cod fillets, cubed

Directions:
1. Turn on the air fryer to 390 degrees.
2. Combine all of the ingredients and put them into a pan that works with the air fryer.
3. After 12 minutes of baking, you can divide this between the four bowls and enjoy.

Nutrition:

Calories 232 | Carbs 5g | Protein 11g | Fat 8g

206. Creamy Chicken

Preparation Time: 10 minutes
Cooking Time: 15 minutes
Servings: 4

Ingredients:
- Pepper and salt
- 1 tsp. Olive oil
- 0.5 tsp. Sweet paprika
- 0.25 cup Coconut cream
- 4 Chicken breasts, cubed

Directions:
1. Turn on the air fryer to 370 degrees.
2. Prepare a pan that fits into the machine with some oil before adding the ingredients inside.
3. Add this to the air fryer and let it bake. After 17 minutes, you can divide between the few plates and serve!

Nutrition:

Calories 250 | Carbs 5g | Protein 11g | Fat 12g

207. Mushroom and Turkey Stew

Preparation Time: 25 minutes
Cooking Time: 25 minutes
Servings: 4

Ingredients:
- Pepper and salt
- 1 tbsp. Parsley, chopped
- 0.25 cup Tomato sauce
- 1 Turkey breast, cubed
- 0.5 lb. Brown mushrooms, sliced

Directions:
1. Turn on the air fryer to 350 degrees.
2. Pick out a pan and mix the tomato sauce, pepper, salt, mushrooms, and turkey together. Add to the air fryer.

3. After 25 minutes, the stew is done—divide between four bowls and top with the parsley.

Nutrition:

Calories 220 | Carbs 5g | Fat 12g | Protein 12g

208. Basil Chicken

Preparation Time: 15 minutes

Cooking Time: 25 minutes

Servings: 4

Ingredients:

- Pepper and salt
- 2 tsp. Smoked paprika
- 0.5 tsp. Dried basil
- 0.5 cup Chicken stock
- 0.5 lb. Chicken breasts, cubed

Directions:

1. Turn on the air fryer to 390 degrees.
2. Bring out a pan and toss the ingredients inside before putting it into the air fryer.
3. After 25 minutes of baking, divide this between a few plates and serve with a side salad.

Nutrition:

Calories 223 | Carbs 5g | Protein 13g | Fat 12g

209. Eggplant Bake

Preparation Time: 20 minutes

Cooking Time: 15 minutes

Servings: 4

Ingredients:

- 2 tsp. Olive oil (2 tsp)
- Pepper and salt
- 4 Spring onions, chopped
- 1 Hot chili pepper, chopped
- 2 Eggplants, cubed
- 4 Garlic cloves, minced
- 0.5 cup Cilantro, chopped
- 0.5 lb. Cherry tomatoes, cubed

Directions:

1. Turn on the air fryer and let it heat up to 380 degrees.
2. Prepare a baking pan that will go into the air fryer and mix all of the ingredients onto it.
3. Place into the air fryer to cook. After 15 minutes, divide between four bowls and serve.

Nutrition:

Calories 232 | Carbs 5g | Fat 12g | Protein 10g

210. Meatball Casserole

Preparation Time: 15 minutes

Cooking Time: 15 minutes

Servings: 6

Ingredients:

1 tbsp. Thyme, chopped

- 0.25 cup Parsley, chopped
- 0.33 lb. Turkey sausage
- 1 Egg, beaten
- 0.66 lb. Ground beef
- 2 tbsp. Olive oil
- 1 Shallot, minced
- 1 tbsp. Dijon mustard
- 3 Garlic cloves, minced
- 2 tbsp. Whole milk
- 1 tbsp. Rosemary, chopped

Directions:

1. Turn on the air fryer to a High setting and then give it time to heat up with some oil inside.
2. Add the garlic and onions and cook for a few minutes to make soft.
3. Add the milk and bread crumbs to a bowl and then mix. Then add in the rest of the ingredients and set aside to soak.
4. Use this mixture, after five minutes, to prepare some small meatballs. Add these to the air fryer.
5. Turn the heat up to 400 degrees to cook. After 10 minutes, take the lid off and shake the basket.
6. Cook another five minutes before serving.

Nutrition:

Calories 168 | Carbs 4g | Protein 12g | Fat 11g

211. Herbed Lamb Rack

Preparation Time: 10 minutes

Cooking Time: 10 minutes

Servings: 2

Ingredients:

- 4 tbsp. Olive oil
- 0.5 tsp. Pepper
- 1 tbsp. Dried thyme
- 2 tbsp. Dried rosemary
- 0.5 tsp. Salt
- 2 tsp. Garlic, minced
- 1 lb. Rack of lamb

Directions:

Turn on the air fryer to 400 degrees. In a bowl, combine the herbs and olive oil well.

Use this to coat the lamb before adding to the basket of the air fryer.

Close the lid, and then let this cook. Halfway through, you can shake the basket to make sure nothing sticks.

After ten minutes, take the lamb out and enjoy.

Nutrition:

Calories 542 | Carbs 3g | Fat 37g | Protein 45g

---

212. Baked Beef

Preparation Time: 1 hour

Cooking Time: 1 hour

Servings: 3

Ingredients:

- 1 bunch Garlic cloves
- 1 bunch Fresh herbs, mixed
- 2 Onions, sliced
- Olive oil
- 3 lbs. Beef
- 2 Celery sticks, chopped
- 2 Carrots, chopped

Directions:

1. Great up a pan and then add the herbs, olive oil, beef roast, and vegetables inside.
2. Turn the air fryer on to 400 degrees and place the pan inside. Let this heat up and close the lid.
3. After an hour of cooking, open the lid and then serve this right away.

Nutrition:

Calories 306 | Carbs 10g | Fat 21g | Protein 32g

---

213. Crispy Pork Chops

Preparation Time: 15 minutes

Cooking Time: 15 minutes

Servings: 6

Ingredients:

- 0.5 tsp. Salt
- 0.5 tsp Onion powder
- 0.25 tsp. Chili powder
- 0.25 tsp. Pepper
- 1 tsp. Smoked paprika
- 1 cup Pork rind
- 3 tbsp. Parmesan, grated
- 5 Boneless pork chops
- 2 Beaten eggs

Directions:

1. Use the pepper and salt to season the pork chops. Blend the rind to make some crumbs.
2. In another bowl, beat the eggs and then coat this onto the pork chops with the crumbs.
3. Take out the air fryer and set it to 400 degrees to heat up.
4. When this is done, add the pork chops into the air fryer and let it heat up. When this is halfway done, flip the pork chops over and cook a little more.
5. After 15 minutes of cooking, turn off the air fryer and serve.

Nutrition:

Calories 391 | Carbs 17g | Fat 18g | Protein 38g

---

214. Turkey Pillows

Preparation Time: 15 minutes

Cooking Time: 15 minutes

Servings: 4

Ingredients:

- 15 slices Turkey breast
- 2 jars Cream cheese
- 1 Egg yolk
- 4 cup Flour
- 0.5 tbsp. Dried granular yeast
- 2 tbsp. Sugar
- 0.75 tsp. Salt
- 0.35 cup Olive oil
- 0.33 cup Water
- 1 cup Milk with an egg inside

Directions:

1. Mix the ingredients for the dough with your hands until smooth. Make it into small balls and put on a floured surface.
2. Open the dough balls with a roller to make it square. Cut into small pieces. Fill with the turkey breast and a bit of cream cheese. Close the points together.
3. Turn on the air fryer to 400 degrees. Place a few of the balls inside and let them cook.
4. After five minutes, take these out and repeat with the rest of the pillows until done.

Nutrition:

Calories 528 | Carbs 23g | Fat 30g | Protein 44g

---

215. Chicken Wings

Preparation Time: 20 minutes

Cooking Time: 25 minutes

Servings: 2

Ingredients:

- 2 tbsp. Chives
- 0.5 tbsp. Salt
- 1 tbsp. Lime
- 0.5 tbsp. Ginger, chopped

- 1 tbsp. Garlic, minced
- 1 tbsp. Chili paste
- 2 tbsp. Honey
- 0.5 tbsp. Cornstarch
- 1 tbsp. Soy sauce
- Oil
- 10 Chicken wings

Directions:

1. Dry the chicken and then cover it with spray. Add into the air fryer that is preheated to 400 degrees.
2. Let this cook for a bit. During that time, add the rest of the ingredients to a bowl and set aside.
3. After 25 minutes, the chicken is done. Add the chicken into a bowl and top with the sauce. Sprinkle the chives on top and serve.

Nutrition:

Calories 81 | Carbs 0g | Fat 5g | Protein 8g

216. Chicken Cordon Bleu

Preparation Time: 60 minutes

Cooking Time: 40 minutes

Servings: 6

Ingredients:

- 1 Garlic clove
- 2 Eggs
- 2 tsp. Butter, melted
- 1 cup Bread, ground
- 0.25 cup Flour
- 2 tsp. Fresh thyme
- 16 slices Swiss cheese
- 8 slices Ham
- 4 Chicken breasts

Directions:

1. Turn on the air fryer to heat to 350 degrees.
2. Flatten out the chicken and then fill with two slices of cheese, ham, and then cheese again. Roll up and use a toothpick to keep together.
3. Mix the garlic, thyme, and bread together with the butter. Beat the eggs and season the flour with pepper and salt.
4. Pass the chicken rolls through the flour, then the egg, and then the breadcrumbs. Add to the air fryer to cook.
5. After 20 minutes, take the chicken out and cool down before serving.

Nutrition:

Calories 387 | Carbs 18g | Fat 20g | Protein 33g

217. Fried Chicken

Preparation Time: 20 minutes

Cooking Time: 25 minutes

Servings: 4

Ingredients:

- 1 Lemon
- 1 Ginger, grated
- Ground pepper, salt, and garlic powder
- 1 lb. Chopped chicken

Directions:

1. Add the chicken to a bowl with the rest of the ingredients. Let it set for a bit to marinate.
2. After 15 minutes, add some oil to the air fryer and let it heat up to 320 degrees.
3. Add the chicken inside to cook for 25 minutes, shaking it a few times to cook through. Serve warm.

Nutrition:

Calories 345 | Carbs 23g | Fat 3g | Protein 3g

218. Chicken and Potatoes

Preparation Time: 1 hour

Cooking Time: 55 minutes

Servings: 2

Ingredients:

- Pepper and salt
- Provencal herbs
- 2 Chicken pieces
- 4 Potatoes
- Olive oil

Directions:

1. Peel the skin from the potatoes and cut into slices. Add some pepper and place into the air fryer.
2. Preheat to 340 degrees. Cover the chicken with the herbs, pepper, salt, and oil and add it in with the potatoes.
3. Cook this until well done. After forty minutes, turn the chicken around and let it cook another 15 minutes before serving.

Nutrition:

Calories 200 | Carbs 18g | Fat 4g | Protein 22g

219. Coconut-Crusted Chicken Tenders

Preparation Time: 15 minutes

Cooking Time: 8 minutes

Servings: 4

Ingredients:

- 3 Eggs
- 1 lb. Chicken tenders

- 1 cup Cornstarch
- 2 cups. Sweetened shredded coconut
- 1 tsp. Cayenne pepper

Directions:
1. Set the Air Fryer temperature at 360° Fahrenheit.
2. Prepare three dishes. In the first one, add the cornstarch and cayenne with any other desired seasonings. In the second bowl, add the eggs. Lastly, add the coconut in the third dish.
3. Dredge the chicken through the cornstarch, egg, and coconut.
4. Lightly spritz the fryer basket with a cooking oil spray as needed.
5. Set the timer for 8 minutes and air-fry until it's golden brown before serving.

Nutrition:
Calories: 390 kcal | Protein: 32.38 g
Fat: 12.14 g | Carbohydrates: 34.67 g

220. Crispy Chicken Sliders

Preparation Time: 10 minutes
Cooking Time: 8 minutes
Servings: 6

Ingredients:
- 1 pkg. Crispy Chicken Strips
- 1 pkg. Sweet Hawaiian Rolls

Optional Ingredients/toppings:
- Spinach leaves
- Tomatoes
- Honey mustard

Directions:
1. Place the six chicken strips in the Air Fryer basket with a coating of olive oil spray. Cook at 390° Fahrenheit for 8 minutes.
2. Slice the rolls in half and top them with honey mustard, spinach, and tomatoes or other toppings of your choice.
3. Slice the chicken strips into chunks and place them on the rolls.

Nutrition:
Calories: 53 kcal | Protein: 3.9 g
Fat: 3.27 g | Carbohydrates: 1.87 g

221. Garlic Herb Turkey Breast

Preparation Time: 1 hour
Cooking Time: 40 minutes
Servings: 6
Ingredients:

- 2 lb. Turkey breast
- 4 tbsp. Melted butter
- 3 cloves Garlic
- 1 tsp. Thyme
- 1 tsp. Rosemary

Directions:
1. Warm the Air Fryer to reach 375° Fahrenheit.
2. Pat the turkey breast dry. Mince the garlic and chop the rosemary and thyme.
3. Melt the butter and mix with the garlic, thyme, and rosemary in a small mixing bowl. Brush the butter over turkey breast.
4. Place in the Air Fryer basket, skin side up, and cook for 40 minutes or until internal temperature reaches 160° Fahrenheit, flipping halfway through.
5. Wait for five minutes before slicing.

Nutrition:
Calories: 321 kcal | Protein: 34.35 g
Fat: 19.32 g | Carbohydrates: 0.56 g

222. Honey-Lime Chicken Wings

Preparation Time: 20 minutes
Cooking Time: 30 minutes
Servings: 4

Ingredients:
- 2 lb. Chicken wings
- 2 tbsp. Lime juice
- .25 cup Honey
- 1 tbsp. Lime zest
- 1 pressed Garlic clove

Directions:
1. Warm the Air Fryer at 360° Fahrenheit.
2. Whisk the garlic, honey, and lime juice and zest. Toss in the wings and cover with the mixture.
3. Prepare the wings in batches. Cook for 25-30 minutes until they're crispy. Shake the basket at 8-minute intervals.
4. Serve and garnish as desired.

Nutrition:
Calories: 375 kcal | Protein: 51.59 g
Fat: 9.56 g | Carbohydrates: 18.67 g

223. Rotisserie-Style, Whole Chicken

Preparation Time: 50 minutes
Cooking Time: 30 minutes
Servings: 4

Ingredients:
- 2 tsp. Olive oil, as needed
- 6-7 lb. Whole chicken

- 1 tbsp. Seasoned salt

Directions:
1. Set the Air Fryer at 350° Fahrenheit.
2. Coat the chicken with oil and a sprinkle of salt.
3. Arrange the chicken in the Air Fryer – skin-side down.
4. Cook for 30 minutes. Flip the chicken over and air-fry for another 30 minutes.
5. Wait for ten minutes before slicing.
6. Note: This recipe is for chickens under 6 lb. for a 3.7-quart Air Fryer.

Nutrition:
Calories: 859 kcal | Protein: 151.45 g
Fat: 23.67 g | Carbohydrates: 0 g

224. Tarragon Chicken

Preparation Time: 15 minutes
Cooking Time: 12 minutes
Servings: 1

Ingredients:
- 1 Skinless/boneless chicken breast
- .125 tsp. freshly cracked ground black pepper
- .5 tsp. Unsalted butter
- .125 tsp. kosher salt
- .25 cup dried tarragon

Also Needed: Aluminum foil (12x14-inch piece)

Directions:
1. Warm the oven in advance to reach 390° Fahrenheit.
2. Arrange the chicken in the foil with the tarragon, butter, salt, and pepper.
3. Loosely wrap the foil for minimal airflow.
4. Air-fry the chicken packs for 12 minutes in the basket.

Nutrition:
Calories: 101 kcal | Protein: 6.53 g
Fat: 8.02 g | Carbohydrates: 0.53 g

225. Beef and Potato

Preparation Time: 5 minutes
Cooking Time: 2 minutes
Servings: 4

Ingredients:
- 3 cups Mashed potatoes
- 1 lb. Ground beef
- 2 Eggs
- 2 tbsp. Garlic powder
- 1 cup Sour cream

Directions:
1. Set the Air Fryer to reach 390° Fahrenheit.
2. Combine all of the fixings in a mixing container. Scoop it into a heat-safe dish.
3. Arrange in the fryer to cook for two minutes.
4. Serve for lunch or a quick dinner.

Nutrition:
Calories: 509 kcal | Protein: 41.36 g
Fat: 25.15 g | Carbohydrates: 27.77 g

226. Beef Roll-Ups

Preparation Time: 20 minutes
Cooking Time: 25 minutes
Servings: 4

Ingredients:
- 6 slices Provolone cheese
- 2 lbs. Beef flank steak
- 3 tbsp. Pesto
- .75 cup Baby spinach
- 3 oz. roasted red bell peppers

Directions:
1. Heat the Air Fryer at 400° Fahrenheit.
2. Slice the steak. Add the pesto and butter evenly on the meat.
3. Layer in the spinach, peppers, and cheese about ¾ of the way down through the roll-up. Roll the mixture. Secure it with skewers or toothpicks.
4. Air-fry for 14 minutes. Turn the beef halfway through the cooking process.
5. Wait for at least ten minutes before slicing to serve.

Nutrition:
Calories: 550 kcal | Protein: 62.48 g
Fat: 30.7 g | Carbohydrates: 2.88 g

227. Breaded Beef Schnitzel

Preparation Time: 15 minutes
Cooking Time: 12 minutes
Servings: 1

Ingredients:
- 2 tbsp. Olive oil
- 1 Thin beef schnitzel
- .5 cup Gluten-free breadcrumbs
- 1 Egg

Directions:
1. Heat the Air Fryer a couple of minutes (356° Fahrenheit).
2. Combine the breadcrumbs and oil in a shallow bowl. Whisk the egg in another mixing container.
3. Dip the beef into the egg, and then the breadcrumbs. Arrange in the basket of the Air Fryer.
4. Air-fry 12 minutes and serve.

Nutrition:
Calories: 126 kcal | Protein: 4.13 g
Fat: 10.76 g | Carbohydrates: 3.34 g

228. Lemon Chicken Breast

Preparation Time: 10 minutes
Cooking Time: 30 minutes
Servings: 4

Ingredients:
- ¼ cup olive oil
- 3 tablespoons garlic, minced
- 1/3 cup dry white wine
- 1 tablespoon lemon zest, grated
- 2 tablespoons lemon juice
- 1 and ½ teaspoons dried oregano, crushed
- 1 teaspoon thyme leaves, minced
- Salt and pepper to taste
- 4 skin-on boneless chicken breasts
- 1 lemon, sliced

Directions:
1. Take baking and add all listed ingredients, add chicken breasts and coat them well.
2. Place lemon slices on top.
3. Spread mustard mixture over toasted bread slices.
4. Press "Power Button" on your Air Fryer and select "Air Fry" mode.
5. Press the Time Button and set time to 30 minutes.
6. Push Temp Button and set temp to 370 degrees F.
7. Press the "Start/Pause" button and start the device.
8. Push the pan into your Air Frye's Cooking basket and cook until done. Serve and enjoy!

Nutrition:
Calories: 388 | Fat: 8 g | Saturated Fat: 1 g | Protein: 13 g
Carbohydrates: 8 g | Fiber: 1 g | Sodium: 339 mg

229. Parmesan Chicken Meatballs

Preparation Time: 10 minutes
Cooking Time: 12 minutes
Servings: 4

Ingredients:
- 1-pound ground chicken
- 1 large egg, beaten
- ½ cup parmesan cheese, grated
- ½ cup pork rinds, ground
- 1 teaspoon garlic powder
- 1 teaspoon paprika
- 1 teaspoon salt
- ½ teaspoon pepper
- ½ cup pork rinds, ground

Directions:
1. Take a bowl and add all listed ingredients.
2. Toss well and mix well.
3. Make small meatballs out of the mixture and roll them into pork rinds, coat them well.
4. Transfer coated meatballs into Air Fryer cooking basket.
5. Press "Power Button" on your Air Fryer and select "Bake" mode.
6. Press the Time Button and set time to 12 minutes.
7. Push Temp Button and set temp to 400 degrees F.
8. Press the "Start/Pause" button and start the device.
9. Push the Air Fryer cooking basket into Oven.
10. Let it cook until the timer runs out, serve, and enjoy!

Nutrition:
Calories: 520 | Fat: 17 g | Saturated Fat: 3 g | Protein: 41 g
Carbohydrates: 55 g | Fiber: 6 g | Sodium: 391 mg

230. Oregano Chicken Meatballs

Preparation Time: 10 minutes
Cooking Time: 25 minutes
Servings: 4

Ingredients:
- 2 pounds chicken breast, minced
- 1 tablespoon avocado oil
- 1 teaspoon smoked paprika
- 1 teaspoon garlic powder
- 1 teaspoon oregano
- ½ teaspoon salt
- Pepper as needed

Directions:
1. Take a bowl and add listed ingredients, mix well.
2. Makes small meatballs out of the mixture and transfer to Air Fryer cooking basket.
3. Transfer coated meatballs into Air Fryer cooking basket.
4. Press "Power Button" on your Air Fryer and select "Air Fry" mode.
5. Press the Time Button and set time to 25 minutes.
6. Push Temp Button and set temp to 375 degrees F.
7. Press the "Start/Pause" button and start the device.
8. Push the Air Fryer cooking basket into the oven.
9. Let it cook until the timer runs out, serve, and enjoy!

Nutrition:
Calories: 325 | Fat: 14 g | Saturated Fat: 2 g | Protein: 26 g
Carbohydrates: 15 g | Fiber: 0.2 g | Sodium: 220 mg

231. Honey and Chicken Drumsticks

Preparation Time: 10 minutes

Cooking Time: 15 minutes

Servings: 4

Ingredients:

- 2 chicken drumsticks, skin removed
- 2 teaspoons olive oil
- 2 teaspoons honey
- ½ teaspoon garlic, minced

Directions:

1. Take a re-sealable zip bag and add olive oil, garlic, and honey, mix well.
2. Add chicken to the bag and let it marinate for 30 minutes.
3. Preheat your Air Fryer to 30 minutes in "AIR FRY" mode.
4. Transfer chicken to Air Fryer cooking basket and cook for 15 minutes. Serve and enjoy!

Nutrition:

Calories: 422 | Fat: 23 g | Saturated Fat: 6 g | Protein: 45 g

Carbohydrates: 7 g | Fiber: 2 g | Sodium: 600 mg

232. Lemon and Chicken Pepper

Preparation Time: 10 minutes

Cooking Time: 15 minutes

Servings: 4

Ingredients:

- 1 chicken breast
- 2 lemon, juiced and rind reserved
- 1 tablespoon chicken seasoning
- 1 teaspoon garlic puree
- Handful of peppercorns
- Salt and pepper to taste

Directions:

1. Preheat your fryer to 352 degrees F on "AIR FRY" mode.
2. Take a large-sized sheet of silver foil and work on top, add all of the seasonings alongside the lemon rind.
3. Layout the chicken breast onto a chopping board and trim any Fat and little bones.
4. Season each side with the pepper and salt.
5. Rub the chicken seasoning on both sides well.
6. Place on your silver foil sheet and rub.
7. Seal it up tightly.
8. Slap it with a rolling pin and flatten it.
9. Place it in your fryer and cook for 15 minutes until the center is fully cooked. Serve and enjoy!

Nutrition:

Calories: 350 | Fat: 33 g | Saturated Fat: 9 g | Protein: 33 g

Carbohydrates: 2 g | Fiber: 0 g | Sodium: 330 mg

233. Chicken Curry on Edamame and Asparagus

Preparation Time: 10 minutes

Cooking Time: 10 minutes

Servings: 4

Ingredients:

- 1 teaspoon cumin, ground
- 12 oz. chicken breast, boneless and skinless
- 2 cups of water
- ¼ teaspoon black pepper
- ¼ cup of light mayonnaise
- ¼ cup plain Greek yogurt
- 1-1/2 teaspoons curry powder
- ½ teaspoon salt
- 1 tablespoon sugar
- 2 cups of cut asparagus
- 4 cups of baby kale mix
- 1 cup edamame, shelled and thawed
- ¼ cup green onion or cilantro, chopped
- ½ cup red onion, chopped

Directions:

1. Sprinkle pepper and cumin over the chicken, cook for 6 minutes. Release pressure naturally and remove the lid to take the chicken out.
2. Keep on your cutting board, shred after 5 minutes and set aside.
3. Whisk together the mayonnaise, yogurt, salt, curt, and sugar in a bowl.
4. Add the edamame and asparagus in the pot, cook for 1 minute.
5. Release pressure and keep the asparagus mix in your colander. Run this under cold water and drain well.
6. Keep equal quantities of your kale mix on 4 plates. Then add the asparagus mixture on top.
7. Mix the onions and chicken to your yogurt mix, tossing to coat well.
8. Spoon equal quantities on each asparagus mixture serving and sprinkle some cilantro.

Nutrition:

Calories 253 | Carbohydrates 17g | Total Fat 9g

Protein 26g | Fiber 5g

234. Cheeseburger 'Mini' Sliders

Preparation Time: 15 minutes

Cooking Time: 10 minutes

Servings: 1

Ingredients:

- 6 slices Cheddar cheese
- 1 lb. Ground beef
- Freshly cracked black pepper and salt (as desired)
- 6 Dinner rolls

Directions:
1. Warm the Air Fryer ahead of fry time to 390° Fahrenheit.
2. Shape six (2.5-oz.) patties and dust with the pepper and salt.
3. Arrange the burgers in the fryer basket and cook for ten minutes.
4. Take them out of the cooker and add the cheese.
5. Return them to the basket for another minute until the cheese melts.

Nutrition:

Calories: 382 kcal | Protein: 35.62 g

Fat: 16.77 g | Carbohydrates: 20.38 g

---

235. Quick and Easy Rib Eye Steak

Preparation Time: 40 minutes

Cooking Time: 35 minutes

Servings: 2

Ingredients:
- 2 lb. Unchilled steak
- 1 tbsp. Olive oil
- Steak Rub: Salt and pepper mix (desired)
- Baking pan also needed to fit into the basket

Directions:
1. Press the "M" button for the French Fries icon. Adjust the time to four minutes at 400° Fahrenheit.
2. Rub the steak with the oil and seasonings. Arrange the steak in the basket and air-fry for 14 minutes. (Flip it over after seven minutes.)
3. Place the rib eye on a platter, and let it rest for ten minutes.
4. Slice it and garnish the way you like it.

Nutrition:

Calories: 1017 kcal | Protein: 129.44 g

Fat: 55.78 g | Carbohydrates: 0 g

---

236. Roast Beef

Preparation Time: 1 hour

Cooking Time: 55 minutes

Servings: 6

Ingredients:
- .5 tsp. Garlic powder
- .5 tsp. Oregano
- 1 tsp. Dried thyme
- 1 tbsp. Olive oil
- 2 lb. Round roast

Directions:
1. Heat the Air Fryer at 330° Fahrenheit.
2. Combine the spices. Brush the oil over the beef, and rub it using the spice mixture.
3. Add to a baking dish and arrange it in the Air Fryer basket for 30 minutes. Turn it over and continue cooking 25 more minutes.
4. Wait for a few minutes before slicing.
5. Serve on your choice of bread or plain with a delicious side dish.

Nutrition:

Calories: 287 kcal | Protein: 45.97 g

Fat: 10.01 g | Carbohydrates: 0.28 g

---

237. Air Fryer Chicken Wings

Preparation Time: 5 minutes

Cooking Time: 20 minutes

Servings: 4

Ingredients:
- 4 (4-oz.) salmon fillets
- 1 tbsp. Grainy mustard
- 2 cloves garlic, finely minced
- 1 tbsp. finely minced shallots
- 2 tsp. fresh thyme leaves, chopped, plus more for garnish
- 2 tsp. fresh rosemary, chopped
- Juice of 1/2 lemon
- Kosher salt
- Freshly ground black pepper
- Lemon slices, for serving

Directions:
1. Take the chicken wing parts out of the refrigerator and pat them dry (if you remove as much moisture as possible, you will get a crispy wing skin).
2. Mix sea salt, black pepper, smoked paprika, garlic powder, onion powder and baking powder in a small bowl or baking dish.
3. Sprinkle the spice mixture on the wings and throw it to cover.
4. Place the wings on the cooking basket. In Ninja Foodie this is known as the "Cook & Crisp" basket.
5. Drizzle the chicken wings with olive oil.
6. Use the Air Crisp setting at 400 degrees on air fryers to cook the wings for 14 minutes on each side. Enjoy hot wings!

Nutrition:

Calories: 32 kcal | Protein: 2 g

Fat: 1.73 g | Carbohydrates: 2.56 g

---

238. Sweet and Spicy Montreal Steak

Preparation Time: 30 minutes

Cooking Time: 6 minutes

Servings: 2

Ingredients:

- 2 boneless Sirloin steaks
- 1 tbsp. Brown sugar
- 1 tbsp. Montreal steak seasoning
- 1 tsp. Crushed red pepper
- 1 tbsp. Olive oil

Directions:

1. Set the temperature of the Air Fryer at 390° Fahrenheit.
2. Prepare the steaks with oil. Rub them with the desired seasonings.
3. Arrange the steaks in the basket and set the timer for three minutes.
4. Flip the steak over and air-fry for another three minutes.
5. Cool and slice it into strips before serving.

Nutrition:

Calories: 1253 kcal | Protein: 126.25 g

Fat: 75.9 g | Carbohydrates: 6.58 g

239. Bacon-Wrapped Pork Tenderloin

Preparation Time: 1 hour

Cooking Time:

Servings: 4 to 6

Ingredients:

- 1 lb. Pork tenderloin
- 1-2 tbsp. Dijon mustard
- 3-4 strips Bacon

Directions:

1. Set the Air Fryer temperature at 360° Fahrenheit.
2. Coat the tenderloin with the mustard and wrap with the bacon.
3. Air-fry them for 15 minutes. Flip and cook 10 to 15 more minutes.
4. Serve with your favorite sides.

Nutrition:

Calories: 133 kcal | Protein: 21.31 g

Fat: 4.65 g | Carbohydrates: 0.41 g

240. Bratwurst and Veggies

Preparation Time: 10 minutes

Cooking Time: 20 minutes

Servings: 2

Ingredients:

- 1 pkg. Bratwurst
- 1 each Red and green bell pepper
- .25 cup Onion - red or purple
- 5 tbsp. Gluten-free Cajun seasoning

Directions:

1. Warm the unit to reach 390° Fahrenheit.
2. Line the Air Fryer with foil, if preferred.
3. Slice and add in the vegetables.
4. Slice the bratwurst into about 0.5-inch size rounds, and place on top of the veggies.
5. Evenly sprinkle the seasoning on top.
6. Air-fry for 10 minutes. Carefully open and stir or mix.
7. Air-fry for another 10 minutes before serving.

Nutrition:

Calories: 84 kcal | Protein: 1.57 g

Fat: 0.06 g | Carbohydrates: 15.89 g

241. Dutch Pancake With Shrimp Salsa

Preparation Time: 5 minutes

Cooking Time: 10 minutes

Servings: 4

Ingredients:

- 1 tablespoon plus 2 teaspoons butter
- 3 eggs
- ½ cup flour
- ½ cup milk
- ⅛ teaspoon salt
- 1 cup salsa
- 1 cup frozen fully cooked small shrimp, thawed

Directions:

1. Preheat the air fryer with a 6-by-6-by-2-inch pan in the basket. Add the butter and heat until it melts.
2. Quickly combine the eggs, flour, milk, and salt in a medium bowl and beat well with an eggbeater until well mixed and frothy.
3. Carefully remove the basket with the pan from the air fryer and tilt so the butter covers the bottom of the pan. Immediately pour the batter into the hot pan and put it back in the fryer.
4. Bake for 12 to 16 minutes or until the pancake is puffed and golden brown.
5. Stir together the salsa and shrimp and top the pancake with this mixture.

Nutrition:

Calories: 213 | Total Fat: 9g | Saturated Fat: 5g

Cholesterol: 198mg | Sodium: 593mg

Carbohydrates: 18g | Fiber: 2g | Protein: 14g

242. Steamed Scallops With Dill

Preparation Time: 5 minutes

Cooking Time: 4 minutes

Servings: 4

Ingredients:
- 1-pound sea scallops
- 1 tablespoon lemon juice
- 2 teaspoons olive oil
- 1 teaspoon dried dill
- Pinch salt
- Freshly ground black pepper

Directions:
1. Check the scallops for a small muscle attached to the side, and pull it off and discard it.
2. Toss the scallops with the lemon juice, olive oil, dill, salt, and pepper. Put into the air fryer basket.
3. Steam for 4 to 5 minutes, tossing the basket once during cooking time, until the scallops are just firm when tested with your finger. The internal temperature should be 145°F at minimum.

Nutrition:

Calories: 121 | Total Fat: 3g | Saturated Fat: 0g

Cholesterol: 37mg | Sodium: 223mg | Carbohydrates: 3g

Fiber: 0g | Protein: 19g

243. Chicken Pita Sandwiches

Preparation Time: 10 minutes

Cooking Time: 10 minutes

Servings: 4

Ingredients:
- 2 boneless, skinless chicken breasts, cut into 1-inch cubes
- 1 small red onion, sliced
- 1 red bell pepper, sliced
- ⅓ cup Italian salad dressing, divided
- ½ teaspoon dried thyme
- 4 pita pockets, split
- 2 cups torn butter lettuce
- 1 cup chopped cherry tomatoes

Directions:
1. Place the chicken, onion, and bell pepper in the air fryer basket. Drizzle with 1 tablespoon of the Italian salad dressing, add the thyme, and toss.
2. Bake for 9 to 11 minutes or until the chicken is 165°F on a food thermometer, tossing once during cooking time.
3. Transfer the chicken and vegetables to a bowl and toss with the remaining salad dressing.
4. Assemble sandwiches with the pita pockets, butter lettuce, and cherry tomatoes.

Nutrition:

Calories: 414 | Total Fat: 19g | Saturated Fat: 4g

Cholesterol: 101mg | Sodium: 253mg

Carbohydrates: 22g | Fiber: 2g | Protein: 36g

244. Chicken À La King

Preparation Time: 10 minutes

Cooking Time: 17 minutes

Servings: 4

Ingredients:
- 2 boneless, skinless chicken breasts, cut into 1-inch cubes
- 8 button mushrooms, sliced
- 1 red bell pepper, chopped
- 1 tablespoon olive oil
- 1 (10-ounce) package refrigerated Alfredo sauce
- ½ teaspoon dried thyme
- 6 slices French bread
- 2 tablespoons softened butter

Directions:
1. Place the chicken, mushrooms, and bell pepper in the air fryer basket. Drizzle with the olive oil and toss to coat.
2. Roast for 10 to 15 minutes or until the chicken is 165°F on a food thermometer, tossing the food once during cooking time.
3. Remove the chicken and vegetables to a 6-inch metal bowl and stir in the Alfredo sauce and thyme. Return to the air fryer and cook for 3 to 4 minutes or until hot.
4. Meanwhile, spread the French bread slices with the butter. When the chicken is done, remove the pan from the basket and add the bread, butter-side up. Toast for 2 to 4 minutes or until light golden brown.
5. Place the toast on a serving plate and top with the chicken.

Nutrition:

Calories: 744 | Total Fat: 32g | Saturated Fat: 15g

Cholesterol: 142mg | Sodium: 3,904mg

Carbohydrates: 64g | Fiber: 2g | Protein: 50g

245. Perfect Pork chops

Preparation Time: 10 minutes

Cooking Time: 16 minutes

Servings: 4

Ingredients:
- 4 boneless pork chops
- 2 tsp olive oil
- ½ tsp granulated onion
- ½ tsp granulated garlic
- ½ tsp parsley
- ½ tsp celery seed
- ½ tsp salt
- ¼ tsp sugar

Directions:

1. Mix together oil, celery seed, parsley, granulated onion, granulated garlic, sugar, and salt in a small bowl
2. Brush seasoning blend all over the pork chops.
3. Arrange pork chops on the air fryer oven pan and cook at 350 F for 8 minutes
4. Cook for 8 minutes more the other side of the chops.
5. Serve and enjoy.

Nutrition:

Calories 279 | Fat 22.3 g | Carbs 0.6 g | Protein 18.1 g

246. Tasty meatballs

Preparation Time: 10 minutes

Cooking Time: 12 minutes

Servings: 8

Ingredients:

- 1 lb. ground beef
- 1 lb. ground pork
- 1 tbsp Worcestershire sauce
- 1/2 cup breadcrumbs
- 1/2 cup crumbled feta cheese
- 2 eggs, lightly beaten
- 1 tbsp minced garlic
- 1 chopped onion
- 1/4 cup fresh parsley, chopped
- 1/4 tsp pepper
- 1 tsp salt

Directions:

1. Mix all ingredients in a bowl until well combined.
2. Use cooking spray over the Air Fryer oven tray pan.
3. Shape small balls from meat mixture, arrange on a pan, and air fry at 400 F for 11 minutes
4. Serve and enjoy.

Nutrition:

Calories 263 | Fat 9 g | Carbs 7.5 g | Protein 35.9 g

247. Good'ol steak

Preparation Time: 1 hour

Cooking Time: 30 minutes

Servings: 8

Ingredients:

- 2 steaks, rinsed and pat dry
- 1 tsp olive oil
- 1/2 tsp garlic powder
- Salt
- Pepper

Directions:

1. Brush steaks with olive oil and spring with salt, garlic powder, and pepper.
2. Preheat your air fryer oven to 400 F.
3. Put the steaks on the air fryer oven pan and air fry for 10-18 minutes turning halfway through.
4. Serve and enjoy.

Nutrition:

Calories 361 Fat 10.9 g Carbs 0.5 g Protein 61.6 g

248. Chicken Curry

Preparation Time: 1 hour and 10 minutes

Cooking Time: 25 minutes

Servings: 5

Ingredients:

For the Chicken:

- 5 pieces skin-on bone-in chicken thighs
- 1/4 cup mayonnaise
- 1 Tablespoon garlic minced
- 1 Tablespoon brown sugar
- 2 Tablespoon soy sauce
- 2 Tablespoon grated ginger
- 1 teaspoon curry powder
- 1/4 teaspoon paprika
- 1/4 teaspoon cumin

Other ingredients:

- 1/2 teaspoon curry powder
- 1/4 teaspoon cumin
- 1/4 teaspoon paprika
- 1/4 cup scallion

Directions:

1. Mix all the ingredients for chicken. Marinate the chicken in this marinade for at least 2 hours or overnight in the refrigerator.
2. Mix 1/2 teaspoon of curry, 1/4 teaspoon of cumin and 1/4 teaspoon of paprika and set aside for later.
3. Take the chicken out of the refrigerator 30 minutes before air frying.
4. Line the fryer basket with a grill mat or a sheet of lightly greased aluminum foil.
5. Put the chicken thighs into the basket skin side down, without stacking, and air fry at 380F (190C) for 10 minutes.
6. Flip the chicken thigh over, now ski side up, and sprinkle some dry seasoning mix over the skin.
7. Air fry at 380F (190C) for another 6-7 minutes until the meat is cooked through, internal temperature exceeds 170F (77C).
8. Sprinkle some scallion to serve

Nutrition:

Calories: 563.3 | Fat: 30.6 g | Saturated Fat: 23.1 g

Carbohydrates: 21.5 g | Fiber: 4.9 g | Protein: 51.9 g

Sugars: 12.5 g | Cholesterol: 130 mg | Sodium: 766.2 mg

Potassium: 1038.3 mg

---

249. Roasted Brussels Sprouts

Preparation Time: 20 minutes

Cooking Time: 10 minutes

Servings: 4

Ingredients:

- 2 tablespoons olive oil
- 1 lb. whole Brussels sprouts, sliced in half
- Salt
- Garlic butter

Directions:

1. Heat an air fryer to 375°F. Cut the Brussels sprouts into halves. Transfer to a bowl, add olive oil and salt. Toss to combine well.
2. Add the Brussels sprouts to the air fryer. Fry and remember to stop and give a shake to your air fryer about halfway through, for 15 minutes total.
3. When the Brussels sprouts are ready, transfer into the bowl. You can add garlic butter for extra flavour. Serve immediately.

Nutrition:

Calories: 135.6 | Fat: 7.2 g | Saturated Fat: 1 g | Fiber: 5.5 g

Carbohydrates: 16.3 g | Protein: 4.6 g | Sugars: 5.3 g |

Cholesterol: 0 mg |Sodium: 669.8 mg| Potassium: 527.9 mg

---

250. Sesame Chicken

Preparation Time: 1 hour

Cooking Time: 50 minutes

Servings: 4

Ingredients:

- Pepper to taste
- Salt to taste
- 3 tbsp Olive oil
- 1 cup Breadcrumbs
- 2 Eggs
- 1 lb. Chicken breast
- Soy sauce as needed to marinate

Directions:

1. Slice the chicken into fillets and add to the bowl with the sesame and soy sauce. Let this marinate for half an hour.
2. Beat the eggs and then pass the chicken through it.
3. Add to the grill of the air fryer at 350 degrees. Let it grill for a bit.
4. After 20 minutes, take the chicken off and let it cool down before serving.

Nutrition:

Calories 375 | Carbs 6g | Fat 18g | Protein 35g

---

251. Pepper Flakes Pork

Preparation Time: 10 minutes

Cooking Time: 25 minutes

Servings: 2

Ingredients:

- ½ teaspoon red pepper flakes, crushed
- Salt and black pepper, to taste
- pounds pork loin
- ½ teaspoon garlic powder
- large red potatoes, chopped

Directions:

1. Place all ingredients except the glaze in a large bowl and toss to coat well. Heat the deep fryer to 325 degrees F. Place the tenderloin in the basket of the deep fryer.
2. Adjust the potatoes around the pork loin.
3. Cook for approximately 25 minutes.

Nutrition:

Calories:260 | Fat: 8g | Carbs: 27g | Protein: 21g

---

252. Marinated Pork Shoulder

Preparation Time: 10 minutes

Cooking Time: 25 minutes

Servings: 4

Ingredients:

- 1 strip of pork shoulder butt with a good amount of fat marbling

    Marinade:

- 1 tbsp. rose wine
- 1 tsp. light soy sauce
- 1 tsp. sesame oil
- tbsp. raw honey

Directions:

1. Combine all the ingredients for the marinade and pour into a Ziploc bag. Put the pork in the bag and make sure that all parts of the pork strip are coated in the marinade. Put in a cool place for 3-24 hours.
2. Take the strip out 30 minutes before you plan to cook it and preheat your hot air fryer to 350 degrees.
3. Put foil on a small pan and brush with olive oil. Place the marinated pork strips in the prepared pan.

4. Adjust the temperature to 350°F and the time to 20 minutes. Broil for 20 minutes.
5. Every 5-10 minutes, glaze with the marinade.
6. Take strips out and let cool for a few minutes before slicing.

Nutrition:

Calories: 289 | Fat: 13g | Protein:33g | Sugar:1g

253. Asian Style Pork

Preparation Time: 2 hours and 10 minutes

Cooking Time: 15 minutes

Servings: 2

Ingredients:

- (1/2-inch-thick) boneless pork chops
- salt and pepper
- 1 tablespoon Asian sweet chili sauce
- 1/2 cup hoisin sauce
- 2 tablespoons cider vinegar

Directions:

1. Mix the hoisin, chilli sauce and vinegar together in a large bowl. Strain a quarter cup of this mixture, then put the pork chops in the bowl and leave them in the fridge for 2 hours. Remove the pork chops and place them on a plate. Evenly sprinkle each side of the pork chop with salt and pepper.
2. Grill at 360 degrees for 14 minutes, turning halfway through. Drizzle with the reserved marinade and serve.

Nutrition:

Calories: 338 | Fat: 21g | Protein:19g | Fiber:1g

254. Mussels & Sausages

Preparation Time: 5 minutes

Cooking Time: 15 minutes

Servings: 2

Ingredients:

- 1 pounds mussels, scrubbed
- 2 ounces black beer
- 2 ounces spicy sausage, chopped
- 1 yellow onion, chopped
- 1 tablespoon paprika

Directions:

1. In a pan that will fit in your hot air fryer, mix all the ingredients together.
2. Place the pan in the hot air fryer and cook the mussels at 400 degrees F for 12 minutes.
3. Distribute the mussels into bowls, serve and enjoy!

Nutrition:

Calories 201 | Fat 6 | Fiber 7 | Carbs 17 | Protein 7

255. Chicken Thighs in Soy Sauce

Preparation Time: 5 minutes

Cooking Time: 20 minutes

Servings: 2

Ingredients:

- 2 garlic cloves, minced
- ½ cup soy sauce
- ½ cup balsamic vinegar
- 4 chicken thighs, boneless
- Salt and black pepper to taste

Directions:

1. Combine the chicken with all the other ingredients in a container that will fit in your deep fryer and toss.
2. Put the pan in the deep fryer and cook at 380 degrees F for 20 minutes.
3. Spread everything out on plates and serve.

Nutrition:

Calories 261 | Fat 7 | Fiber 5 | Carbs 15 | Protein 16

256. Lemon Drumsticks

Preparation Time: 10 minutes

Cooking Time: 28 minutes

Servings: 2

Ingredients:

- 1/3 cup lemon juice
- 1-pound drumstick
- ½ cup water
- ½ cup hot sauce
- 1 tbsp butter

Directions:

1. Put all the ingredients in the cooking and crisping basket and place the basket in the air fryer.
2. Set the pressure cooker lid on the cooker and close the pressure valve to the sealing position. Adjust the pressure cooker function to high heat and set the timer for 5 minutes
3. Quickly release the pressure immediately after the end of the cooking process by carefully opening the pressure cooker valve.
4. Serve hot.

Nutrition:

Calories 414 | Fat 26g | Carbohydrates 3g | Protein 42g.

257. Chicken In Salsa Verde

Preparation Time: 5 minutes

Cooking Time: 25 minutes

Servings: 2

Ingredients:

- 1 teaspoon ground coriander
- 1 teaspoon cilantro
- 1 tablespoon paprika
- 1-pound boneless chicken breasts
- ounces Salsa Verde

Directions:

1. Round the boneless chicken breasts with paprika, ground black pepper and coriander. Adjust the pressure cooker to "pressure" mode.
2. Put the boneless chicken in the pressure cooker. Spread the salsa verde over the meat and stir well.
3. Shut the lid of the pressure cooker and cook for 30 minutes.
4. At the end of the cooking time, release the pressure and transfer the chicken to a mixing bowl. Mince the chicken well. Serve.

Nutrition:

Calories: 160 | Fat: 4g | Carbs: 5g | Protein: 26g

258. Madeira Beef Cubes

Preparation Time: 5 minutes

Cooking Time: 25 minutes

Servings: 6

Ingredients:

- 1 yellow onion, thinly sliced
- 1 chili pepper, sliced
- Salt and black pepper to the taste
- 1 cup Madeira
- 1 and ½ pounds beef meat, cubed

Directions:

1. Place the turning rack in the hot air fryer, put the baking dish in it and mix all the ingredients in it.
2. Cook the mixture in the baking mode at 380 degrees F for 25 minutes, spread it in bowls and serve.

Nutrition:

Calories 295 | Fat 16 | Fiber 9 | Carbs 20 | Protein 15.

259. Juicy BBQ Tofu

Preparation Time: 10 minutes

Cooking Time: 50 minutes

Servings: 2

Ingredients:

- Oil for greasing
- 1 block tofu, extra firm
- 1 ½ cups BBQ sauce

Directions:

1. Set the temperature to 400°F and preheat the hot air fryer.
2. Push down the tofu and cut it into 1" cubes.
3. Place them on a greased baking tray.
4. Spread a layer of BBQ sauce over them and cook in the hot air fryer for 20 minutes. Set aside.
5. Pour ½ cup of BBQ sauce into a glass pot. The sauce should spread evenly in the pan. Lay the cooked tofu cubes on top and add another layer of the sauce.
6. Put them back in the hot air fryer and cook for 30 minutes.
7. Enjoy!

Nutrition:

Calories: 173 | Fat: 10g | Carbs 9g | Protein: 16g

260. Veggie Plate

Preparation Time: 10 minutes

Cooking Time: 30 minutes

Servings: 2

Ingredients:

- 2 tbsp. soy sauce, low sodium
- Cooking spray
- 1 tsp garlic powder
- 2 cups Brussel sprouts
- 2 cups sweet potato

Directions:

1. Lay the sweet potatoes in the hot air fryer. Add a light layer of oil to toss.
2. Add 1 teaspoon of garlic powder on top and toss.
3. Adjust the temperature to 400 F and cook for 15 minutes. Turn after 5 minutes.
4. Put the Brussels sprouts in the cooking basket and spray with a layer of oil and the remaining garlic powder. Turn the Brussels sprouts well and cook at 400 F for 5 minutes.
5. Sprinkle some soy sauce and shake to coat the vegetables evenly.
6. Adjust to the same temperature and cook for 5 minutes. Test it when it reaches 2 minutes and toss the contents.

7. The cooking time depends on the type of vegetable. As soon as the vegetables are cooked, they are soft and brown.

Nutrition:

Calories: 261 | Fat: 8g | Carbs: 28g | Protein: 14g

261. Corned Beef

Preparation Time: 10 minutes

Cooking Time: 55 minutes

Servings: 2

Ingredients:

- 1 pounds corned beef brisket
- 1 medium onion, chopped
- 2 tbsp. Dijon mustard
- cups of water

Directions:

1. Set the temperature to 400° F and preheat the hot air fryer for 5 minutes.
2. Cut the beef brisket into cubes.
3. Put all the ingredients in a baking tray that fits in the hot air fryer.
4. Leave to cook for 50 minutes at a temperature of 400 F. Enjoy!:

Nutrition:

Calories: 320 | Fat: 22g | Carbs: 10g | Protein: 21g

262. Creamy Pork Chops

Preparation Time: 5 minutes

Cooking Time: 20 minutes

Servings: 4

Ingredients:

- Salt and black pepper
- ½ cup breadcrumbs
- 2 tbsp sour cream (you can add more)
- 2 pounds pork chops, center-cut
- 4 tbsp flour

Directions:

1. Dust the chops with flour. Sprinkle with the cream and rub in lightly to coat them well.
2. Spread the breadcrumbs in a bowl and sprinkle over each pork chop. Drizzle the chops with oil and place them in the basket of your air fryer.
3. Bake for 14 minutes at 380 F, turning once halfway through. Then serve them with salad, coleslaw or potatoes.

Nutrition:

Calories: 250 | Carbs: 13 g | Fat: 13 g | Protein: 24 g

263. Spicy Pork Belly

Preparation Time: 10 minutes

Cooking Time: 3 hours

Servings: 2

Ingredients:

- ¾ tsp garlic powder
- 1 tsp salt
- ½ tsp white pepper
- 1 ½ lb pork belly, blanched
- 1 tsp five spice seasoning

Directions:

1. When you have blanched the pork belly, leave it to air dry for 2 hours at room temperature.
2. Blot it with paper towels if there is excess water. Heat the hot air fryer to 330F.
3. Grab a skewer and pierce the skin as many times as possible to make sure it is crispy. In a small bowl, mix together the spices and rub them into the pork.
4. Put the pork in the hot air fryer and cook for 30 minutes. Increase the temperature to 350 F and cook for another 30 minutes.
5. Leave to cool slightly before serving.

Nutrition:

Calories: 280 | Carbs: 14 g | Fat: 17 g | Protein: 29 g

264. Cinnapple Pork Tenderloins

Preparation Time: 5 minutes

Cooking Time: 50 minutes

Servings: 4

Ingredients:

- 1 tbsp soy sauce
- Salt and black pepper
- 4 pork tenderloins
- 1 apple, wedged
- 1 cinnamon quill

Directions:

1. Place the pork, apple, cinnamon, soy sauce, salt and black pepper in a bowl; mix to coat well. Leave to rest at room temperature for 25-35 minutes.
2. Add pork and apples and a little marinade to deep fryer.
3. Cook at 380 F for 14 minutes, flipping once halfway through. Serve hot!

Nutrition:

Calories: 200 | Carbs: 10 g | Fat: 10 g | Protein: 18 g

265. Juicy Beef & Mushrooms

Preparation Time: 3 hours

Cooking Time: 20 minutes

Servings: 4

Ingredients:

- 4 tbsp bulgogi marinade
- 2 pounds beef
- 1 tbsp diced onion
- ½ cup sliced mushrooms

Directions:

1. Cut the beef into bite-sized pieces and place in a bowl. Include the bulgogi and mix to completely cover the beef. Put a lid on the bowl and place it in the fridge to marinate for 3 hours. Heat the hot air fryer to 350F.
2. Place the beef in a baking dish and stir in the mushrooms and onions. Broil for 10 minutes until nice and tender. Set aside and serve with roast potatoes and a green salad.

Nutrition:

Calories: 220 | Carbs: 12 g | Fat: 11 g | Protein: 23 g

266. Beef Liver

Preparation Time: 15 minutes

Cooking Time: 30 minutes

Servings: 2

Ingredients:

- 1 cup warm milk
- Salt and black pepper to taste
- 2 buns
- ½ lb of beef liver
- eggs as needed

Directions:

1. Slice the liver and place in the fridge for 15 minutes. Split the bread rolls into pieces and soak them in milk for 10 minutes.
2. Place the liver in a blender and add the egg yolks, bread mixture and spices. Chop the ingredients and pour them into the ramekins.
3. Place the ramekins in the basket of the deep fryer; cook at 350 F for 20 minutes.

Nutrition:

Calories: 230 | Carbs: 15 g | Fat: 11 g | Protein: 26 g

267. Real Wiener Beef Schnitzel

Preparation Time: 5 minutes

Cooking Time: 30 minutes

Servings: 4

Ingredients:

- Salt and black pepper to taste
- 1 cup breadcrumbs
- 3 eggs, beaten
- 2 pounds beef schnitzel cutlets
- 1 cup flour

Directions:

1. Cover the beef cutlets in flour and remove excess flour. Immerse the coated cutlets in the egg mixture. Flavour with salt and black pepper.
2. Next, dip in the breadcrumbs and coat well.
3. Generously drizzle with oil and cook for 10 minutes at 360 F, flipping once halfway through.

Nutrition:

Calories: 195 | Carbs: 12 g | Fat: 11 g | Protein: 18 g

268. Bacon Wrapped Pork

Preparation Time: 15 minutes

Cooking Time: 30 minutes

Servings: 4

Ingredients:

- bacon strips
- 1 tablespoon honey
- 1 (1½ pound) pork tenderloin
- tablespoons Dijon mustard

Directions:

1. Cover the fillet with mustard and honey.
2. Tape strips of bacon around the pork tenderloin.
3. Put the pork tenderloin in a greased air fry basket.
4. Place the air fry basket in the centre of the Instant Omni Plus Toaster Oven.
5. Push "Air Fry" and then adjust the temperature to 360 degrees F.
6. Turn the timer to 30 minutes and push "Start".
7. Once the display shows "Turn Food", turn the pork fillet over.
8. Once the cooking time is finished, take the air fryer basket out of the toaster oven.
9. Put the pork fillet on a cutting board for about 10 minutes before slicing.
10. Cut the fillet into slices of the desired size with a sharp knife and serve.

Nutrition:

Calories 386 | Total Fat 16.1 g | Saturated Fat 5.7 g

Cholesterol 164 mg | Sodium 273 mg | Total Carbs 4.8 g

Fiber 0.3 g | Sugar 4.4 g | Protein 52.6 g | Cholesterol 15 mg |
Sodium 798 mg | Total Carbs 20.3 g | Fiber 2.6 g Sugar 1.7 g |
Protein 43.9 g

POULTRY

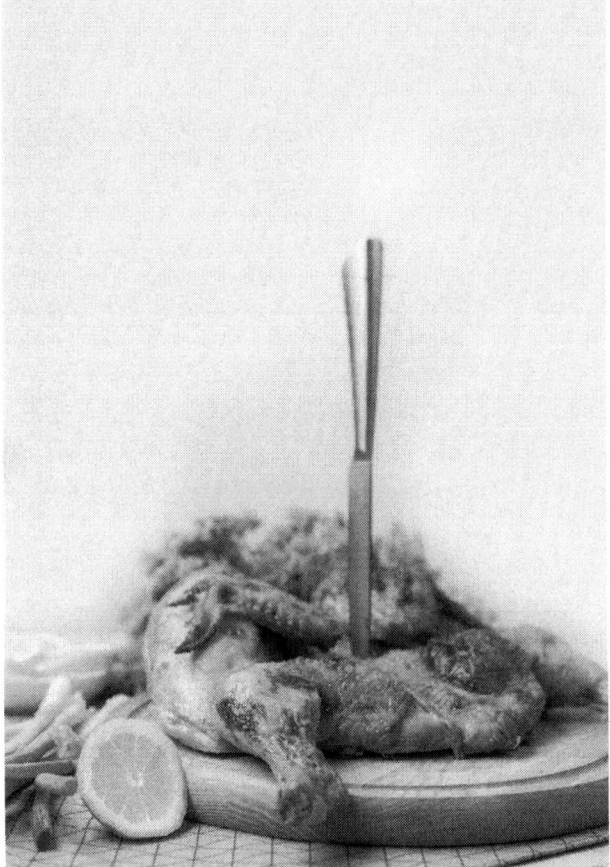

269. Asian Chicken Wings

Preparation Time: 2 hours and 5 minutes

Cooking Time: 10 minutes

Servings: 4

Ingredients:

- 2-tbsp. soy sauce
- Salt and black pepper to the taste.
- 4 chicken wings
- 2-tbsp. honey
- 3-tbsp. lime juice

Directions:

1. Combine honey with soy sauce, salt, black and lime juice in a bowl, whisk well, add chicken pieces, toss and refrigerate for 2 hours.
2. Place chicken in hot air fryer, cook at 370 °F for 6 minutes on each side, raise heat to 400 °F and cook for another 3 minutes. Serve hot.

Nutrition:

Calories: 372; | Fat: 9g; | Fiber: 10g; | Carbs: 37g;

Protein: 24g

270. Healthy Chicken & Asparagus

Preparation Time: 5 minutes

Cooking Time: 25 minutes

Servings: 4

Ingredients:

- Salt and black pepper to the taste.
- 1 tablespoon rosemary, chopped.
- 1 teaspoon cumin, ground.
- asparagus spears
- 8 chicken wings, halved

Directions:

1. Blot chicken wings dry, season with salt, pepper, cumin and rosemary, place in basket of hot air fryer and cook at 360 °F for 20 minutes.
2. Heat a pan over medium heat, add asparagus, cover with water and steam for a few minutes; place in a bowl filled with ice water, drain and arrange on plates. Place the chicken wings on the side and serve.

Nutrition:

Calories: 270; | Fat: 8g; | Fiber: 12g; | Carbs: 24g;

Protein: 22g

271. Sweet Duck Breasts

Preparation Time: 5 minutes

Cooking Time: 30 minutes

Servings: 2

Ingredients:

- ½-tsp. apple vinegar
- 1 teaspoon honey
- 1 teaspoon tomato paste
- 1 smoked duck breast, halved.
- 1 tablespoon mustard

Directions:

1. Combine honey with tomato paste, mustard and vinegar in a bowl, beat well, add duck breast pieces, swirl well
2. Place in hot air fryer and cook at 370 °F for 15 minutes.
3. Take duck breast out of fryer, put in honey mixture, swirl again, put back in fryer and cook at 370 °F for another 6 minutes. Arrange on plates and serve with a salad.

Nutrition:

Calories: 274; | Fat: 11g; | Fiber: 13g; | Carbs: 22g;

Protein: 13g

272. Lemony Turkey

Preparation Time: 10 minutes

Cooking Time: 45 minutes

Serving: 6

Ingredients:

- 1/2 teaspoon salt
- 2 teaspoon lemon pepper
- 2 tablespoon Worcestershire sauce
- 2 lbs. turkey breast
- 2 tablespoons oil

Directions:

1. Mix everything together in a bowl and coat the turkey generously.
2. Put the turkey in the basket of the air fryer.
3. Push the "Power" button of the air fryer and turn the wheel to choose the "Air fry" mode.
4. Push the "Time" button and rotate the dial again to adjust the cooking time to 45 minutes.
5. Next, press the Temp button and turn the wheel to set the temperature to 375 degrees F.
6. After preheating, put the air fry basket in and close the lid.
7. Serve warm.

Nutrition:

Calories 391 | Total Fat 2.8 g | Saturated Fat 0.6 g

Cholesterol 330 mg | Sodium 62 mg | Total Carbs 36.5 g

Fiber 9.2 g | Sugar 4.5 g | Protein 6.6

273. Mustard Chicken Thighs

Preparation Time: 10 minutes

Cooking Time: 30 minutes

Serving: 4

Ingredients:

- 1 clove minced garlic
- 2 tablespoons French mustard
- 2 tablespoons maple syrup
- 2 tablespoons Dijon mustard
- 4 large chicken thighs, bone-in

Directions:

1. Combine the chicken with everything in a bowl and coat well.
2. Put the chicken in the baking dish with the marinade.
3. Push the "Power" button of the Air Fry oven and turn the dial to choose the "Bake" mode.
4. Push the "Time" button and rotate the dial again to set the cooking time to 30 minutes.
5. Next, press the Temp button and turn the wheel to set the temperature to 370 degrees F.
6. After preheating, put the baking dish in and close the lid.
7. Serve warm.

Nutrition:

Calories 301 | Total Fat 15.8 g | Saturated Fat 2.7 g

Cholesterol 75 mg | Sodium 189 mg | Total Carbs 31.7 g

Fiber 0.3 g | Sugar 0.1 g | Protein 28.2 g

274. Mozzarella Chicken Bake

Preparation Time: 10 minutes

Cooking Time: 25 minutes

Serving: 6

Ingredients:

- 1 cup Mozzarella cheese, shredded
- 1 tablespoon fresh basil, chopped
- ½ (14 oz) can tomatoes, diced
- ¾ lbs. chicken breasts
- 2 tablespoons pesto sauce

Directions:

1. Put the flattened chicken breasts in a baking dish and spread with pesto.
2. Pour tomatoes, cheese and basil on top of each chicken piece.
3. Push the "Power button" of the Air Fry oven and rotate the wheel to select the "Bake" mode.
4. Push the "Time" button and rotate the dial again to set the cooking time to 25 minutes.
5. Next, press the Temp button and turn the wheel to set the temperature to 355 degrees F.
6. After preheating, place the casserole dish inside and close the lid. Serve warm.

Nutrition:

Calories 537 | Total Fat 19.8 g | Saturated Fat 1.4 g

Cholesterol 10 mg | Sodium 719 mg | Total Carbs 25.1 g

Fiber 0.9 g | Sugar 1.4 g | Protein 37.8 g

275. Pesto & Tomato Chicken

Preparation Time: 10 minutes

Cooking Time: 35 minutes

Serving: 3

Ingredients:

- 3 mozzarella cheese slices
- 2 medium fresh tomatoes, sliced

- 3 chicken breasts
- 1 (6 oz.) jar basil pesto

Directions:

1. Distribute the tomato slices in a baking dish and top with chicken.
2. Put the pesto and cheese on the chicken and spread them evenly.
3. Push the "Power" button of the Air Fry oven and rotate the wheel to select the "Air Fry" mode.
4. Push the "Time" button and rotate the dial again to set the cooking time to 30 minutes.
5. Next, press the Temp button and turn the wheel to adjust the temperature to 350 degrees F.
6. After preheating, put the casserole dish in and close the lid.
7. Once baked, turn the oven to broil mode and broil them for 5 minutes. Serve warm.

Nutrition:

Calories 452 | Total Fat 4 g | Saturated Fat 2 g

Cholesterol 65 mg | Sodium 220 mg | Total Carbs 23.1 g

Fiber 0.3 g | Sugar 1 g | Protein 26g

276. Simple Grilled Chicken

Preparation Time: 30 minutes

Cooking Time: 30 minutes

Servings: 6

Ingredients:

- Garlic salt and pepper
- 6 tablespoons ranch dressing
- 6 chicken thigh fillets

Directions:

1. Brush both sides of the chicken with ranch dressing.
2. Dust with garlic salt and pepper.
3. Adjust your Fryer to grill if it has one.
4. Or set it to medium preheat.
5. Place the chicken on the grill rack.
6. Cook for 15 minutes on each side.

Nutrition:

Calories: 475 kcal | Protein: 33.16 g | Fat: 36.43 g

Carbohydrates: 1.66 g

277. Chestnut Turkey Meatballs

Preparation Time: 24 minutes

Cooking Time: 13 minutes

Servings: 4

Ingredients:

- ¼ cup water chestnuts, finely chopped
- ¼ cup panko bread crumbs
- 1 ½ tablespoons low-sodium soy sauce
- 2 tablespoons peanut oil
- 1 egg, beaten
- ½ teaspoon ground ginger
- 1-pound ground turkey
- 1 small onion, minced

Directions:

1. Put the onion and peanut oil in a 6×6×2-inch baking dish. Stir well.
2. Put the pan in the hot air fryer and put the lid of the hot air fryer on. Carefully cook the onion in the preheated fryer at 375ºF for 1 to 2 minutes, or until soft and translucent. Put the cooked onions in a large bowl.
3. Pour the water chestnuts, soy sauce, ground ginger and breadcrumbs into the onion. Whisk in the beaten egg and whisk well, then add the turkey. Mix until the mixture is well blended.
4. Scoop the mixture out onto the cutting board and shape into 1-inch meatballs.
5. Put the meatballs in the pan and drizzle them with the oil.
6. Position the pan in the hot air fryer and put the lid of the hot air fryer on. Cook the meatballs in batches at 400ºF for 10 to 12 minutes, or until they are cooked through.
7. Take the meatballs out of the pan and place them on a plate. Leave them to cool for 3 minutes before serving.

Nutrition:

Calories: 683 | Total Fat: 33.29g | Total Carbs: 3.23g

Fiber: 0.6g | Protein: 24.77g | Sugar: 1.17g

278. Orangy Spicy Chicken

Preparation Time: 15 minutes

Cooking Time: 15 minutes

Servings: 4

Ingredients:

- ¼ cup chicken stock
- 3 teaspoons curry powder
- 1 yellow bell pepper, cut into 1½-inch pieces
- 1 tablespoon cornstarch
- ¾ pound boneless, skinless chicken thighs, cut into 1-inch pieces
- 1 small red onion, sliced
- 1 tablespoon olive oil
- ¼ cup orange juice

- tablespoons honey

Directions:

1. Arrange the red onion, chicken thighs and peppers in the basket of the deep fryer and drizzle with olive oil.
2. Place the lid of the deep fryer and cook the chicken thighs in the preheated deep fryer at 37 °C for 12 to 14 minutes. Flip the chicken thighs when "TURN FOOD" is displayed on the lid screen midway through the cooking time, or until the chicken reaches 1650F.
3. Put the chicken and vegetables in a 6-inch metal bowl. Put the chicken broth, curry powder, honey, orange juice and cornstarch into the bowl. Mix well.
4. Put the metal bowl in the basket and put the lid of the deep fryer on. Cook for another 3 minutes.
5. Take the bowl out of the basket. Leave to cool for 3 minutes before serving.

Nutrition:

Calories: 746 | Total Fat: 22.98g | Saturated Fat: 16.852g

Total Carbs: 25.2g | Fiber: 2.1g | Protein: 12.61g

Sugar: 14.48g | Sodium: 471mg

279. Breaded Chicken bites

Preparation Time: 15 minutes

Cooking Time: 15 minutes

Servings: 4

Ingredients:

- 4 tablespoons bread crumbs
- Cooking spray
- Salt and pepper to taste
- 4 tablespoons panko bread crumbs
- 1-pound boneless, skinless chicken breasts
- 2 eggs
- Chicken seasoning or rub

Directions:

1. Cut the chicken breast into 1-inch cutlets on your chopping board.
2. Mix the chicken cutlets, chicken seasoning, salt and pepper in a large bowl. Toss until completely coated. Put to one side.
3. In a separate bowl, whisk the eggs. Mix the breadcrumbs with the panko in a third bowl.
4. Bread the chicken cutlets in the beaten eggs and then in the breadcrumbs to coat them well.
5. Put the breaded chicken cutlets in the basket of the deep fryer and spray them with cooking spray.
6. Place the lid of the deep fryer on and cook them in batches in the preheated deep fryer at 400°F for 4 minutes. When the lid display shows "TURN FOOD" during the cooking time, give the fryer basket a shake and cook for another 4 minutes.
7. Put the cooked chicken cutlets into a serving bowl. Leave them to cool for 3 minutes and serve.

Nutrition:

Calories: 508 | Total Fat: 24g. Saturated Fat: 1g

Cholesterol: 147mg | Sodium: 267mg

Carbohydrates: 67g | Fiber: 1g | Protein: 24g

280. Buffalo Yogurt Chicken

Preparation Time: 36 minutes

Cooking Time: 15 minutes

Servings: 4

Ingredients:

- 1 tablespoon sweet paprika
- 1 tablespoon garlic pepper
- 1 cup panko bread crumbs
- ¼ cup egg substitute
- 1-pound skinless, boneless chicken breasts, cut into 1-inch strips
- ½ cup plain fat-free Greek yogurt
- 1 tablespoon hot sauce
- 1 teaspoon hot sauce
- 1 tablespoon cayenne pepper

Directions:

1. Combine the breadcrumbs, sweet paprika, cayenne pepper and garlic pepper in a bowl. Put to one side.
2. Beat together the Greek yoghurt, egg substitute and 1 tablespoon plus 1 teaspoon hot sauce in a second bowl.
3. Dunk the chicken strips in the buffalo sauce and then coat them with the breadcrumb mixture.
4. Put the well coated chicken strips in the basket of the hot air fryer. Place the lid of the fryer and cook the chicken strips in the preheated fryer at 400°F for 15 minutes or until they are well browned.
5. Flip the chicken strips when the halfway cooked.
6. Take the chicken out of the basket and serve on a plate.

Nutrition:

Calories: 234, | Fat: 4.6g, | Carbohydrates: 22.1g

Protein: 31.2g | Cholesterol: 65mg | Sodium: 696mg

281. Barbecue Lemon Chicken

Preparation Time: 10 minutes

Cooking Time: 12 minutes

Servings: 4

Ingredients:

- ¼ cup barbecue sauce, gluten-free

- 2 tablespoons lemon juice
- 2 cloves garlic, minced
- 4 boneless, skinless chicken thighs

Directions:

1. Combine the chicken, cloves, barbecue sauce and lemon juice in a medium bowl. Leave to marinate for 10 minutes.
2. Place the marinated chicken thighs in the basket of the hot air fryer and shake off any excess sauce. You may have to do this in batches to avoid overcrowding.
3. Place the lid on the fryer and grill the chicken thighs in the heated fryer at 375°F for 12 minutes.
4. Turn the chicken thighs over halfway through cooking, or until the chicken reaches at least 165°F with a meat thermometer placed in the centre of the chicken.
5. Remove to a platter and repeat with the remaining chicken thighs. Serve warm.

Nutrition:

Calories: 113 | Total Fat: 12.31g | Saturated Fat: 8.531g

Total Carbs: 27g | Fiber: 0.2g | Protein: 6.61g

Sugar: 2.874g | Sodium: 803mg

282. Chicken Popcorn

Preparation time: 10 minutes

Cooking time: 10 minutes

Servings: 6

Ingredients:

- 1/2 cups pork rind, crushed
- 1 tsp onion powder
- 1 tsp paprika
- Salt
- 1/2 tsp garlic powder
- 1/4 cup coconut flour
- Pepper
- 1 1/2 lb. Chicken breasts, cut into small chunks
- eggs

Directions:

1. Combine the coconut flour, pepper and salt in a small bowl.
2. Beat the eggs in another bowl until combined.
3. In another bowl, mix together the pork panko, paprika, garlic powder and onion powder.
4. Place the chicken pieces in a large bowl. Scatter the coconut flour mixture over the chicken and toss well.
5. Dunk the chicken pieces in the egg mixture, coat with the pork panko mixture and transfer to a plate.
6. Coat the basket of the deep fryer with cooking spray.
7. Heat the deep fryer to 400 degrees.
8. Add half of the prepared chicken to the fryer basket and cook for 10-12 minutes. Give the basket a shake halfway through.
9. Continue to cook the other half in the same way. Serve and enjoy.

Nutrition:

Calories 265 | Fat 11 g | Carbohydrates 3 g | Sugar 0.5 g

Protein 35 g | Cholesterol 195 mg

283. Delicious Rotisserie Chicken

Preparation time: 10 minutes

Cooking time: 20 minutes

Servings: 6

Ingredients:

- 1 1/2 tsp garlic powder
- Salt
- 1/4 tsp cayenne
- 1/2 tbsp dried thyme
- 1 tsp paprika
- 1 1/2 tsp dried oregano
- Pepper
- 2 lbs. Chicken, cut into eight pieces
- tsp onion powder

Directions:

1. Spice the chicken with pepper and salt.
2. Combine spices and herbs in a bowl and rub the spice mixture over the chicken pieces.
3. Coat the basket of the deep fryer with cooking spray.
4. Put the chicken in the fryer basket and cook at 350 degrees for 10 minutes.
5. Turn the chicken to the other side and cook for an additional 10 minutes or until the internal temperature of the chicken reaches 165 degrees.
6. Serve and enjoy.

Nutrition:

Calories 350 | Fat 7 g | Carbohydrates 1.8 g | Sugar 0.5 g

Protein 66 g | Cholesterol 175 mg

284. Asian Style Teriyaki Chicken

Preparation time: 10 minutes

Cooking time: 30 minutes

Servings: 2

Ingredients:

- 1-1/2 teaspoons cold water
- 2 skinless chicken thighs
- 2 tablespoons cider vinegar

- 1/4 cup soy sauce
- 1/8 teaspoon ground black pepper
- 1-1/2 teaspoons cornstarch
- 1/4 cup white sugar
- 1/4 teaspoon ground ginger
- 1/2 clove garlic, minced

Directions:

1. Grease the baking tin of the hot air fryer lightly with cooking spray. Include all the ingredients and toss well to coat. Divide the chicken in a single layer on the bottom of the pan.
2. Cook on 390oF for 15 minutes.
3. Flip the chicken as you coat it with the sauce, coating it well.
4. Continue to cook for a further 15 minutes at 330oF.
5. Serve and enjoy.

Nutrition:

Calories:267 | Carbs: 19.9g | Protein: 24.7g | Fat: 9.8g

285. Mozzarella Rolls

Preparation time: 10 minutes

Cooking time: 10 minutes

Servings: 4

Ingredients:

- 4 slices turkey breast
- 4 chive shoots
- 1 tomato, sliced
- ½ cup fresh basil
- 1 cup sliced fresh mozzarella

Directions:

1. Heat your hot air fryer to 390°F.
2. Put the slices of mozzarella, tomato and basil on each turkey slice.
3. Make sure you roll up the turkey so that the stuffing is well contained and secure it by tying a chive sprout around each slice.
4. Put in the hot air fryer and cook for 10 minutes. If desired, serve with a salad.

Nutrition:

Calories: 3616 kcal | Protein: 506.27 g | Fat: 160.48 g

Carbohydrates: 1.21 g

286. Sage Turkey rolls

Preparation time: 25 minutes

Cooking time: 15 minutes

Servings: 2

Ingredients:

- ½ tsp. garlic, pureed
- 1 medium egg
- 1 tsp. sage
- tbsp. friendly bread crumbs
- ½ small onion, diced
- pepper to taste
- 1 pound turkey mince
- Salt to taste

Directions:

1. Place all the ingredients in a bowl and mix well.
2. Use equal portions of the mixture and shape each one into a small ball. Put in the hot air fryer and cook for 15 minutes at 350°F.
3. To serve, serve with tartar sauce and potato puree.

Nutrition:

Calories: 516 kcal | Protein: 22.1 g | Fat: 30.22 g

Carbohydrates: 37.75 g

287. Moroccan Style Chicken

Preparation time: 15 minutes

Cooking time: 15 minutes

Servings: 2

Ingredients:

- Pinch of cinnamon
- Pinch of red pepper
- 1 carrot
- Pinch of cumin
- ½ lb. shredded chicken
- Pinch of sea salt
- 1 broccoli, chopped
- 1 cup broth

Directions:

1. Coat the shredded chicken with cumin, red pepper, sea salt and cinnamon in a bowl.
2. Chop the carrots into small pieces. Add the carrot and broccoli to the bowl with the chicken.
3. Pour in the broth and mix everything well. Leave aside for about 30 minutes.
4. Place in the hot air fryer. Cook at 390°F for about 15 minutes. Serve hot.

Nutrition:

Calories: 212 kcal | Protein: 30.03 g | Fat: 7.1 g

Carbohydrates: 5.96 g

FISH DISHES

288. Spicy Shrimp

Preparation time: 5 minutes

Baking time: 5 minutes

Servings: 8

Ingredients:

- 2 teaspoons old bay seasoning
- 1 teaspoon cayenne pepper
- 1 teaspoon smoked paprika
- 4 tablespoons olive oil
- 2-pounds tiger shrimp
- Salt, to taste

Directions:

1. Add all the ingredients in a large bowl. Mix well.
2. Preheat the air fryer to 390 degrees F and grease the air fryer basket.
3. Place shrimps in the air fryer basket and cook for about 5 minutes.
4. Take out and serve hot.
5. Tip: Top with chili sauce to enhance its taste.

Nutrition:

Calories 174 | Total Fat 8.3g | Saturated Fat 1.4g

Cholesterol 221mg | Sodium 434mg | Total Carbs 0.3g

Fiber 0.2g | Sugar 0.1g | Protein 23.8g | Potassium 217mg

289. Lemon Tuna

Preparation time: 10 minutes

Cooking time: 12 minutes

Servings: 4

Ingredients:

- 1 tablespoon fresh lime juice
- 1 egg
- 3 tablespoons canola oil
- 2 tablespoons hot sauce
- 2 teaspoons Dijon mustard
- 2 tablespoons fresh parsley, chopped
- ½ pound water packed plain tuna
- ½ cup breadcrumbs
- Salt and freshly ground black pepper, to taste

Directions:

1. Add tuna fish, parsley, mustard, crumbs, citrus juice and hot sauce in a bowl. Mix well.
2. Now, add oil, salt and eggs in the bowl and make patties from the mixture.
3. Refrigerate and preheat the air fryer to 360 degrees F.
4. Place the patties in the air fryer basket and cook for 12 minutes. Take out and serve hot.
5. Tip: Refrigerate the patties for at least 3 hours.

Nutrition:

Calories 315 | Total Fat 18.7g | Saturated Fat 2.1g

Cholesterol 53mg | Sodium 729mg | Total Carbs 25g

Fiber 1.1g | Sugar 1.2g | Protein 10.7g | Potassium 79mg

290. Lemony & Spicy Coconut Crusted Prawns

Preparation time: 20 minutes

Cooking time: 7 minutes

Servings: 4

Ingredients:

- ½ cup unsweetened coconut, shredded
- ¼ teaspoon lemon zest
- ¼ teaspoon cayenne pepper
- Vegetable oil, as required
- ¼ teaspoon red pepper flakes, crushed
- ½ cup flour

- ½ cup breadcrumbs
- 1-pound prawns, peeled and de-veined
- 2 egg whites
- Salt and black pepper, to taste

Directions:
1. Take a shallow dish and mix salt, flour and pepper in it.
2. Crack eggs in another shallow dish. Beat well.
3. In the third shallow dish, add coconut, breadcrumbs, lime zest, salt and cayenne pepper. Mix well.
4. Now, preheat the air fryer to 395 degrees F.
5. Dip shrimp into flour mixture, then in the egg mixture and roll them evenly into the breadcrumb mixture.
6. Place them in the air fryer basket and drizzle vegetable oil over them.
7. Cook for about 7 minutes and take out. Serve and enjoy!
8. Tip: Using more breadcrumbs will make shrimps crispier.

Nutrition:
Calories 773 | Total Fat 60.7g | Saturated Fat 14.4g
Cholesterol 239mg | Sodium 433mg | Total Carbs 25.5g
Fiber 2.1g | Sugar 1.6g | Protein 31.5g | Potassium 307mg

291. Tuna Stuffed Potatoes

Preparation time: 15 minutes
Cooking time: 30 minutes
Servings: 4

Ingredients:
- 1½-pounds tuna, drained
- 2 tablespoons plain Greek yogurt
- ½ tablespoon olive oil
- 4 starchy potatoes, soaked for 30 minutes
- 1 tablespoon capers
- 1 teaspoon red chili powder
- 1 scallion, chopped and divided
- Salt and freshly ground black pepper, to taste

Directions:
1. Preheat the air fryer to 355 degrees F.
2. Place the potatoes in the air fryer basket and cook for about 30 minutes.
3. Take out and place on a flat surface.
4. Meanwhile, add yogurt, tuna, red chili powder, scallion, salt and pepper in a bowl. Mix well.
5. Cut each potato from top side lengthwise and press the open side of potato halves slightly.
6. Stuff potato with tuna mixture and sprinkle with capers. Dish out and serve.
7. Tip: Top with mint and oregano to enhance taste.

Nutrition:
Calories 1387 | Total Fat 54g | Saturated Fat 11.6g
Cholesterol 203mg | Sodium 489mg | Total Carbs 35.7g
Fiber 2.7g | Sugar 4.8g | Protein 180.7g | Potassium 2926mg

292. Packet Lobster Tail

Preparation Time: 27 minutes
Cooking Time: 12 minutes
Servings: 2

Ingredients:
- 2 (6-oz. lobster tails, halved
- 2 tbsp. salted butter; melted.
- 1 tsp. dried parsley.
- ½ tsp. Old Bay seasoning
- Juice of ½ medium lemon.

Directions:
1. Place the two halved tails on a sheet of aluminum foil. Drizzle with butter, Old Bay seasoning and lemon juice.
2. Seal the foil packets, completely covering tails. Place into the air fryer basket.
3. Adjust the temperature to 375 Degrees F and set the timer for 12 minutes. Once done, sprinkle with dried parsley and serve immediately.

Nutrition:
Calories: 234 | Protein: 23g | Fiber: 1g | Fat: 19g |Carbs: 7g

293. Shrimp and Green Beans

Preparation Time: 20 minutes
Cooking Time: 15 minutes
Servings: 4

Ingredients:
- ½ lb. green beans; trimmed and halved
- 1 lb. shrimp; peeled and deveined
- ¼ cup ghee; melted
- 2 tbsp. cilantro; chopped.
- Juice of 1 lime
- A pinch of salt and black pepper

Directions:
1. In a pan that fits your air fryer, mix all the ingredients, toss.
2. Introduce in the fryer and cook at 360°F for 15 minutes shaking the fryer halfway. Divide into bowls and serve.

Nutrition:
Calories: 222 | Fat: 8g | Fiber: 3g | Carbs: 5g | Protein: 10g

294. Crab Dip

Preparation Time: 18 minutes
Cooking Time: 8 minutes
Servings: 4

Ingredients:

- 8 oz. full-fat cream cheese; softened.
- 2 (6-oz. cans lump crabmeat
- ¼ cup chopped pickled jalapeños.
- ¼ cup full-fat sour cream.
- ¼ cup sliced green onion
- ½ cup shredded Cheddar cheese
- ¼ cup full-fat mayonnaise
- 1 tbsp. lemon juice
- ½ tsp. hot sauce

Directions:

1. Place all Ingredients: into a 4-cup round baking dish and stir until fully combined. Place dish into the air fryer basket.
2. Adjust the temperature to 400 Degrees F and set the timer for 8 minutes. Dip will be bubbling and hot when done. Serve warm.

Nutrition:

Calories: 441 | Protein: 18g | Fiber: 6g | Fat: 38g |Carbs: 2g

295. Buttered Shrimp Skewers

Preparation Time: 10 minutes
Cooking Time: 6 minutes
Servings: 2

Ingredients:

- 8 shrimps
- 4 garlic cloves
- Black pepper and Salt
- 8 green bell pepper
- 1 tbsp. rosemary
- 1 tbsp. butter

Directions:

1. Mix shrimp with garlic, pepper, salt, butter, bell pepper slices, and rosemary, toss to coat in a bowl and allow for 10 minutes.
2. Place 2 bell pepper slices and 2 shrimp on a skewer. Repeat for the remaining shrimp and bell pepper pieces.
3. Place them all in your air fryer basket and cook at 360°F for 6 minutes. Share on plates and serve.

Nutrition:

Calories: 170 | Total Fat: 7.5g | Sodium: 257mg | Fiber: 0.8g
Total Carbs: 4.4g | Sugars: 0.1g | Protein: 20.6g

296. Sesame Shrimp

Preparation Time: 15 minutes
Cooking Time: 12 minutes
Servings: 4

Ingredients:

- 1 lb. shrimp; peeled and deveined
- 1 tbsp. olive oil
- 1 tbsp. sesame seeds, toasted
- ½ tsp. Italian seasoning
- A pinch of salt and black pepper

Directions:

1. Take a bowl and mix the shrimp with the rest of the Ingredients: and toss well.
2. Put the shrimp in the air fryer's basket, cook at 370°F for 12 minutes, divide into bowls and serve.

Nutrition:

Calories: 199 | Fat: 11g | Fiber: 2g | Carbs: 4g | Protein: 11g

297. Salmon and Cauliflower Rice

Preparation Time: 30 minutes
Cooking Time: 15 minutes
Servings: 4

Ingredients:

- 4 salmon fillets; boneless
- ½ cup chicken stock
- 1 cup cauliflower, riced
- 1 tbsp. butter; melted
- 1 tsp. turmeric powder
- Salt and black pepper to taste

Directions:

1. In a pan that fits your air fryer, mix the cauliflower rice with the other Ingredients: except the salmon and toss.
2. Arrange the salmon fillets over the cauliflower rice, put the pan in the fryer and cook at 360°F for 25 minutes, flipping the fish after 15 minutes.
3. Divide everything between plates and serve .

Nutrition:

Calories: 241 | Fat: 12g | Fiber: 2g | Carbs: 6g | Protein: 12g

298. Tilapia and Salsa

Preparation Time: 20 minutes
Cooking Time: 15 minutes
Servings: 4

Ingredients:

- 4 tilapia fillets; boneless
- 12 oz. canned tomatoes; chopped.
- 2 tbsp. green onions; chopped.
- 2 tbsp. sweet red pepper; chopped.
- 1 tbsp. balsamic vinegar
- 1 tbsp. olive oil
- A pinch of salt and black pepper

Directions:

1. Arrange the tilapia in a baking sheet that fits the air fryer and season with salt and pepper.
2. In a bowl, combine all the other ingredients, toss and spread over the fish.
3. Introduce the pan in the fryer and cook at 350°F for 15 minutes.
4. Divide the mix between plates and serve.

Nutrition:

Calories: 221 | Fat: 12g | Fiber: 2g | Carbs: 5g | Protein: 14g

299. Garlic Tilapia

Preparation Time: 25 minutes

Cooking Time: 20 minutes

Servings: 4

Ingredients:

- 4 tilapia fillets; boneless
- 1 bunch kale; chopped.
- 2 garlic cloves; minced
- 3 tbsp. olive oil
- 1 tsp. fennel seeds
- ½ tsp. red pepper flakes, crushed
- Salt and black pepper to taste

Directions:

1. In a pan that fits the fryer, combine all the ingredients, put the pan in the fryer and cook at 360°F for 20 minutes.
2. Divide everything between plates and serve.

Nutrition:

Calories: 240 | Fat: 12g | Fiber: 2g | Carbs: 4g | Protein: 12g

300. Trout and Mint

Preparation Time: 21 minutes

Cooking Time: 16 minutes

Servings: 4

Ingredients:

- 1 avocado, peeled, pitted and roughly chopped
- 4 rainbow trout
- 1/3 pine nuts
- 1 cup olive oil+ 3 tbsp.
- 1 cup parsley; chopped
- 3 garlic cloves; minced
- ½ cup mint; chopped
- Zest of 1 lemon
- Juice of 1 lemon
- A pinch of salt and black pepper

Directions:

1. Pat dry the trout, season with salt and pepper and rub with 3 tbsp. oil

2. Put the fish in your air fryer's basket and cook for 8 minutes on each side. Divide the fish between plates and drizzle half of the lemon juice all over.
3. In a blender, combine the rest of the oil with the remaining lemon juice, parsley, garlic, mint, lemon zest, pine nuts and the avocado and pulse well. Spread this over the trout and serve.

Nutrition:

Calories: 240 | Fat: 12g | Fiber: 4g | Carbs: 6g | Protein: 9g

301. Salmon and Coconut Sauce

Preparation Time: 25 minutes

Cooking Time: 20 minutes

Servings: 4

Ingredients:

- 4 salmon fillets; boneless
- 1/3 cup heavy cream
- ¼ cup lime juice
- ½ cup coconut; shredded
- ¼ cup coconut cream
- 1 tsp. lime zest; grated
- A pinch of salt and black pepper

Directions:

1. Take a bowl and mix all the Ingredients: except the salmon and whisk.
2. Arrange the fish in a pan that fits your air fryer, drizzle the coconut sauce all over, put the pan in the machine and cook at 360°F for 20 minutes.
3. Divide between plates and serve.

Nutrition:

Calories: 227 | Fat: 12g | Fiber: 2g | Carbs: 4g | Protein: 9g

302. Simple Salmon

Preparation Time: 22 minutes

Cooking Time: 12 minutes

Servings: 2

Ingredients:

- 2 (4-oz. salmon fillets, skin removed
- 1 medium lemon.
- 2 tbsp. unsalted butter; melted.
- ½ tsp. dried dill
- ½ tsp. garlic powder.

Directions:

1. Place each fillet on a 5" × 5" square of aluminum foil. Drizzle with butter and sprinkle with garlic powder.

2. Zest half of the lemon and sprinkle zest over salmon. Slice other half of the lemon and lay two slices on each piece of salmon. Sprinkle dill over salmon.
3. Gather and fold foil at the top and sides to fully close packets. Place foil packets into the air fryer basket. Adjust the temperature to 400 Degrees F and set the timer for 12 minutes.
4. Salmon will be easily flaked and have an internal temperature of at least 145 Degrees F when fully cooked.

Nutrition:

Calories: 252 | Protein: 29g | Fiber: 4g | Fat: 15g |Carbs: 2g

303. Cajun Spiced Salmon

Preparation time: 10 minutes

Cooking time: 8 minutes

Servings: 8

Ingredients:

4 tablespoons Cajun seasoning

4 salmon steaks

Directions:

- Add Cajun seasoning in a bowl and rub salmon evenly with it.
- Preheat the air fryer to 385 degrees F.
- Arrange air fryer grill pan and place salmon steaks on it.
- Cook for about 8 minutes and flip once in the middle way.
- Take out and serve hot.
- Tip: Set aside salmon steaks for at least 15 minutes before placing them in the air fryer.

Nutrition:

Calories 118 | Total Fat 5.5g | Saturated Fat 0.8g

Cholesterol 39mg | Sodium 114mg | Total Carbs 0g

Fiber 0g | Sugar 0g | Protein 17.3g | Potassium 342mg

304. Tangy Salmon

Preparation time: 10 minutes

Cooking time: 7 minutes

Servings: 8

Ingredients:

- 4 tablespoons Cajun seasoning
- 8 salmon fillets
- 4 tablespoons fresh lemon juice

Directions:

1. Season salmon fillets with Cajun seasoning and set aside for 15 minutes.
2. Preheat the air fryer to 360 degrees F and arrange grill pan in it.
3. Place salmon fillets on the grill pan and cook for about 7 minutes.
4. Drizzle with lemon juice and serve.

5. Tip: Salmon fillets should be ¾-inch thick

Nutrition:

Calories 237 | Total Fat 11.1g | Saturated Fat 1.6g

Cholesterol 78mg | Total Carbs 0.2g | Sugar 0.2g

Fiber 0g |Sodium 155mg | Potassium 693mg |Protein 34.7g

305. Sesame Seeds Coated Fish

Preparation time: 20 minutes

Cooking time: 14 minutes

Servings: 28

Ingredients:

- ½ cup sesame seeds, toasted
- ½ teaspoon dried rosemary, crushed
- 8 tablespoons olive oil
- 14 frozen fish fillets (white fish of your choice)
- 6 eggs
- ½ cup breadcrumbs
- 8 tablespoons plain flour
- Salt and freshly ground black pepper, to taste

Directions:

1. Take three dishes, place flour in one, crack eggs in the other and mix remaining ingredients except fillets in the third one.
2. Now, coat fillets in the flour and dip in the beaten eggs.
3. Then, dredge generously with the sesame seeds mixture.
4. Meanwhile, preheat the air fryer to 390 degrees F and line the air fryer basket with the foil.
5. Arrange fillets in the basket and cook for about 14 minutes, flipping once in the middle way. Take out and serve hot.
6. Tip: Use shallow dishes.

Nutrition:

Calories 179 | Total Fat 9.3g | Saturated Fat 1.6g

Cholesterol 53mg | Total Carbs 15.8g | Sugar 0.7g

Fiber 1g | Sodium 247mg | Potassium 32mg | Protein 7.7g

306. Parsley Catfish

Preparation time: 5 minutes

Cooking time: 25 minutes

Servings: 04

Ingredients:

- 4 catfish fillets
- 1/4 cup Louisiana Fish fry
- 1 tablespoon olive oil
- 1 tablespoon chopped parsley optional
- 1 lemon, sliced
- Fresh herbs, to garnish

Directions:

1. Preheat air fryer to 400 degrees F.

2. Rinse the fish fillets and pat them try.
3. Rub the fillets with the seasoning and coat well.
4. Spray oil on top of each fillet.
5. Place the fillets in the air fryer basket.
6. Cover the lid and cook for 10 minutes.
7. Flip the fillets and cook more for another 10 minutes.
8. Flip the fish and cook for 3 minutes until crispy.
9. Garnish with parsley, fresh herbs, and lemon. Serve warm.

Nutrition:

Calories 248 | Total Fat 15.7 g | Saturated Fat 2.7 g

Cholesterol 75 mg | Sodium 94 mg | Total Carbs 0.4 g

Fibre 0g | Sugar 0 g | Protein 24.9 g

307. Seasoned Salmon

Ingredients:

Preparation time: 5 minutes

Cooking time: 7 minutes

Total time: 12 minutes

Servings: 2

Ingredients:

- 2 wild caught salmon fillets, 1-1/12-inches thick
- 2 teaspoons avocado oil or olive oil
- 2 teaspoons paprika
- Salt and coarse, to taste
- Black pepper, to taste
- Green herbs, to garnish

Directions:

1. Clean the salmon and let it rest for 1 hour at room temperature.
2. Season the fish with olive oil, salt, pepper, and paprika.
3. Arrange the fish in the air fryer basket.
4. Cook for 7 minutes at 390 degrees.
5. Once done, remove the fish from the fryer.
6. Garnish with fresh herbs. Serve warm.

Nutrition:

Calories 249 | Total Fat 11.9 g | Saturated Fat 1.7 g

Cholesterol 78 mg | Sodium 79 mg | Total Carbs 1.8 g

Fibre 1.1 g | Sugar 0.3 g | Protein 35 g

308. Ranch Fish Fillets

Preparation time: 05 minutes

Cooking time: 13 minutes

Servings: 4

Ingredients:

- 3/4 cup breadcrumbs or Panko or crushed cornflakes
- 1 packet dry ranch-style dressing mix
- 2 1/2 tablespoons vegetable oil
- 2 eggs beaten
- 4 tilapia salmon or other fish fillets
- Herbs and chillies to garnish

Directions:

1. Preheat the air fryer to 180 degrees F.
2. Mix ranch dressing with panko in a bowl.
3. Whisk eggs in a shallow bowl.
4. Dip each fish fillet in the egg then coat evenly with the panko mixture.
5. Place the fillets in the air fryer.
6. Cook for 13 minutes.
7. Serve warm with herbs and chillies.

Nutrition:

Calories 301 | Total Fat 12.2 g | Saturated Fat 2.4 g

Cholesterol 110 mg | Sodium 276 mg | Total Carbs 15 g

Fibre 0.9 g | Sugar 1.4 g | Protein 28.8 g

309. Montreal Fried Shrimp

Preparation time: 5 minutes

Cooking time: 8 minutes

Servings: 6

Ingredients:

- 1-pound raw shrimp peeled and deveined
- 1 egg white 3 tablespoon
- 1/2 cup all-purpose flour
- 3/4 cup panko breadcrumbs
- 1 teaspoon paprika
- 1 tablespoon McCormick's Grill Mates Montreal Chicken Seasoning or to taste
- Salt and pepper to taste
- Cooking spray

Directions:

1. Preheat the Air Fryer to 400 degrees F.
2. Toss the shrimp with Montreal seasonings.
3. Whisk egg whites in a medium sized bowl.
4. Keep the breadcrumbs and flour in separate bowls.
5. First dredge each shrimp in the flour, then dip into the egg whites, and then coat with the breadcrumbs.
6. Place the coated shrimps in the air dryer and spray the cooking oil over them.
7. Air fry for about 4 minutes then flip the shrimps.
8. Continue cooking for another 4 minutes. Serve warm.

Nutrition:

Calories 248 | Total Fat 2.4 g | Saturated Fat 0.1 g

Cholesterol 320 mg | Sodium 350 mg | Total Carbs 12.2 g

Fibre 0.7 g | Sugar 0.7 g | Protein 44.3 g

310. Shrimp Scampi

Preparation time: 5 minutes
Cooking time: 8 minutes
Servings: 4

Ingredients:
- 1 tablespoon lemon juice
- 4 tablespoons butter
- 1 lb defrosted shrimp
- 1 teaspoon chives, dried
- 1 tablespoon fresh basil leaves, minced
- 2 tablespoons chicken stock
- 1 tablespoon garlic, minced
- 2 teaspoons red pepper flakes

Directions:
1. Melt butter in a 6-inch hot pan.
2. Add garlic and red pepper flakes to sauté for 2 minutes.
3. Transfer the pan to the air fryer.
4. Add the entire remaining ingredients to the pan except basil.
5. Cook for 5 minutes with occasional stirring.
6. Mix well and remove the hot pan from the fryer.
7. Let the shrimp rest for 1 minute.
8. Mix gently and garnish with basil. Serve warm.

Nutrition:
Calories 372 | Total Fat 11.1 g | Saturated Fat 5.8 g
Cholesterol 610 mg | Sodium 749 mg | Total Carbs 0.9 g
Fibre 0.2 g | Sugar 0.2 g | Protein 63.5 g

311. Buttered Scallops

Preparation time: 10 minutes
Cooking time: 5 minutes
Servings: 8

Ingredients:
- 4 tablespoons butter, melted
- 3-pounds sea scallops
- 2 tablespoons fresh thyme, minced
- Salt and freshly ground black pepper, to taste

Directions:
1. Add butter, sea scallops, thyme, salt and pepper in a bowl. Toss to coat well.
2. Preheat the air fryer to 385 degrees F and grease the air fryer basket.
3. Place scallops in the basket and cook for 5 minutes.
4. Take out and serve hot.
5. Tip: Pour melted butter on the scallops to enhance their taste.

Nutrition:
Calories 203 | Total Fat 7.1g | Saturated Fat 3.8g
Cholesterol 71mg | Sodium 335mg | Total Carbs 4.5g
Fiber 0.3g | Sugar 0g | Protein 28.7g | Potassium 555mg

312. Ham Wrapped Prawns

Preparation time: 15 minutes
Cooking time: 14 minutes
Servings: 4

Ingredients:
- 2 garlic cloves, minced
- 1 tablespoon paprika
- 8 king prawns, peeled, deveined and chopped
- 4 ham slices, halved
- 2 tablespoons olive oil
- Salt and freshly ground black pepper, to taste

Directions:
1. Preheat the air fryer to 430 degrees F and wrap each prawn with a ham slice.
2. Arrange in the air fryer basket and cook for about 4 minutes.
3. Dish out and meanwhile place bell pepper in the air fryer basket.
4. Cook for about 10 minutes and transfer in a bowl.
5. Cover the bowl with a foil and set aside for 15 minutes.
6. Now, place bell pepper, garlic, paprika and oil in a blender.
7. Blend till a puree is formed and serve with ham wrapped prawns.
8. Tip: Cook the prawns until they become golden brown.

Nutrition:
Calories 553 | Total Fat 33.6g | Saturated Fat 12.7g
Cholesterol 16mg | Sodium 405mg | Total Carbs 2.6g
Fiber 1.1g | Sugar 7.2g | Protein 5g | Potassium 127mg

313. Nacho Chips Crusted Prawns

Preparation time: 10 minutes
Cooking time: 8 minutes
Servings: 8

Ingredients:
- 2 large eggs
- 36 prawns, peeled and deveined
- 1½-pounds Nacho flavored chips, crushed finely

Directions:
1. Add nacho chips in a bowl and crush well.
2. Add eggs in another bowl and beat well.
3. Preheat the air fryer to 350 degrees F.
4. Dip each prawn in the egg mixture and then in the crushed nachos.
5. Place them in the air fryer and cook for about 8 minutes.
6. Take out and serve hot.

7. Tip: More crushed nachos will make prawns crispier.

Nutrition:

Calories 1090 | Total Fat 55.2g | Saturated Fat 22.4g

Cholesterol 305mg | Sodium 2511mg | Total Carbs 101.9g

Fiber 0g | Sugar 0.1g | Protein 49.2g | Potassium 658mg

---

314. Fish Tacos

Preparation Time: 10 minutes

Cooking Time: 9 minutes

Servings: 4

Ingredients:

- 4 cod fillets, cut into 1-inch cubes
- Salt and black pepper to taste
- ½ lime, juiced
- ½ cup all-purpose flour
- 1 large egg, lightly beaten
- 1 cup panko breadcrumbs
- Olive oil for brushing
- 4 medium corn tortillas
- ½ cup shredded red cabbage
- 1 medium avocado, pitted, peeled, and chopped
- 2 tbsp chopped fresh cilantro
- 1 cup sour cream
- Lime wedges for serving

Directions:

1. Insert the dripping pan in the bottom part of the air fryer and preheat the oven at Air Fry mode at 400 F for 2 to 3 minutes. Lightly brush the rotisserie basket with some olive oil and set aside.
2. Season the fish with salt, black pepper, and lime juice.
3. Pour the flour onto a plate and the breadcrumbs onto another. Dredge the fish pieces lightly on the flour, then in the eggs, and the breadcrumbs. Put the coated fish in the rotisserie basket and fit into the oven using the rotisserie lift.
4. Set the timer for 9 minutes or until the fish pieces are golden brown.
5. To serve, lay the tortillas individually on a clean, flat surface and add the fish pieces. Top with the cabbage, avocado, cilantro, sour cream, and lime wedges. Serve immediately.

Nutrition:

Calories 275 | Total Fat 11.34g | Total Carbs 19.39g

Fiber 25g | Protein 23.37g

---

315. Grilled Tilapia with Portobello Mushrooms

Preparation Time: 20 minutes

Cooking Time: 5 minutes

Servings: 2

Ingredients:

- 2 tilapia fillets
- 1 tablespoon avocado oil
- 1/2 teaspoon red pepper flakes, crushed
- 1/2 teaspoon dried sage, crushed
- 1/4 teaspoon lemon pepper
- 1/2 teaspoon sea salt
- 1 teaspoon dried parsley flakes
- 4 medium-sized Portobello mushrooms
- A few drizzles of liquid smoke

Directions:

1. Toss all ingredients in a mixing bowl, except for the mushrooms.
2. Transfer the tilapia fillets to a lightly greased grill pan. Preheat your Air Fryer to 400 degrees F and cook the tilapia fillets for 5 minutes.
3. Now, turn the fillets over and add the Portobello mushrooms. Continue to cook for 5 minutes longer or until mushrooms are tender and the fish is opaque. Serve immediately.

Nutrition:

Calories 320 | Fat 11.4g | Carbs 29.1g | Protein 49.3g

Sugars 4.2g

---

316. Authentic Mediterranean Calamari Salad

Preparation Time: 15 minutes

Cooking Time: 5 minutes

Servings: 3

Ingredients:

- 1-pound squid, cleaned, sliced into rings
- 2 tablespoons sherry wine
- 1/2 teaspoon granulated garlic
- Salt, to taste
- 1/2 teaspoon ground black pepper
- 1/2 teaspoon basil
- 1/2 teaspoon dried rosemary
- 1 cup grape tomatoes
- 1 small red onion, thinly sliced
- 1/3 cup Kalamata olives, pitted and sliced
- 1/2 cup mayonnaise
- 1 teaspoon yellow mustard
- 1/2 cup fresh flat-leaf parsley leaves, coarsely chopped

Directions:

1. Start by preheating the Air Fryer to 400 degrees F. Spritz the Air Fryer basket with cooking oil.
2. Toss the squid rings with the sherry wine, garlic, salt, pepper, basil, and rosemary. Cook in the preheated Air Fryer for 5 minutes, shaking the basket halfway through the cooking time.

3. Work in batches and let it cool to room temperature. When the squid is cool enough, add the remaining ingredients.
4. Gently stir to combine and serve well chilled. Bon appétit!

Nutrition:
Calories 457 | Fat 31.3g | Carbs 18.4g
Protein 21g | Sugars 9.2g

317. Shrimp Scampi Linguine

Preparation Time: 25 minutes
Cooking Time: 20 minutes
Servings: 4

Ingredients:

1 ½ pounds shrimp, shelled and deveined
1/2 tablespoon fresh basil leaves, chopped
2 tablespoons olive oil
2 cloves garlic, minced
1/2 teaspoon fresh ginger, grated
1/4 teaspoon cracked black pepper
1/2 teaspoon sea salt
1/4 cup chicken stock
2 ripe tomatoes, pureed
8 ounces linguine pasta
1/2 cup parmesan cheese, preferably freshly grated

Directions:

1. Start by preheating the Air Fryer to 395 degrees F. Place the shrimp, basil, olive oil, garlic, ginger, black pepper, salt, chicken stock, and tomatoes in the casserole dish.
2. Transfer the casserole dish to the cooking basket and bake for 10 minutes.
3. Bring a large pot of lightly salted water to a boil. Cook the linguine for 10 minutes or until al dente; drain.
4. Divide between four serving plates. Add the shrimp sauce and top with parmesan cheese. Bon appétit!

Nutrition:
Calories 560 | Fat 11g | Carbs 47.3g
Protein 59.3g | Sugars 1.6g

318. Sunday Fish with Sticky Sauce

Preparation Time: 20 minutes
Cooking Time: 11 minutes
Servings: 2

Ingredients:

- 2 pollack fillets
- Salt and black pepper, to taste
- 1 tablespoon olive oil
- 1 cup chicken broth
- 2 tablespoons light soy sauce
- 1 tablespoon brown sugar
- 2 tablespoons butter, melted
- 1 teaspoon fresh ginger, minced
- 1 teaspoon fresh garlic, minced
- 2 corn tortillas

Directions:

1. Pat dry the pollack fillets and season them with salt and black pepper; drizzle the sesame oil all over the fish fillets.
2. Preheat the Air Fryer to 380 degrees F and cook your fish for 11 minutes. Slice into bite-sized pieces.
3. Meanwhile, prepare the sauce. Add the broth to a large saucepan and bring to a boil. Add the soy sauce, sugar, butter, ginger, and garlic. Reduce the heat to simmer and cook until it is reduced slightly.
4. Add the fish pieces to the warm sauce. Serve on corn tortillas and enjoy!

Nutrition:
Calories 573 | Fat 38.3g | Carbs 31.5g
Protein 26.2g | Sugars 7g

319. Tasty Air Fried Cod

Preparation Time: 10 minutes
Cooking Time: 12 minutes
Servings: 4

Ingredients:

- 7 oz. 2 cod fish
- Sesame oil
- Salt and black pepper
- 1 cup water
- 1 tsp. dark soy sauce
- 4 tbsp. light soy sauce
- 1 tbsp. sugar
- 3 tbsp. olive oil
- 4 ginger slices
- 3 spring onions
- 2 tbsp. coriander

Directions:

1. Season fish with pepper, salt, sprinkle sesame oil, rub well and allow for 10 minutes.
2. Add fish to air fryer. Cook at 356°F for 12 minutes.
3. Heat a pot with the water over medium heat. Add sugar and light and dark soy sauce. Allow to simmer. Take off heat.
4. Heat pan with the olive oil over medium heat. Add green onions and ginger. Cook for a few minutes. Take off heat.
5. Divide fish on plates. Top with ginger and green onions. Drizzle soy sauce mix. Sprinkle coriander and serve.

Nutrition:
Calories: 524 | Total Fat: 27.5g | Sodium: 252mg

Total Carbs: 56.2g | Fiber: 2.3g | Sugars: 20.3g

Protein: 26.6g

320. Delicious Catfish

Preparation Time: 10 minutes

Cooking Time: 20 minutes

Servings: 4

Ingredients:

- 4 catfish fillets
- Black pepper and Salt
- A pinch of sweet paprika
- 1 tbsp. parsley
- 1 tbsp. lemon juice
- 1 tbsp. olive oil

Directions:

1. Season catfish fillets with salt, paprika, pepper, drizzle oil, rub well. Then put in air fryer basket and cook at 400°F for 20 minutes. Flip the fish after 10 minutes of time.
2. Share fish on plates. Sprinkle parsley and drizzle some lemon juice over it, serve.

Nutrition:

Calories: 247 | Total Fat: 15.7g | Sodium: 86mg

Total Carbs: 0.2g | Fiber: 0.1g | Sugars: 0.1g | Protein: 25g

321. Cod Fillets with Fennel and Grapes Salad

Preparation Time: 10 minutes

Cooking Time: 15 minutes

Servings: 2

Ingredients:

- 2 black cod fillets
- 1 tbsp. olive oil
- Black pepper and Salt
- 1 fennel bulb
- 1 cup grapes
- ½ cup pecans

Directions:

1. Sprinkle half of the oil over fish fillets, season with pepper and salt, rub well, place fillets in air fryer basket. Then cook for 10 minutes' time at 400°F and put in the plate.
2. Mix pecans with grapes, fennel, the rest of the oil, salt, and pepper, toss to coat, in a bowl. Add to pan that fits air fryer. Cook at 400° F for 5 minutes.
3. Share cod on plates, add grapes and fennel mix on the side then serve.

Nutrition:

Calories: 602 | Total Fat: 50.4g | Sodium: 132mg

Total Carbs: 21.4g | Fiber: 7g | Sugars: 8.5g | Protein: 21.7g

322. Tabasco Shrimp

Preparation Time: 10 minutes

Cooking Time: 10 minutes

Servings: 4

Ingredients:

- 1 lb. shrimp
- 1 tbsp. red pepper flakes
- 2 tbsp. olive oil
- 1 tbsp. Tabasco sauce
- 2 tbsp. water
- 1 tbsp. oregano
- Black pepper and salt
- ½ tbsp. parsley
- ½ tbsp. smoked paprika

Directions:

1. Mix oil with water, pepper flakes, Tabasco sauce, oregano, parsley, pepper, salt, paprika and shrimp and toss well to coat in a bowl
2. Place shrimp to preheated air fryer at 370° F and cook for 10 minutes. Shake fryer once.
3. Share shrimp on plates then serve by a side salad.

Nutrition:

Calories: 206 | Total Fat: 9.4g | Sodium: 301mg

Total Carbs: 3.7g | Fiber: 1.2g | Sugars: 0.3g| Protein: 26.3g

323. Asian Salmon

Preparation Time: 60 minutes

Cooking Time: 20 minutes

Servings: 2

Ingredients:

- 2 medium salmon fillets
- 6 tbsp. light soy sauce
- 3 tbsp. mirin
- 1 tbsp. water
- 6 tbsp. honey

Directions:

1. Mix soy sauce with honey, water, and mirin, whisk very well, in a bowl, add salmon, rub well. Leave it in a fridge for an hour.
2. Place salmon to air fryer. Cook at 360° F for 15 minutes' time. Flip it after 7 minutes.
3. Put the soy marinade in pan, heat above medium heat, whisk very well. Cook for 2 minutes the put off heat.
4. Share salmon on plates, sprinkle marinade over and serve.

Nutrition:

Calories: 473 | Total Fat: 11g | Sodium: 976mg | Fiber: 0.1g
Total Carbs: 77.3g | Sugars: 66.8g | Protein: 37.9g

324. Asian Coconut Shrimp

Preparation Time: 10 minutes
Cooking Time: 8 minutes
Servings: 4

Ingredients:

- ½ cup all-purpose flour
- 2 large eggs
- 2/3 cup unsweetened coconut flakes
- 1/3 cup panko breadcrumbs
- 24 medium shrimps
- Salt and black pepper to taste
- Olive oil

Directions:

1. Insert the dripping pan in the bottom part of the air fryer and preheat the oven at Air Fry mode at 400 F for 2 to 3 minutes. Lightly brush the rotisserie basket with some olive oil and set aside.
2. Pour the flour into a shallow plate, whisk the eggs in a bowl, and mix the coconut flakes with breadcrumbs on another plate.
3. Season the shrimps with salt, black pepper, and dredge lightly in the flour. Proceed to coat in the eggs and then, generously, in the breadcrumb's mixture.
4. Spray the coated shrimps with some olive oil and arrange it in the rotisserie basket. Fit the basket in the oven using the rotisserie lift and set the timer for 8 minutes or until the shrimps are golden brown.
5. When ready, transfer the shrimps to serving plates and serve warm with sweet coconut dipping sauce.

Nutrition:

Calories 190 | Total Fat 7.16g | Total Carbs 20.88g
Fiber 2g | Protein 10.32g

325. Mahi Mahi with Herby Buttery Drizzle

Preparation Time: 10 minutes
Cooking Time: 12 minutes
Servings: 4

Ingredients:

- 4 (6 oz) Mahi Mahi fillets
- Salt and black pepper to taste
- Olive oil for spraying
- 2/3 cup butter, melted
- 1 tbsp chopped fresh parsley
- ½ tbsp chopped fresh dill

Directions:

1. Insert the dripping pan in the bottom part of the air fryer and preheat the oven at Bake mode at 400 F for 2 to 3 minutes.
2. Season the Mahi Mahi fillets with salt, black pepper, and grease lightly with some olive oil. Lay the fish on the cooking tray and fit onto the middle rack of the oven.
3. Close the lid and set the timer for 12 minutes.
4. Once the fish cooks, transfer to a serving platter. Whisk the butter with the parsley and dill and drizzle the mixture on the fish before serving. Enjoy immediately.

Nutrition:

Calories 529 | Total Fat 46.54g | Total Carbs 9.25g
Fiber 5.6g | Protein 20.26g

326. Classic Lemon Pepper Haddock

Preparation Time: 10 minutes
Cooking Time: 12 minutes
Servings: 4

Ingredients:

- ¼ cup all-purpose flour
- 2 egg whites
- 1/3 cup panko breadcrumbs
- 2 tsp lemon pepper
- 2 egg whites
- 4 (8 oz) haddock fillets
- Salt to taste
- 2 slices lemon
- Chopped parsley to garnish

Directions:

1. Insert the dripping pan in the bottom part of the air fryer and preheat the oven at Air Fry mode at 400 F for 2 to 3 minutes.
2. Pour the flour in a shallow plate, mix the breadcrumbs and lemon peppers in another shallow dish, whisk the egg whites lightly in a medium bowl, and season the fish lightly with salt.
3. Dredge the fish lightly in the flour, then coat in the egg whites, and then generously in the breadcrumb's mixture.
4. Lay the fish on the cooking tray, grease lightly with cooking spray, and fit onto the middle rack of the oven. Close the air fryer and set the timer for 12 minutes.
5. Once the fish cooks, transfer to a serving platter and serve immediately with the lemon and parsley garnish.

Nutrition:

Calories 208 | Total Fat 1.22g | Total Carbs 10.95g
Fiber 1.1g | Protein 36.88g

327. Fried Scallops with Saffron Cream Sauce

Preparation Time: 5 minutes
Cooking Time: 2 minutes

Servings: 4

Ingredients:
- Olive oil for greasing
- 24 scallops, cleaned
- 2/3 cup heavy cream
- 1 tbsp freshly squeezed lemon juice
- ¼ tsp dried crushed saffron threads

Directions:
1. Insert the dripping pan in the bottom part of the air fryer and preheat the oven at Air Fry mode 400 F for 2 to 3 minutes.
2. Lightly brush the rotisserie basket with some olive oil and fill with the scallops.
3. Close and fit the basket in the oven using the rotisserie lift and set the timer for 2 minutes or until the scallops are golden brown on the outside.
4. Meanwhile, in a medium bowl, quickly whisk the heavy cream lemon juice and saffron threads.
5. When the scallops are ready, transfer to a serving plate and drizzle the sauce on top. Enjoy immediately.

Nutrition:
Calories 77 | Total Fat 7.73g | Total Carbs 1.05g
Fiber 0g | Protein 1.15g

328. Easy Crab Cakes

Preparation Time: 10 minutes
Cooking Time: 10 minutes
Servings: 4

Ingredients:
- 8 oz lump crab
- 1 medium red bell pepper, deseeded and diced
- 2 scallions, finely chopped
- 2 tbsp mayonnaise
- 2 tbsp panko breadcrumbs
- 1 tbsp Dijon mustard
- 1 tsp old bay seasoning
- Olive oil for spraying
- 4 lemon wedges for serving

Directions:
1. Insert the dripping pan in the bottom part of the air fryer and preheat the oven at Bake mode at 370 F for 2 to 3 minutes.
2. Meanwhile, in a medium bowl, mix all the ingredients except for the olive oil and lemon wedges until evenly distributed. From 4 to 6 firm patties from the mixture, arrange on the cooking tray, and grease lightly with some olive oil. You may do this in two batches.
3. Fit the cooking tray on the middle rack and close the oven. Set the timer to 10 minutes and cook until the timer reads to the end, and the crab cakes are golden brown and well compacted.
4. Remove the crab cakes from the oven and serve with the lemon wedges.

Nutrition:
Calories 246 | Total Fat 6.19g | Total Carbs 13.65g
Fiber 1.5g | Protein 33.16g

329. Sweet Asian Style Salmon

Preparation Time: 10 minutes
Cooking Time: 12 minutes
Servings: 4

Ingredients:
- 2 garlic cloves, minced
- 1 tbsp fresh ginger paste
- 2 tsp fresh orange zest
- ½ cup fresh orange juice
- ¼ cup soy sauce
- 3 tbsp plain vinegar
- 1 tbsp olive oil
- Salt to taste
- 4 (5 oz) salmon fillets

Directions:
1. In a large bowl, mix all the ingredients except for the fish and place the fish in the sauce. Spoon the sauce well on top and cover the bowl with a plastic wrap. Allow marinating at room temperature for 30 minutes.
2. After 30 minutes, insert the dripping pan in the bottom part of the air fryer and preheat the oven at Bake mode at 400 F for 2 to 3 minutes.
3. Using tongs, remove the fish from the sauce, making sure to shake off some marinade of the fish and place the cooking tray. You can work in two batches.
4. Slide the tray onto the top rack of the oven, close the oven, and set the timer for 12 minutes, flipping the fish after 6 minutes.
5. Once ready, transfer the fish to serving plates and serve warm with steamed greens.

Nutrition:
Calories 132 | Total Fat 7.39g | Total Carbs 8.72g
Fiber 0.5g | Protein 7.2g

330. Zesty Ranch Fish Fillets

Preparation Time: 10 minutes
Cooking Time: 13 minutes
Servings: 4

Ingredients:
- ¾ cup finely crushed cornflakes or panko breadcrumbs
- 3 tbsp dry ranch-style dressing mix
- 1 tsp fresh lemon zest

- 2 ½ tbsp olive oil
- 2 eggs, beaten
- 4 white fish fillets
- Lemon wedges to garnish

Directions:

1. Insert the dripping pan in the bottom part of the air fryer and preheat the oven at Air Fry mode at 400 F for 2 to 3 minutes.
2. Mix the cornflakes, dressing mix, lemon zest, and oil on a shallow plate and then pour the eggs on another.
3. Working in two batches, dip the fish into the egg, drip off excess egg, and coat well in the cornflake's mixture on both sides.
4. Place the fish on the cooking tray and fix the tray on the middle rack of the oven. Close the oven and set the timer for 13 minutes and cook until the fish is golden brown and the fish flaky within.
5. Transfer to a serving plate and serve with the lemon wedges.

Nutrition:

Calories 409 | Total Fat 23.84g | Total Carbs 3.79g
Fiber 0.5g | Protein 42.55g

331. Dill Fish Chops

Preparation Time: 10 minutes
Cooking Time: 11 minutes
Servings: 4

Ingredients:

- 4 (5 oz) cod fillets, cut into 2-inch cubes
- ½ cup tapioca starch
- 2 eggs
- 1 cup almond flour
- 1 ½ dried fish seasoning
- 1 ½ dried dill
- Salt and black pepper to taste
- ½ tsp mustard powder
- Olive oil for greasing

Directions:

1. Insert the dripping pan in the bottom part of the air fryer and preheat the oven at Air Fry mode at 390 F for 2 to 3 minutes.
2. Pour the tapioca starch on a shallow plate, beat the eggs in a medium bowl, and mix the almond flour, fish seasoning, dill, salt, black pepper, and mustard powder on another plate.
3. Lightly coat the fish cubes in the starch, then dip in the eggs, and coat generously in the mustard mixture until well coated on all sides.
4. Spray the coated fish with a little olive oil and put it in the rotisserie basket. Fit the basket in the oven using the rotisserie ling and close the oven. Set the timer for 11 minutes and cook until the fish is golden brown on the outside.
5. Transfer the crusted fish onto serving plates and serve warm with your favorite sauce.

Nutrition:

Calories 206 | Total Fat 4.02g, | Total Carbs 18.18g
Fiber 0.4g | Protein 22.79g

332. Easy Fish Sticks with Chili Ketchup Sauce

Preparation Time: 10 minutes
Cooking Time: 12 minutes
Servings: 4

Ingredients:

- 8 fish sticks, store bought
- ½ cup tomato ketchup
- 1 tbsp Sriracha sauce
- 1 tbsp chopped fresh parsley to garnish
- Sliced pickles for serving

Directions:

1. Insert the dripping pan in the bottom part of the air fryer and preheat the oven at Air Fry mode at 390 F for 2 to 3 minutes.
2. Arrange the fish sticks on the cooking tray and fit onto the middle rack of the oven. Close and set the timer for 12 minutes and cook until the fish sticks are golden brown and crispy.
3. Meanwhile, in a small bowl, mix the tomato ketchup, Sriracha sauce, and parsley until well combined and set aside for serving.
4. When the fish is ready, transfer onto serving plates and serve warm with the sauce and pickles.

Nutrition:

Calories 341 | Total Fat 2.53g
Total Carbs 1.13g | Fiber 0.4g | Protein 73.57g

333. Basil Cod

Preparation Time: 20 minutes
Cooking Time: 15 minutes
Servings: 4

Ingredients:

- 4 cod fillets; boneless
- 2 tbsp. olive oil
- 1 tsp. basil; dried
- 1 tsp. red pepper flakes
- ½ tsp. hot paprika
- Salt and black pepper to taste

Directions:

1. Take a bowl and mix the cod with all the other Ingredients: and toss.

2. Put the fish in your air fryer's basket and cook at 380°F for 15 minutes. Divide the cod between plates and serve.

Nutrition:

Calories: 194 | Fat: 7g | Fiber: 2g

Carbs: 4g | Protein: 12g

---

334. Lime Baked Salmon

Preparation Time: 22 minutes

Cooking Time: 12 minutes

Servings: 2

Ingredients:

- 2 (3-oz. salmon fillets, skin removed
- ¼ cup sliced pickled jalapeños
- ½ medium lime, juiced
- 2 tbsp. chopped cilantro
- 1 tbsp. salted butter; melted.
- ½ tsp. finely minced garlic
- 1 tsp. chili powder

Directions:

1. Place salmon fillets into a 6-inch round baking pan. Brush each with butter and sprinkle with chili powder and garlic.
2. Place jalapeño slices on top and around salmon. Pour half of the lime juice over the salmon and cover with foil. Place pan into the air fryer basket. Adjust the temperature to 370 Degrees F and set the timer for 12 minutes.
3. When fully cooked, salmon should flake easily with a fork and reach an internal temperature of at least 145 Degrees F.
4. To serve, spritz with remaining lime juice and garnish with cilantro.

Nutrition:

Calories: 167 | Protein: 18g | Fiber: 7g | Fat: 9g | Carbs: 6g

---

335. Sea Bass and Fennel.

Preparation Time: 25 minutes

Cooking Time: 20 minutes

Servings: 2

Ingredients:

- ¼ cup black olives, pitted and sliced
- 2 sea bass, fillets
- ¼ cup basil; chopped.
- 1 fennel bulb; sliced
- Juice of 1 lemon
- 1 tbsp. olive oil
- A pinch of salt and black pepper

Directions:

1. In a pan that fits the air fryer, combine all the ingredients.

2. Introduce the pan in the machine and cook at 380°F for 20 minutes, shaking the fryer halfway.
3. Divide between plates and serve!

Nutrition:

Calories: 254 | Fat: 10g | Fiber: 4g | Carbs: 6g | Protein: 11g

---

336. Snapper and Spring Onions

Preparation Time: 19 minutes

Cooking Time: 14 minutes

Servings: 4

Ingredients:

- 4 snapper fillets; boneless and skin scored
- 6 spring onions; chopped.
- Juice of ½ lemon
- 3 tbsp. olive oil
- 2 tbsp. sweet paprika
- A pinch of salt and black pepper

Directions:

1. Take a bowl and mix the paprika with the rest of the Ingredients: except the fish and whisk well.
2. Rub the fish with this mix, place the fillets in your air fryer's basket and cook at 390°F for 7 minutes on each side.
3. Divide between plates and serve with a side salad.

Nutrition:

Calories: 241 | Fat: 12g | Fiber: 4g | Carbs: 6g | Protein: 13g

---

337. Herbed Trout and Asparagus

Preparation Time: 25 minutes

Cooking Time: 14 minutes

Servings: 4

Ingredients:

- 4 trout fillets; boneless and skinless
- 1 bunch asparagus; trimmed
- ¼ cup mixed chives and tarragon
- 2 tbsp. ghee; melted
- 2 tbsp. olive oil
- 1 tbsp. lemon juice
- A pinch of salt and black pepper

Directions:

1. Mix the asparagus with half of the oil, salt and pepper, put it in your air fryer's basket, cook at 380°F for 6 minutes and divide between plates.
2. Take a bowl and mix the trout with salt, pepper, lemon juice, the rest of the oil and the herbs and toss.
3. Put the fillets in your air fryer's basket and cook at 380°F for 7 minutes on each side.

4. Divide the fish next to the asparagus, drizzle the melted ghee all over and serve.

Nutrition:

Calories: 240 | Fat: 12g | Fiber: 4g | Carbs: 6g | Protein: 9g

338. Coco Shrimp

Preparation Time: 11 minutes

Cooking Time: 6 minutes

Servings: 2

Ingredients:

- 8 oz. medium shelled and deveined shrimp
- ¼ cup unsweetened shredded coconut
- 2 tbsp. salted butter; melted.
- ½ tsp. Old Bay seasoning

Directions:

1. Take a large bowl, toss the shrimp in butter and Old Bay seasoning.
2. Place shredded coconut in bowl. Coat each piece of shrimp in the coconut and place into the air fryer basket.
3. Adjust the temperature to 400 Degrees F and set the timer for 6 minutes. Gently turn the shrimp halfway through the cooking time. Serve immediately.

Nutrition:

Calories: 252 | Protein: 19g | Fiber: 0g | Fat: 18g |Carbs: 8g

339. Shrimp and Zucchinis

Preparation Time: 20 minutes

Cooking Time: 15 minutes

Servings: 4

Ingredients:

- 1 lb. shrimp; peeled and deveined
- 2 zucchinis; cut into medium cubes
- 1 tbsp. lemon juice
- 1 tbsp. olive oil
- 1 tbsp. garlic; minced
- A pinch of salt and black pepper

Directions:

1. In a pan that fits the air fryer, combine all the Ingredients, toss, put the pan in the machine and cook at 370°F for 15 minutes.
2. Divide between plates and serve right away.

Nutrition:

Calories: 221 | Fat: 9g | Fiber: 2g | Carbs: 15g | Protein: 11g

340. Trout and Zucchinis

Preparation Time: 20 minutes

Cooking Time: 15 minutes

Servings: 4

Ingredients:

- 3 zucchinis, cut in medium chunks
- 4 trout fillets; boneless
- ¼ cup tomato sauce
- 1 garlic clove; minced
- ½ cup cilantro; chopped
- 1 tbsp. lemon juice
- 2 tbsp. olive oil
- Salt and black pepper to taste

Directions:

1. In a pan that fits your air fryer, mix the fish with the other Ingredients, toss, introduce in the fryer and cook at 380°F for 15 minutes.
2. Divide everything between plates and serve right away.

Nutrition:

Calories: 220 | Fat: 12g | Fiber: 4g | Carbs: 6g | Protein: 9g

341. Flounder Fillets

Preparation Time: 25 minutes

Cooking Time: 20 minutes

Servings: 4

Ingredients:

- 4 flounder fillets; boneless
- 1 cup parmesan; grated
- 2 tbsp. olive oil
- 4 tbsp. butter; melted
- A pinch of salt and black pepper

Directions:

1. Take a bowl and mix the parmesan with salt, pepper, butter and the oil and stir well.
2. Arrange the fish in a pan that fits the air fryer, spread the parmesan mix all over, introduce in the fryer and cook at 400°F for 20 minutes.
3. Divide between plates and serve with a side salad.

Nutrition:

Calories: 251 | Fat: 14g | Fiber: 5g | Carbs: 6g | Protein: 12g

342. Garlic Lemon Shrimp

Preparation Time: 11 minutes

Cooking Time: 6 minutes

Servings: 2

Ingredients:

- 8 oz. medium shelled and deveined shrimp
- 1 medium lemon.
- 2 tbsp. unsalted butter; melted.

- ½ tsp. minced garlic
- ½ tsp. Old Bay seasoning

Directions:

1. Zest lemon and then cut in half. Place shrimp in a large bowl and squeeze juice from ½ lemon on top of them.
2. Add lemon zest to bowl along with remaining ingredients. Toss shrimp until fully coated
3. Pour bowl contents into 6-inch round baking dish. Place into the air fryer basket.
4. Adjust the temperature to 400 Degrees F and set the timer for 6 minutes. Shrimp will be bright pink when fully cooked. Serve warm with pan sauce.

Nutrition:

Calories: 190 | Protein: 14g | Fiber: 4g | Fat: 18g | Carbs: 9g

343. Crab Cakes

Preparation Time: 15 minutes

Cooking Time: 10 minutes

Servings: 4

Ingredients:

- ¼ cup red bell pepper, seeded and chopped finely
- 2 scallions, chopped finely
- 2 tablespoons mayonnaise
- 2 tablespoons breadcrumbs
- 1 tablespoon Dijon mustard
- 1 teaspoon old bay seasoning
- 8 ounces lump crabmeat, drained

Directions:

1. In a large bowl, add all the ingredients except crabmeat and mix until well combined.
2. Gently fold in the crabmeat.
3. Make 4 equal-sized patties from the mixture.
4. Arrange the patties onto a lightly greased cooking tray.
5. Arrange the drip pan in the bottom of your Air Fryer.
6. Select "Air Fry" and then adjust the temperature to 370 degrees F.
7. Set the timer for 10 minutes and press the "Start".
8. When the display shows "Add Food" insert the cooking rack in the center position.
9. When the display shows "Turn Food" do nothing.
10. When cooking time is complete, remove the tray from the machine and serve hot.

Nutrition:

Calories 91 | Total Fat 7.4 g | Saturated Fat 0.4 g

Cholesterol 34 mg | Sodium 603 mg | Total Carbs 6.4 g

Fiber 0.6 g | Sugar 1.3 g | Protein 9.1 g

344. Remarkable Fish and Chips with Sauce

Preparation Time: 10 minutes

Cooking Time: 35 minutes

Servings: 4

Ingredients:

- 4 cod fish fillets
- 1 teaspoon of olive oil
- 1 cup of flour
- 1 cup of panko breadcrumbs
- 2 beaten eggs
- 2 potatoes, cut into ½-inch strips
- 1 tablespoon of olive oil
- 1 teaspoon of salt

Sauce Ingredients:

- ¼ cup of mayonnaise
- 1 tablespoon of freshly chopped dill
- 1 tablespoon of freshly chopped tarragon
- 2 tablespoons of sour cream
- 2 tablespoons of finely chopped dill pickle
- 2 tablespoons of finely chopped red onion

Directions:

1. Soak the potato pieces in a bowl of water for 30 minutes. After 30 minutes, drain it into a colander and pat it dry using a cloth.
2. Preheat your air fryer to 360 degrees Fahrenheit.
3. Using a large bowl, add and mix the potato strips, olive oil, salt and toss it until it is properly covered.
4. Place the potato strips inside your air fryer and cook it for 20 to 25 minutes, while still shaking it at a regular interval of 6 minutes until the potatoes reaches its golden-brown color and crispy texture state. After that, remove and set it aside.
5. Then for the fish: Using a bowl, add the flour, pick another bowl, add the eggs and stir properly, then using another separate bowl, add the breadcrumbs and olive oil.
6. Dredge the cod fillets in the flour, dip it in the egg mixture, and then cover it with the breadcrumbs.
7. Grease your air fryer basket with a nonstick cooking spray and add the battered cod fillets.
8. Cook it for 10 minutes or until it has a golden-brown color, carefully remove it from your air fryer basket and allow it to cool off.
9. For the sauce: Using a bowl, add all the mayonnaise, dill, tarragon, sour cream, dill pickle, the red onion, and stir it until it is properly mixed. Serve and enjoy!

Nutrition:

Calories: 250 | Fat: 8g | Protein: 13g | Fiber: 2g

Carbohydrates: 3g

345. Grand Air-Fried Coconut Shrimp

Preparation Time: 10 minutes
Cooking Time:
Servings: 4
Ingredients:
- 1 pound of peeled and deveined shrimp
- 1 cup of shredded coconut
- 1 cup of panko breadcrumbs
- 2 eggs
- 1/3 cup of flour
- 1 teaspoon of salt
- 1 teaspoon of black pepper

Directions:
1. Preheat your air fryer to 360 degrees Fahrenheit.
2. Using a bowl, add and mix the flour, salt, and black pepper. Then using a second bowl, add the eggs and beat it properly. Pick a third bowl, add and mix the shredded coconut and breadcrumbs.
3. Dredge each shrimp in the flour, dip it into the egg wash and then cover it with the coconut breadcrumb mixture.
4. Grease your air fryer basket with a nonstick cooking spray and add the shrimp.
5. Cook it for 10 to 15 minutes at a 360 degrees Fahrenheit or until it has a golden-brown color. Serve and enjoy!

Nutrition:
Calories: 250 | Fat: 14g | Protein: 9g | Fiber: 1.6g | Carbohydrates: 4g

346. Splendid Salmon Patties

Preparation Time: 10 minutes
Cooking Time: 15 minutes
Servings: 2
Ingredients:
- 1 (14-ounce) can have drained canned salmon
- ¼ cup of chopped onion
- ¼ cup of ground oats
- ¼ cup of wheat flour
- 1 egg
- ¼ cup of mayonnaise
- 1 tablespoon of parsley
- 1 teaspoon of salt
- 1 teaspoon of black pepper
- 1 cup of breadcrumbs

Directions:
1. Preheat your air fryer to 390 degrees Fahrenheit.
2. Using a bowl, add and mix the canned salmon, onion, ground oats, wheat flour, egg, parsley, salt, black pepper and the mayonnaise properly.
3. Divide the salmon mixture into 4 patties and cover it with the breadcrumbs.
4. Add the salmon patties inside your air fryer and cook it for 8 to 10 minutes or until it has a golden-brown color. Serve and enjoy!

Nutrition:
Calories: 260, | Fat: 15g | Protein: 16g | Dietary Fiber: 1g | Carbohydrates: 14g

347. Japanese-Style Fried Prawns

Preparation Time: 10 minutes
Cooking Time: 15 minutes
Servings: 2
Ingredients:
- 1 pound of peeled and deveined prawns
- 1 cup of rice flour
- 1 cup of panko breadcrumbs
- 2 eggs
- 1 teaspoon of ground ginger
- 1 tablespoon of paprika
- 1 teaspoon of salt
- 1 teaspoon of black pepper
- 1 teaspoon of garlic powder

Directions:
1. Preheat your air fryer to 380 degrees Fahrenheit.
2. Using a bowl, add the prawns, salt, black pepper, garlic powder, ground ginger and toss until it is properly mixed.
3. Then using another bowl, add the rice flour, paprika and mix it well. Pick a second bowl, add the eggs and beat it properly. Then using a third bowl, add the panko breadcrumbs.
4. Dredge the seasoned prawns into the flour, dip it into the egg wash, and then cover it with the panko breadcrumbs.
5. Grease your air fryer basket with a nonstick cooking spray and add the prawns.
6. Cook it for 8 minutes or until it has a golden-brown color and repeat if necessary. Serve and enjoy!

Nutrition:
Calories: 210 | Fat: 8g | Protein: 40g | Fiber: 0g | Carbohydrates: 4g

348. Great Air-Fried Soft-Shell Crab

Preparation Time: 10 minutes
Cooking Time: 10 minutes
Servings: 2
Ingredients:

- 2 soft-shell crabs
- 1 cup of flour
- 2 beaten eggs
- 1 cup of panko breadcrumbs
- 1 teaspoon of onion powder
- 1 teaspoon of garlic powder
- 1 teaspoon of salt
- 1 teaspoon of black pepper

Directions:

1. Preheat your air fryer to 360 degrees Fahrenheit.
2. Using a bowl, add the flour, pick a second bowl, add the eggs and mix properly. Then using a third bowl, mix the panko breadcrumbs and the seasonings properly.
3. Grease your air fryer basket with a nonstick cooking spray and add the crabs inside.
4. Cook it inside your air fryer for 8 minutes or until it has a golden-brown color.
5. Thereafter, carefully remove it from your air fryer and allow it to cool off. Serve and enjoy!

Nutrition:

Calories: 380 | Fat: 16g | Protein: 24g | Carbohydrates: 9g
Fiber: 5g

349. Stunning Air-Fried Clams

Preparation Time: 10 minutes
Cooking Time: 15 minutes
Servings: 2

Ingredients:

- 1 (10-ounce) can of whole baby clams, drained and shucked
- 2 beaten eggs
- 1 cup of flour
- 1 cup of panko breadcrumbs
- 1 teaspoon of salt
- 1 teaspoon of black pepper
- 1 teaspoon of garlic powder
- 1 teaspoon of onion powder
- 1 teaspoon of cayenne pepper
- 1 tablespoon of dried oregano

Directions:

1. Preheat your air fryer to 390 degrees Fahrenheit.
2. Using a bowl, add the flour, pick a second bowl, add the eggs and mix properly. Then using a third bowl, add and mix the panko breadcrumbs, seasonings, and the herbs properly.
3. Dredge the clams in the flour, immerse it into the egg wash and then cover it with the breadcrumb mixture.
4. Place the clams inside your air fryer and cook it for 2 minutes or until it has a golden-brown color, while being cautious of overcooking.
5. Thereafter, carefully remove it from your air fryer and allow it to cool. Serve and enjoy!

Nutrition:

Calories: 225 | Fat: 12g | Protein: 15g | Carbohydrates: 3g | Fiber: 0.5g

350. Mind-Blowing Air-Fried Crawfish with Cajun Dipping Sauce

Preparation Time: 10 minutes
Cooking Time: 10 minutes
Servings: 4

Ingredients:

- 1 pound of cooked craw-fish tail meat
- 1 beaten egg
- 4 chopped green onions
- 1 teaspoon of melted butter
- 1 teaspoon of salt
- 1 teaspoon of cayenne pepper
- 1 teaspoon of black pepper
- 1/3 cup of panko breadcrumbs
- 1/3 cup of bread flour
- Sauce Ingredients:
- ¾ cup of mayonnaise
- ½ cup of ketchup
- 1 teaspoon of horseradish

Directions:

1. Preheat your air fryer to 380 degrees Fahrenheit.
2. Using a bowl, add the eggs, green onion, butter, salt, cayenne pepper, black pepper and salt.
3. Add the panko breadcrumbs, bread flour and pour in the crawfish, stirring it until it is properly covered.
4. Grease your air fryer basket with a nonstick cooking spray.
5. Add the battered crawfish inside your air fryer and cook it for 5 minutes or until it has a golden-brown color.
6. Thereafter, using a bowl, add the mayonnaise, ketchup, horseradish and mix properly. Serve and enjoy!

Nutrition:

Calories: 205 | Fat: 16.7g | Protein: 26g | Fiber: 0.3g
Carbohydrates: 8.8g

351. Southern-Air-Fried Catfish

Preparation Time: 10 minutes
Cooking Time: 15 minutes
Servings: 4

Ingredients:

- 4 skinless catfish fillets
- 1 teaspoon of salt

- 1 teaspoon of black pepper
- 1 cup of cornmeal
- 1 cup of flour

Directions:

1. Preheat your air fryer to 360 degrees Fahrenheit.
2. Using a bowl, add the cornmeal, flour, salt, black pepper and mix it properly.
3. Dredge the catfish fillets in the seasoned cornmeal mixture.
4. Grease your air fryer with a non-stick cooking spray and add the catfish fillets.
5. Cook the catfish for 8 minutes at a 360 degrees Fahrenheit or until it turns brown. Serve and enjoy!

Nutrition:

Calories: 350 | Fat: 15g | Protein: 25g | Fiber: 0g | Carbohydrates: 36g

352. Wondrous Creole Fried Shrimp with Sriracha Sauce

Preparation Time: 10 minutes

Cooking Time: 10 minutes

Servings: 4

Ingredients:

- 1 pound of peeled and deveined shrimp
- ½ cup of cornmeal
- ½ cup of breadcrumbs
- 1 beaten egg
- 1 tablespoon of hot sauce
- 1 tablespoon of mustard
- 2 tablespoons of creole seasoning
- 1 teaspoon of onion powder
- 1 teaspoon of garlic powder
- 1 teaspoon of black pepper
- 1 teaspoon of salt
  Siracha Sauce Ingredients:
- 1 cup of mayonnaise
- 3 tablespoons of sriracha sauce
- 1 tablespoon of soy sauce
- 1 teaspoon of black pepper

Directions:

1. Preheat your air fryer to 360 degrees Fahrenheit.
2. Using a bowl, add the eggs, hot sauce, mustard, 1 tablespoon of creole seasoning, onion powder, garlic powder, black pepper, salt, the shrimp and toss until it is properly covered.
3. Using another bowl, add the breadcrumbs, flour, 1 tablespoon of creole seasoning, the shrimp and cover it properly.
4. Grease your air fryer basket with a nonstick cooking spray and add the shrimp.
5. Cook for it for 5 minutes or until it has a golden-brown color, while being careful not to overcook.
6. Thereafter, carefully remove it from your air fryer and allow it to cool.
7. Pick a separate bowl, add and mix all the sauce ingredients properly. Serve!

Nutrition:

Calories: 200 | Fat: 12g | Protein: 15g | Carbohydrates: 7g Fiber: 0.6g

353. Lemon & Orange Grilled Branzini

Preparation Time: 5 minutes

Cooking Time: 15 minutes

Servings: 4

Ingredients:

- oranges, juice freshly squeezed
- lemons, juice freshly squeezed
- 4 branzini fillets
- Salt and pepper to taste

Directions:

1. Put all the ingredients in a Ziploc bag. Store them in the fridge for 2 hours.
2. Heat the hot air fryer to 3900 F.
3. Insert the grill pan attachment into the hot air fryer.
4. Put the fish on the grill pan and continue cooking for 15 minutes or until the fish is flaky.

Nutrition:

Calories: 318; | Carbs: 20.8g; | Protein: 23.5g; | Fat: 15.6g

354. Creamy Breaded Salmon

Preparation Time: 5 minutes

Cooking Time: 20 minutes

Servings: 4

Ingredients:

- 1-2 cups breadcrumbs
- 4 salmon fillets
- 2 eggs, beaten
- 1 cup Swiss cheese, shredded

Directions:

1. Heat your hot air fryer to 390°Fahrenheit. Immerse each salmon fillet in the eggs. Cover with Swiss cheese.
2. Coat in breadcrumbs so that the entire fish is covered. Place in an ovenproof dish and cook for 20 minutes.

Nutrition:

Calories: 296, | Total Fat: 9.2g, | Carbs: 8.7g, | Protein: 15.2g

355. Buttery Pesto Salmon

Preparation Time: 5 minutes
Cooking Time: 15 minutes
Servings: 4

Ingredients:
- ¼ cup pesto
- 1 tbsp. unsalted butter; melted.
- 1 ½-inch-thick salmon fillets: about 4 oz. each
- ¼ cup sliced almonds, roughly chopped

Directions:
1. Combine the pesto and almonds in a small bowl. Put to one side. Put the fillets in a round casserole dish 6 inches in diameter.
2. Butter each fillet and spread half of the pesto mixture on the top of each fillet. Put the dish in the basket of the deep fryer. Turn the temperature to 390 ° F and turn the timer to 12 minutes.
3. The salmon will release easily when it is fully cooked and has reached an internal temperature of at least 145 degrees F.

Nutrition:
Calories: 433; | Protein: 23.3g; | Fiber: 2.4g; | Fat: 34.0g; Carbs: 6.1g | Protein: 30 g

356. Breaded Cod Bites

Preparation Time: 5 minutes
Cooking Time: 20 minutes
Servings: 4

Ingredients:
- 1 cup Almond flour:
- 1 cup Gluten-free breadcrumbs:
- 1 lb. Cod fillet
- 3 Eggs
- 4 tbsp. Olive oil

Directions:
1. Set the temperature of the hot air fryer to 390° Fahrenheit.
2. Slice the cod into nuggets.
3. Make three bowls. Beat the eggs into one. In another, combine the oil and breadcrumbs. Add the almond flour to the last one.
4. Coat each of the nuggets with the flour, a dip in the eggs and the breadcrumbs.
5. Place the prepared nuggets in the basket and set the timer for 20 minutes. Serve.

Nutrition:
Calories: 220 | Carbs: 10 g | Fat: 12 g | Protein: 23 g

357. Tasty Lobster Tail

Preparation Time: 5 minutes
Cooking Time: 10 minutes
Servings: 2

Ingredients:
- 1 tablespoon minced fresh chives
- 2 (4- to 6-ounce) frozen lobster tails
- 1 teaspoon salt
- 1 tablespoon minced garlic
- 2 tablespoons unsalted butter, melted

Directions:
1. Getting the ingredients ready
2. Put the butter, garlic, salt and chives in a bowl and mix together.
3. Cut out the lobster tail with butterflies: Start at the fleshy end of the tail and cut off the middle of the top shell with kitchen scissors. Quit when you reach the fanned-out, wide part of the tail.
4. Gently spread the meat and shell apart along the cut line, but leave the meat where it connects to the wide part of the tail. Carefully separate the meat from the bottom of the shell with your hand.
5. Raise the meat up and out of the shell (leave it attached at the wide end). Shut the shell under the meat so that the meat is on top of the shell.
6. Lay the lobster in the basket of the deep fryer and brush the meat generously with the butter mixture.
7. Air fry. Adjust the temperature of your AF to 380°F. Turn on the timer and steam for 4 minutes.
8. Crack open the air fryer and flip the lobster tails over. Baste them with more of the butter mixture. Adjust the timer again and steam for another 4 minutes. The lobster is ready when the meat is opaque.

Nutrition:
Calories: 255; | Fat: 13g; | Carbohydrate: 2g; | Protein: 32g; | Sodium: 1453mg

358. Pecan-Crusted Catfish Fillets

Preparation Time: 5 minutes
Cooking Time: 12 minutes
Servings: 4

Ingredients:
- 4 (4-ounce) catfish fillets
- Fresh oregano to garnish
- ½ cup pecan meal
- 1 teaspoon fine sea salt
- ¼ teaspoon ground black pepper

Directions:

1. Ready the ingredients. Lubricate the basket of the hot air fryer with avocado oil. Heat the deep fryer to 375°F. Mix the pecan flour, salt and pepper in a large bowl.
2. One at a time, sprinkle the mixture over the catfish fillets so they are well coated. Press the pecan flour into the fillets with your hands.
3. Drizzle the fish with avocado oil and place them in the basket of the air fryer.
4. Air fry. Continue cooking the coated catfish for 12 minutes, or until slightly flaky and no longer translucent in the centre, turning halfway through.
5. Decorate with oregano sprigs and pecan halves, if desired.

Nutrition:
Calories 162; | Fat 11g; | Protein 17g; | Total carbs 1g; | Fiber 1g

359. Creamy Pesto Scallops

Preparation Time: 10 minutes
Cooking Time: 7 minutes
Servings: 4

Ingredients:
- 1 tbsp olive oil
- Salt and Pepper
- 1 lb. Scallops
- 3 tbsp heavy cream
- 1/4 cup basil pesto

Directions:
1. Coat the multi-level deep fryer basket with cooking spray.
2. Add the scallops with pepper and salt and place in the air fryer basket.
3. Close the pot with the lid of the air fryer and select the air frying mode, then adjust the temperature to 320 F and the timer to 5 minutes. Flip the scallops after 3 minutes.
4. In the meantime, in a small pan, heat the olive oil over medium heat. Pour in the pesto and cream and cook for 2 minutes. Take off the heat.
5. Put the scallops in the mixing bowl. Add the pesto sauce over the scallops and toss well.
6. Serve and enjoy.

Nutrition:
Calories 171 | Fat 8.5 g | Carbohydrates 3.5 g | Sugar 0 g
Protein 19.4 g | Cholesterol 53 mg

360. Lemony Parmesan Shrimp

Preparation Time: 10 minutes
Cooking Time: 5 minutes
Servings: 4

Ingredients:
- 1 lb. Shrimp, deveined and cleaned
- 1/4 cup salad dressing
- 1 tbsp garlic, minced
- 1 oz parmesan cheese, grated
- 1 tbsp lemon juice

Directions:
1. Sprinkle the multi-level air frying basket of the deep fryer with cooking spray.
2. Put the prawns in the frying basket and set the basket in the air fryer.
3. Cover the pot with the lid of the air fryer and select the air frying mode, adjust the temperature to 400 F and the timer to 5 minutes.
4. Add the shrimps to the mixing bowl. Pour remaining ingredients over shrimp and mix for 1 minute.
5. Serve and enjoy.

Nutrition:
Calories 219 | Fat 8.4 g | Carbohydrates 6.3 g | Sugar 1 g
Protein 28.4 g | Cholesterol 248 mg

361. Honey & Vinegar Salmon

Preparation Time: 10 minutes
Cooking Time: 3 minutes
Servings: 2

Ingredients:
- 2 tbsp balsamic vinegar
- 1 cup of water
- 1 1/2 tbsp honey
- Salt and Pepper
- 2 salmon fillets

Directions:
1. Season the salmon with pepper and salt.
2. Stir together the vinegar and honey.
3. Coat the fish fillets with the vinegar and honey mixture.
4. Pour water into the deep fryer and put trivets in the basket.
5. Arrange the fish fillets on the trivet.
6. Shut the fryer and cook on manual high pressure for 3 minutes.
7. Once cooked, relieve the pressure using the quick release method and open the lid.
8. Decorate with parsley and serve.

Nutrition:
Calories 278 | Fat 7.8 g | Carbohydrates 3.3 g | Sugar 0.5 g
Protein 46.8 g | Cholesterol 341 mg

VEGETABLES

362. Carrot Sticks

Preparation Time: 5 Minutes

Cooking Time: 12-15 Minutes

Ingredients:
- ½ Teaspoon Sea Salt
- 1 Tablespoon Olive Oil
- 5 Large Carrots

Directions:
1. Warm your hot air fryer to 390. Then wash and peel your carrots. Cut them so that they form French fries.
2. Mix the carrot sticks with the olive oil and salt and spread them evenly.
3. Put them in the deep fryer and fry them for twelve minutes. When they are not as crispy as you want them, keep cooking for another two to three minutes.
4. Serve them with sour cream, ketchup or simply with your favourite main dish.

Nutrition:

Calories: 140 | Fat: 3 | Carbs: 6 | Protein: 7

363. Cheesy Broccoli

Preparation Time: 5 Minutes

Cooking Time: 9 Minutes

Ingredients:
- Sharp Cheddar Cheese, Shredded
- 1 Head Broccoli, Washed & Chopped
- 1 Tablespoon Olive oil
- Salt & Pepper to Taste

Directions:
1. First, set your deep fryer to 360°.
2. Mix the broccoli with the olive oil and sea salt.
3. Put it in the deep fryer and cook for six minutes.
4. Remove it and cover it with cheese, which will cook for another three minutes.
5. Serve it with a protein of your choice.

Nutrition:

Calories: 170 | Fat: 5 | Carbs: 9 | Protein: 7

364. Fried bananas

Preparation Time: 5 minutes

Cooking Time: 10 minutes

Servings: 2

Ingredients:
- ¼ teaspoon kosher salt
- 3 tablespoons ghee, melted
- 2 ripe plantains, peeled and cut at a diagonal into ½-inch-thick pieces

Directions:
1. Ready the ingredients. Mix the plantains in a bowl with the ghee and salt.
2. Air fry. Place the plantain pieces in the basket of the air fryer. Turn the air fryer on to 400°F for 8 minutes. Plantains are done when they are soft and tender on the inside and have lots of crispy, sweet, brown bits on the outside.

Nutrition:

Calories: 180 | Fat: 5 | Carbs: 10 | Protein: 7

365. Tasty Wrapped Asparagus

Preparation Time: 5 minutes

Cooking Time: 10 minutes

Servings: 4

Ingredients:
- ½ cup Ranch Dressin for serving
- 3 tablespoons chopped fresh chives, for garnish
- 4 slices bacon or beef bacon
- 1 pound asparagus, trimmed (about 24 spears)

Directions:

1. Ready the ingredients. Lubricate the basket of the air fryer with avocado oil. Heat the hot air fryer to 400°F.
2. Split the bacon down the middle to make long, thin strips. Using 1 slice of bacon, wrap around 3 asparagus spears and secure each end with a toothpick. Again, repeat the process with the remaining bacon and asparagus.
3. Air fry. Lay the asparagus bundles in a single layer in the air fryer. (If using a smaller air fryer, deep fry in several layers if necessary). Fry for 8 minutes for thin spears, 10 minutes for medium to thick spears, or until asparagus is slightly charred at the ends and bacon is crisp.
4. Serve with Ranch dressing and top with chives. Serve fresh at best.

Nutrition:

Calories 241; | Fat 22g; | Protein 7g; | Total carbs 6g; | Fiber 3g

366. Balsamic Brussels Sprouts

Preparation Time: 5 minutes
Cooking Time: 15 minutes
Servings: 4

Ingredients:

- 3tablespoons olive oil
- 2cups Brussels sprouts, halved
- ¼ teaspoon salt
- 1 tablespoon balsamic vinegar

Directions:

1. Ready the ingredients. Heat the hot air fryer for 5 minutes. Combine all the ingredients in a bowl until the courgette fries have been well coated.
2. Air fry. Put in the basket of the hot air fryer. Seal and cook at 350°F for 15 minutes.

Nutrition:

Calories: 82; | Fat: 6.8g; | Protein: 1.5g

367. Healthy Thyme Mushrooms

Preparation Time: 5 minutes
Cooking Time: 10 minutes
Servings: 4

Ingredients:

- ½ teaspoon fine sea salt
- 3 tablespoons unsalted butter, melted
- 2 cloves garlic, minced
- 3 sprigs fresh thyme leaves
- 1 (8-ounce) package button mushrooms, sliced

Directions:

1. Ready the ingredients. Lubricate the basket with avocado oil. Heat the hot air fryer to 400°F.
2. Put all the ingredients in a medium bowl. Using a spoon or your hands, coat the mushroom slices.
3. Air fry. Put the mushrooms in the basket in a single layer; work in batches if necessary. Broil for 10 minutes, or until lightly crisped and brown. Before serving, garnish with thyme sprigs.
4. Warm mushrooms in reheated fryer at 350°F for 5 minutes, or until cooked through

Nutrition:

Calories 82; | Fat 9g; | Protein 1g; | Total carbs 1g; | Fiber 0.2g

368. Jicama Fries

Preparation Time: 10 minutes
Cooking Time: 5 minutes
Servings: 4

Ingredients:

- ½ large Jicama
- ¾ C. arrowroot flour
- Eggs
- 1 tbsp. dried thyme

Directions:

1. Get the ingredients ready. Cut the jicama into fries.
2. Beat the eggs and pour over the fries. Toss to coat.
3. Mix together a pinch of salt, thyme and arrowroot flour. Add the egg-coated jicama to the dry mixture and swirl to coat well.
4. Air fry. Coat the basket of the air fryer with olive oil and place the fries inside. Adjust the temperature to 350°F and the time to 5 minutes. Flip halfway through cooking.

Nutrition:

Calories: 211; | Fat: 19g; | Carbs: 16g; | Protein:9g

369. Eggplant stacks

Preparation Time: 5 minutes
Cooking Time: 15 minutes
Servings: 4

Ingredients:

- 1 medium eggplant; cut into ¼-inch slices
- ¼ cup fresh basil, sliced
- 2tbsp. Olive oil
- 4oz. Fresh mozzarella; cut into ½-oz. Slices
- 2large tomatoes; cut into ¼-inch slices

Directions:

1. Place four aubergine slices in a round casserole dish (6 inch) on the bottom. Put a slice of tomato on each aubergine round, then mozzarella, then aubergine. Continue repeating as needed.
2. Sprinkle with olive oil. Line the tray with foil and place the tray in the basket of the deep fryer. Adjust the temperature to 350 degrees F and set the timer for 12 minutes.
3. When done, the aubergine will be tender. Garnish with fresh basil to serve.

Nutrition:

Calories: 195; | Protein: 8.5g; | Fiber: 5.2g; | Fat: 12.7g; Carbs: 12.7g

370. Juicy Spaghetti Squash

Preparation Time: 5 minutes
Cooking Time: 50 minutes
Servings: 4

Ingredients:

- 1tsp. Dried parsley.
- ½tsp. Garlic powder.
- 1 tbsp. Coconut oil
- ½ large spaghetti squash
- 2tbsp. Salted butter; melted

Directions:

1. Paint the skin of the spaghetti squash with coconut oil. Put the skin side down and brush the inside with butter. Dust with garlic powder and parsley.
2. Put the pumpkin, skin side down, in the basket of the deep fryer. Adjust the temperature to 350 degrees and set the timer for 30 minutes.
3. After the beep, turn the squash over, skin side up, and cook for another 15 minutes until fork-tender. Serve warm.

Nutrition:

Calories: 182; | Protein: 1.9g; | Fiber: 3.9g; | Fat: 11.7g; Carbs: 18.2g

371. Blue Cheese & Beets Salad

Preparation Time: 10 minutes
Cooking Time: 15 minutes
Servings: 6

Ingredients:

- 1 tablespoon olive oil
- ¼ cup blue cheese, crumbled
- 6 beets, peeled and quartered
- Salt and black pepper to the taste

Directions:

1. Place beetroot in hot air fryer, cook at 350 degrees F for 14 minutes and place in a bowl. Include blue cheese, salt, pepper and oil, toss and serve. Enjoy!

Nutrition:

Calories 100 | Fat 4 | Fiber 4 | Carbs 10 | Protein 5

372. Avocado chips

Preparation Time: 5 minutes
Cooking Time: 5 minutes
Servings: 6

Ingredients:

- ½ C. panko breadcrumbs
- ½ tsp. salt
- Bean liquid (aquafaba) from a 15-ounce can of white or garbanzo beans
- 1 avocado

Directions:

1. Skin, pit and slice the avocado. Combine the salt and breadcrumbs in a bowl.
2. Put the aquafaba in another bowl. Bread the avocado slices first in aquafaba and then in panko, making sure they are evenly coated.
3. Put coated avocado slices in a single layer in the hot air fryer.
4. Broil at 390 degrees for 5 minutes, tossing after 5 minutes. Serve with your favourite keto dipping sauce!

Nutrition:

Calories: 102 | Fat: 22g | Protein: 9g | Sugar: 1g

373. Italian Spaghetti Squash

Preparation Time: 5 minutes
Cooking Time: 15 minutes
Servings: 10

Ingredients:

- 1 spaghetti squash
- ½ tsp. salt
- 1 thinly sliced scallion
- ¼ tsp. pepper

Directions:

1. Rinse the pumpkin and cut it lengthwise. Scratch out the seeds.
2. Using a fork, remove the spaghetti flesh thread by thread and discard the skin.
3. Put the squash in a clean towel and wring out as much moisture as possible. Put in a bowl and cut through the flesh a few times with a knife to make it smaller. Combine the pepper, salt and spring onions with the pumpkin and stir well.

4. Shape into "tots" with your hands and place in the deep fryer. Drizzle with olive oil.
5. Fry for 15 minutes at 350 degrees until golden and crispy!

Nutrition:

Calories: 231 | Fat: 18g | Protein: 5g | Sugar: 0g

374. Cinnamon flavoured Fries

Preparation Time: 10 minutes

Cooking Time: 10 minutes

Servings: 2

Ingredients:

- 1 tbsp. coconut oil
- 1 tbsp. powdered unprocessed sugar
- 2tsp. cinnamon
- 1 pinch of salt
- 10ounces pre-cut butternut squash fries

Directions:

1. Put all the ingredients in a plastic bag.
2. Spread the fries with the other ingredients until they are coated and the sugar is dispersed.
3. Place coated fries in a single layer in the hot air fryer. Broil at 390 degrees for 10 minutes until crispy.

Nutrition:

Calories: 175 | Fat: 8g | Protein: 1g | Sugar: 5g

375. Broccoli & Sweet Potato

Preparation Time: 5 minutes

Cooking Time: 20 minutes

Servings: 4

Ingredients:

- 2 tbsps Vegetable oil
- Salt and ground black pepper, as required
- 2 Medium sweet potatoes, peeled and cut in 1-inch cubes
- 1 Broccoli head, cut in 1-inch florets

Directions:

1. Oil a baking dish that will fit in the air fryer oven. Put all the ingredients in a bowl and toss to distribute them well.
2. Transfer the vegetable mixture to the prepared casserole dish in a single layer. Put the casserole dish on the bottom of the cooking chamber of the air fryer.
3. Choose "Roast" option and then adjust the temperature to 415 °F. Set the time to 20 minutes and press "Start".
4. If the display shows "Turn Food", turn the vegetables. After the cooking time is finished, take the baking dish out of the oven. Serve hot.

Nutrition:

Calories 170 | Carbs 25.2g | Fat 7.1g,

SOUPS & STEWS

376. Chicken Soup

Preparation Time: 10 minutes
Cooking Time: 17 minutes
Servings: 4

Ingredients:

- 29 ounces canned diced tomatoes
- 1 teaspoon garlic powder
- 1 tablespoon chili powder
- 3 garlic cloves, peeled and minced
- 16 ounces chunky salsa
- 1 tablespoon onion powder
- 32 ounces canned black beans, drained
- 4 chicken breasts, skinless and boneless
- 1 onion, peeled and chopped
- 29 ounces chicken stock
- 15 ounces frozen corn
- Salt and ground black pepper, to taste
- 2 tablespoons extra virgin olive oil
- 2 tablespoons dried parsley

Directions:

1. Set the hot air fryer to sauté mode, pour in the oil and heat. Add the onion, mix and cook for 5 minutes. Add the garlic, stir and cook for a minute.
2. Pour in the chicken breasts, tomatoes, salsa, peppers, onion powder, stock, salt, garlic powder, parsley and chilli powder, mix, then cover and cook for 8 minutes on the soup setting.
3. Of course, let off the pressure for 10 minutes, cover the fryer, put the chicken breasts on a chopping board, shred with 2 forks and return to the pot.
4. Next, add the beans and corn, switch the hot air fryer to manual mode and cook for 2 to 3 minutes. Distribute into soup bowls and serve.

Nutrition:

Calories: 210 | Protein: 26 g. | Fat: 4.4 g. | Carbs: 18 g.

377. Cheesy Potato Soup

Preparation Time: 10 minutes
Cooking Time: 10 minutes
Servings: 6

Ingredients:

- 1/8 teaspoon red pepper flakes
- 3 ounces cream cheese, cubed
- 1 cup cheddar cheese, shredded
- 28 ounces chicken stock
- 6 bacon slices, cooked and crumbled
- 2 cups half and half
- 2 tablespoons dried parsley
- 6 cups potatoes, cubed
- 2 tablespoons butter
- 1 cup corn
- 2 tablespoons cornstarch
- 2 tablespoons water
- ½ cup yellow onion, chopped
- Salt and ground black pepper, to taste

Directions:

1. Set the air fryer to sauté mode, add the butter and melt it. Add the onion, stir and cook for 5 minutes. Add half the stock, salt, pepper, red pepper flakes and parsley and stir. Place the potatoes in the steamer basket, cover the Airfryer and cook for 4 minutes on the steaming setting.
2. Of course, let off the pressure, cover the airfryer and put the potatoes in a bowl. Combine the cornflour with water in another bowl and stir well.
3. Switch the hot air fryer to manual mode, add the cornflour slurry, cream cheese and grated cheese and stir well. Put in the rest of the stock, the corn, the bacon, the potatoes and the half and half. Give it a stir, bring to a simmer, ladle into bowls and serve.

Nutrition:

Calories: 188 | Protein: 9 g. | Fat: 7.14 g. | Carbs: 22 g.

---

378. Split Pea Soup

Preparation Time: 10 minutes

Cooking Time: 20 minutes

Servings: 6

Ingredients:

- 2cups water
- 16 ounces split peas, rinsed
- ½ cup carrots, peeled and chopped
- ½ cup celery, chopped
- ¼ teaspoon red pepper flakes
- 1 pound chicken sausage, ground
- ½ cup half and half
- 2 garlic cloves, peeled and minced
- 29 ounces chicken stock
- Salt and ground black pepper, to taste
- 1 yellow onion, peeled and chopped
- 2tablespoons butter

Directions:

1. Switch the air fryer to sauté mode, add the sausage, fry it on all sides and transfer it to a plate. Put the butter in the air fryer and melt it. Next, add the celery, onions and carrots, stir and cook for 4 minutes.
2. Mix in the garlic, stir and cook for 1 minute. Pour in the water, stock, peas and red pepper flakes, mix, then cover and cook on the "soup" setting for 10 minutes. Relieve the pressure, blend the mixture with a hand blender and switch the fryer to manual mode.
3. Next, add the sausage, salt, pepper and half and half, mix, simmer and ladle into soup bowls.

Nutrition:

Calories: 30 | Protein: 20 g. | Fat: 11 g. | Carbs: 14 g.

---

379. Veggy Corn Soup

Preparation Time: 10 minutes

Cooking Time: 15 minutes

Servings: 4

Ingredients:

- 1-quart chicken stock
- 1 tablespoon fresh chives, chopped
- 2 garlic cloves, peeled and minced
- 6 ears of corn, cobs reserved, kernels cut off,
- Extra virgin olive oil
- Salt and ground black pepper, to taste
- 2 leeks, chopped
- 2 tablespoons butter
- 4 tarragon sprigs, chopped
- 2 bay leaves

Directions:

1. Switch the air fryer to sauté mode, put in the butter and melt it. Pour in the leeks and garlic, mix and cook for 4 minutes.
2. Then add the sweetcorn, corn on the cob, bay leaves, tarragon and broth to cover everything, then cover the air fryer and cook on the "soup" setting for 15 minutes. Relieve the pressure, open the fryer, get rid of the bay leaves and corn on the cob and transfer everything to a blender.
3. Pulsate well to get a smooth soup, pour in the rest of the stock and blend again. Put salt and pepper in, mix well, distribute in soup bowls and serve cold sprinkled with chives and olive oil.

Nutrition:

Calories: 300 | Protein: 13 g. | Fat: 8.3 g. | Carbs: 50 g.

---

380. Aromatic Butternut Squash Cream

Preparation Time: 10 minutes

Cooking Time: 16 minutes

Servings: 6

Ingredients:

- 1½ pounds butternut squash, baked, peeled and cubed
- ½ teaspoon Italian seasoning
- 3 tablespoons butter
- 1½ cup half and half
- 1/8 teaspoon red pepper flakes
- 1/8 teaspoon nutmeg, grated
- 29 ounces chicken stock
- ½ cup celery, chopped
- ½ cup green onions, chopped
- 1 garlic clove, peeled and minced
- ½ cup carrots, peeled and chopped
- Green onions, chopped, for serving
- 15 ounces canned diced tomatoes
- 1 cup orzo, already cooked
- Salt and ground black pepper, to taste
- 1 cup chicken meat, already cooked and shredded

Directions:

1. Adjust the air fryer to sauté mode, add the butter and melt it. Put in the celery, carrots and onions, mix and cook for 3 minutes.
2. Pour in the garlic, stir and cook for 1 minute.
3. Put in the squash, tomatoes, stock, Italian seasoning, salt, pepper, red pepper flakes and nutmeg. Mix, cover the fryer and simmer on the "soup" stage for 10 minutes.
4. Relieve the pressure, put the lid on and blend everything with a hand blender. Turn the fryer on manual mode, add the half

and half, orzo and chicken, mix and cook the soup for 3 minutes.
5. Distribute the soup into bowls, scatter green onions on top and serve.

Nutrition:

Calories: 130 | Protein: 6 g. | Fat: 2.3 g. | Carbs: 18 g.

381. Beef Soup with Rice

Preparation Time: 10 minutes
Cooking Time: 15 minutes
Servings: 6

Ingredients:

- 28 ounces beef stock
- 15 ounces canned garbanzo beans, rinsed
- 1 celery stalk, chopped
- 1 yellow onion, peeled and chopped
- 1 potato, cubed
- 3 garlic cloves, peeled and minced
- 14 ounces canned crushed tomatoes
- Salt and ground black pepper, to taste
- 1 pound ground beef
- 12 ounces spicy tomato juice
- 2 carrots, peeled and sliced thin
- 1 tablespoon vegetable oil
- ½ cup white rice
- ½ cup frozen peas

Directions:

1. Switch the air fryer to sauté mode, include the beef, mix, fry until browned and place on a plate.
2. Put the oil in the air fryer and heat. Put in the celery and onion, mix and fry for 5 minutes. Put in the garlic, mix and cook for 1 minute.
3. Put in the tomato juice, stock, tomatoes, rice, beans, carrots, potatoes, beef, salt and pepper, mix and cook, covered, on the "Manual" setting for 5 minutes.
4. Depressurize, uncover and set the hot air fryer to manual mode. Add the more salt and pepper, if desired, and the peas, mix, bring to the boil, pour into bowls and serve hot.

Nutrition:

Calories: 230 | Protein: 3 g. | Fat: 7 g. | Carbs: 10 g.

382. Noodle Soup with Chicken

Preparation Time: 10 minutes
Cooking Time: 12 minutes
Servings: 6

Ingredients:

- Salt and ground black pepper, to taste
- 6 cups chicken stock
- 1 celery stalk, chopped
- cups chicken, already cooked and shredded
- 1 yellow onion, peeled and chopped
- 4 carrots, peeled and sliced
- Egg noodles, already cooked
- 1 tablespoon butter

Directions:

1. Set the air fryer to sauté mode, add the butter and heat.
2. Put in the onion, mix and cook for 2 minutes. Put in the celery and carrots, mix and cook for 5 minutes.
3. Put in the chicken and stock, mix, cover the fryer and cook on the "soup" setting for 5 minutes. Depressurize, open the fryer, season with salt and pepper and stir.
4. Distribute the noodles in soup bowls, pour the soup over them and serve.

Nutrition:

Calories: 100 | Protein: 7 g. | Fat: 1 g. | Carbs: 4 g.

383. Original Tuscan Soup

Preparation Time: 10 minutes
Cooking Time: 17 minutes
Servings: 8

Ingredients:

- 1 cup yellow onion, peeled and chopped
- Salt and ground black pepper, to taste
- 3 tablespoons cornstarch
- 1 pound chicken sausage, ground
- 12 ounces evaporated milk
- 2 cup spinach, chopped
- 1 tablespoon butter
- 40 ounces chicken stock
- 6 bacon slices, chopped
- 1 cup Parmesan, shredded
- 3 garlic cloves, peeled and minced
- Red pepper flakes
- 3 potatoes, cubed

Directions:

1. Change the deep fryer to sauté mode, put in the bacon, mix, fry until crispy and transfer to a plate. Put the sausage in the deep fryer, stir, fry until browned on all sides and also place on a plate.
2. Add the butter to the hot air fryer and melt. Put in the onion, mix and fry for 5 minutes.
3. Put in the garlic, mix and cook for a minute. Put in ⅓ of the stock, salt, pepper and red pepper flakes and stir. Transfer the potatoes to the steam basket of the airfryer, cover and cook for 4 minutes on the "steam" setting.

4. Relieve the pressure, remove the Airfryer and place the potatoes in a bowl.
5. Pour the remaining stock into the airfryer along with the cornflour mixed with the condensed milk, mix and set the airfryer to manual mode. Include the cheese, sausage, bacon, potatoes, spinach and more salt and pepper if necessary, mix, distribute the dish into bowls and serve.

Nutrition:

Calories: 170 | Protein: 10 g. | Fat: 4 g. | Carbs: 24 g.

384. Italian Minestrone

Preparation Time: 10 minutes

Cooking Time: 15 minutes

Servings: 8

Ingredients:

- 1 cup corn kernels
- 1 cup Asiago cheese, grated
- 4 garlic cloves, peeled and minced
- 1 onion, peeled and chopped
- 3 pounds tomatoes, cored, peeled, and chopped
- 1 cup uncooked pasta
- 1 tablespoon extra virgin olive oil
- 1 zucchini, chopped
- 1 celery stalk, chopped
- 15 ounces canned kidney beans
- 2 carrots, peeled and chopped
- 29 ounces chicken stock
- 2 tablespoons fresh basil, chopped
- 1 teaspoon Italian seasoning
- Salt and ground black pepper, to taste
- 2 cups baby spinach

Directions:

1. Set the air fryer to sauté mode, pour in the oil and heat. Put in the onion, mix and fry for 5 minutes. Put in the carrots, garlic, celery, sweetcorn and courgettes, mix and cook for 5 minutes. Pour in the tomatoes, stock, Italian seasoning, pasta, salt and pepper, mix and cook, covered, for 4 minutes on the "soup" stage. Of course, depressurize, remove the lid, add the beans, basil and spinach. If desired, add a little more salt and pepper, divide into bowls, top with the cheese and serve.

Nutrition:

Calories –110 | Protein: 5 g. | Fat: 2 g. | Carbs: 18 g.

385. Wild Rice Soup with Chicken

Preparation Time: 10 minutes

Cooking Time: 15 minutes

Servings: 6

Ingredients:

- 1 tablespoon dried parsley
- Salt and ground black pepper, to taste
- 1 cup carrots, chopped
- 1 cup yellow onion, peeled and chopped
- 1 cup half and half
- Red pepper flakes
- tablespoons butter
- 2 chicken breasts, skinless, boneless and chopped
- 4 ounces cream cheese, cubed
- 1 cup celery, chopped
- 28 ounces chicken stock
- 6 ounces wild rice
- 2 tablespoons cornstarch
- 2 tablespoons water
- 1 cup milk

Directions:

1. Adjust the air fryer to sauté mode, put in the butter and melt it.
2. Put in the carrot, onion and celery, mix and cook for 5 minutes.
3. Add the rice, chicken, stock, parsley, salt and pepper, mix, cover and cook for 5 minutes on the 'soup' setting.
4. Relieve the pressure, cover, pour in the cornflour mixed with water, mix and set the fryer to manual mode.
5. Add the cheese, milk and half and half, mix, heat, put the soup in bowls and serve.

Nutrition:

Calories: 200 | Protein: 5 g. | Fat: 7 g. | Carbs: 19 g.

386. Celery and Tomato Soup

Preparation Time: 10 minutes

Cooking Time: 6 minutes

Servings: 8

Ingredients:

- 29 ounces chicken stock
- 2 garlic cloves, peeled and minced
- Salt and ground black pepper, to taste
- 1 cup half and half
- ¼ cup fresh basil, chopped
- 1 yellow onion, peeled and chopped
- 3 pounds tomatoes, peeled, cored, and cut into quarters
- 3 tablespoons butter
- ½ cup Parmesan cheese, shredded
- 2 celery stalks, chopped
- 1 tablespoon tomato paste
- 1 carrot, peeled and chopped

Directions:

1. Switch the air fryer to sauté mode, put in the butter and melt it. Put in the onion, carrots and celery, mix and cook for 3 minutes.
2. Put in the garlic, then stir and cook for 1 minute. Include the tomatoes, tomato paste, stock, basil, salt and pepper, stir and cook, covered, on the "soup" stage for 5 minutes.
3. Depressurize, uncover the fryer and puree the soup with a hand blender. Pour in the cheese and half and half, mix, set the air fryer to manual mode and heat everything up.
4. Distribute the soup into soup bowls and serve.

Nutrition:

Calories: 280 | Protein: 24 g. | Fat: 8 g. | Carbs: 32 g.

387. Delicious Tomato Soup

Preparation Time: 10 minutes

Cooking Time: 45 minutes

Servings: 6

Ingredients:

- For the roasted tomatoes:
- 2 tablespoons extra virgin olive oil
- ½ teaspoon red pepper flakes
- Salt and ground black pepper, to taste
- 14 garlic cloves, peeled and crushed
- 3 pounds cherry tomatoes, cut into halves

For the soup:

- 2 cups chicken stock
- ½ tablespoon dried basil
- Salt and ground black pepper, to taste
- 1 cup heavy cream
- 3 tablespoons tomato paste
- 2 celery ribs, chopped
- 2 tablespoons olive oil
- 1 teaspoon garlic powder
- 1 teaspoon onion powder
- ½ teaspoon red pepper flakes
- 1 red bell pepper, seeded and chopped
- 1 yellow onion, peeled and chopped

For serving:

- ½ cup Parmesan cheese, grated
- Fresh basil leaves, chopped

Directions:

1. Transfer the tomatoes and garlic to a baking tray, sprinkle with 2 tablespoons of oil, season with salt, pepper and a ½ teaspoon of red pepper flakes, toss, place in the oven at 425ºF and roast for 25 minutes.
2. Take the tomatoes out of the oven and put them aside.
3. Turn the air fryer to sauté mode, add the oil and heat. Place the onion, paprika, celery, salt, pepper, garlic powder, onion powder, basil and the remaining red pepper flakes, mix and fry for 3 minutes. Include the tomato paste, roasted tomatoes and garlic and stir.
4. Pour in the stock, cover the fryer and cook on the manual setting for 10 minutes.
5. Relieve the pressure, uncover the fryer and switch it to sauté mode. Pour in the heavy cream and blend everything with a hand blender.
6. Distribute in bowls, top with basil and cheese and serve.

Nutrition:

Calories: 150 | Protein: 4 g. | Fat: 1 g. | Carbs: 3 g.

388. Sriracha Carrot Soup

Preparation Time: 10 minutes

Cooking Time: 16 minutes

Servings: 4

Ingredients:

- 1 pound carrots, peeled and chopped
- 1 tablespoon vegetable oil
- 1 tablespoon Sriracha
- Cilantro leaves, chopped, for serving
- 1 garlic clove, peeled and minced
- 1 onion, peeled and chopped
- 14 ounces canned coconut milk
- 1 small ginger piece, peeled and grated
- Salt and ground black pepper, to taste
- 1 tablespoon butter
- 2 cups chicken stock
- ¼ teaspoon brown sugar

Directions:

1. Switch the air fryer to sauté mode, add the butter and oil and heat.
2. Put in the onion, mix and cook for 3 minutes.
3. Pour in the ginger and garlic, mix and cook for 1 minute.
4. Put in the sugar, carrots, salt and pepper, stir and cook for 2 minutes.
5. Pour in the Sriracha, coconut milk and stock, mix, cover and cook for 6 minutes on the "soup" stage.
6. Relieve the pressure naturally for 10 minutes, uncover the fryer, blend the soup with a hand blender, add more salt and pepper if needed and distribute into soup bowls.
7. Put the coriander on top and serve.

Nutrition:

Calories: 60 | Protein: 2 g. | Fat: 1 g. | Carbs: 12 g.

389. Cabbage & Celery Soup

Preparation Time: 10 minutes

Cooking Time: 10 minutes

Servings: 4

Ingredients:

- 1 cabbage head, chopped
- 12 ounces soy burger
- Salt and ground black pepper, to taste
- 4 cups chicken stock
- 12 ounces baby carrots
- 2 tablespoons olive oil
- 3 celery stalks, chopped
- ½ onion, peeled and chopped
- ¼ cup cilantro, chopped
- 1 packet vegetable soup mix
- 3 teaspoons garlic, peeled and minced

Directions:

1. Combine the cabbage, celery, carrots, onion, soup mix, soy burger, stock, olive oil and garlic in the hot air fryer, mix, cover and simmer in soup mode for 5 minutes.
2. Relieve the pressure, open the fryer, add salt, pepper and coriander, mix well again, distribute in soup bowls and serve.

Nutrition:

Calories: 100 | Protein: 10 g. | Fat: 1 g. | Carbs: 10 g.

390. Creamy Chicken Asparagus Soup

Preparation Time: 10 minutes

Cooking Time: 25 minutes

Servings: 4

Ingredients:

- 6 cups chicken stock
- ½ cup crème fraiche
- Salt and ground white pepper, to taste
- 2 pounds green asparagus, trimmed, tips cut off and cut into medium pieces
- 1 yellow onion, peeled and chopped
- 3 tablespoons butter
- ¼ teaspoon lemon juice

Directions:

1. Put the air fryer on sauté mode, add the butter and melt it.
2. Put in the asparagus, salt and pepper, stir and cook for 5 minutes.
3. Pour in 5 cups of the stock, cover the fryer and cook in soup mode for 15 minutes.
4. Depressurize, cover the fryer and put the soup in a blender. Blend several times and put it back into the fryer.
5. Turn the fryer to manual mode, add the crème fraîche, the remaining stock, salt, pepper and lemon juice, heat the soup to boiling, distribute it in soup bowls and serve.

Nutrition:

Calories: 80 | Protein: 6.3 g. | Fat: 8 g. | Carbs: 16 g.

391. Vegan Noodle Soup

Preparation Time: 5 minutes

Cooking Time: 10 minutes

Servings: 4

Ingredients:

- Tomato: 1, diced
- Dried oregano: 1 tsp.
- Ground black pepper
- Sweet onion: 1, chopped
- Celery: 4 stalks, chopped into bite-sized pieces
- Broccoli florets: 1 cup
- Carrots: 4, chopped into bite-sized pieces
- Garlic: 2 cloves, minced
- Chopped fresh parsley, for garnish
- Water: 1 to ½ cups, plus more as needed
- Vegetable stock: 4 cups, plus more as needed
- Bay leaf: 1
- Crackers, for serving
- Salt: 1 to 2 tsp.
- Lemon zest for garnish
- Dried pasta: 1 cup
- Sweet potatoes: 2, peeled and chopped
- Dried thyme: 1 tsp.
- Dried basil: 1 tsp.

Directions:

1. Combine water, stock, pasta, salt, pepper, basil, thyme, oregano, bay leaf, garlic, tomatoes, broccoli, onions, sweet potatoes, carrots and celery in the deep fryer.
2. Put a lid on the hot air fryer.
3. Broil for 3 minutes on the highest setting.
4. Let go of the lid naturally and then quickly.
5. Take the lid off and stir the soup.
6. Dispose of the bay leaf, garnish the soup and serve.

Nutrition:

Calories: 120 | Protein: 8 g.| Fat: 10 g. | Carbs: 22 g.

392. Carrot Soup with Cashew Sour Cream

Preparation Time: 5 minutes

Cooking Time: 10 minutes

Servings: 2

Ingredients:

- Vegetable stock: 1 ¼ cups
- Cashew sour cream for garnish
- Sweet onion: ½, chopped
- Salt: ½ tsp.

- Carrots: 7 chopped
- Fresh ginger: 1-inch, peeled and chopped
- Fresh herbs for garnish
- Sweet paprika: ½ tsp.
- Ground black pepper

Directions:
1. Combine the paprika, salt, broth, onion, ginger and carrots in the hot air fryer. Add pepper to taste.
2. Put a lid on the hot air fryer.
3. Broil for 3 minutes on the highest setting.
4. Take out naturally and then take out quickly.
5. Open and blend with a hand blender until smooth.
6. Decorate and serve.

Nutrition:
Calories: 85 | Protein: 6.7 g. | Fat: 8.5 g. | Carbs: 18 g.

393. Vegan Soup

Preparation Time: 5 minutes
Cooking Time: 4 minutes
Servings: 4

Ingredients:
- Fresh basil: ¼ cup, plus more for garnishing
- Tomatoes: 3 pounds, quartered
- Nutritional yeast: ¼ cup
- Garlic: 2 cloves, minced
- Carrot: 1, chopped
- Vegan butter: 2 Tbsp.
- Salt and ground black pepper
- Celery: 1 stalk, chopped
- Small sweet onion: 1, chopped
- Nondairy milk: ½ to 1 cup
- Vegetable stock: 3 cups

Directions:
1. Put sauté on the deep fryer, give butter and melt it.
2. Put in garlic and onion and stir-fry for 3 to 4 minutes.
3. Next, add the celery and carrot and fry for a further 2 minutes. Continue stirring all the time.
4. Pour in the stock and deglaze the pot.
5. Put in the salt, yeast, basil and tomatoes. Mix.
6. Put a lid on the hot air fryer.
7. Broil for 4 minutes on the highest setting.
8. Let go naturally rather than quickly.
9. Open and puree with a hand blender until smooth.
10. Mix in the milk. Season to taste and adjust seasonings.
11. Decorate and serve.

Nutrition:
Calories: 70 | Protein: 5.6 g. | Fat: 7.4g. | Carbs: 13 g.

394. Mushroom Tofu Soup

Preparation Time: 5 minutes
Cooking Time: 4 minutes
Servings: 4

Ingredients:
- White button mushrooms: 1 ½ pound, sliced
- Silken tofu: ½ cup
- Chopped fresh thyme for garnishing
- Garlic: 2 cloves, minced
- Dried thyme: 2 tsp.
- Sea salt -1 tsp.
- Vegan butter: 2 Tbsp.
- Small sweet onion: 1, chopped
- Vegetable stock: 1 ¾ cup

Directions:
1. Put the sauté on the airfryer. Heat the butter and stir in the onion. Fry them for 2 minutes, adding the stir-fry. Include the salt, dried thyme, garlic and mushrooms. Stir-fry for another 2 minutes and press cancel.
2. Mix in the stock. Cover the deep fryer.
3. Broil for 5 minutes on the highest setting.
4. In the meantime, process the tofu in a food processor until smooth. Leave to one side.
5. Release naturally, then quickly release.
6. Open and blend with a hand blender until smooth.
7. Decorate and serve.

Nutrition:
Calories: 80 | Protein: 6.2 g. | Fat: 9 g. | Carbs: 17 g.

395. Sweet Potato & Tomato Stew

Preparation Time: 5 minutes
Cooking Time: 4 minutes
Servings: 4

Ingredients:
- Paprika: 1 tsp.
- Water: 1 ¼ cups, plus more as needed
- Sweet potatoes: 2, peeled and cubed
- Roma tomatoes: 2, chopped
- Salt: 1 to 1 ½ tsp.
- Avocado oil: 2 Tbsp.
- Lite coconut milk: 1 (14-ounce) can, shaken well
- Chopped kale: 1 to 2 cups
- Ground turmeric: 1 tsp.
- Sweet onion: ½, diced
- Ground cumin: ½ tsp.
- Dried oregano: ½ tsp.

- Chili powder: 1 to 2 dashes
- Garlic: 2 cloves, minced

Directions:

1. Choose sauté on the airfryer and pour in oil.
2. Put in the onion and stir-fry for 3 minutes.
3. Add in chilli powder, oregano, cumin, paprika, turmeric, salt, garlic and sweet potato. Stir-fry for 1 minute.
4. Pour in the water, tomatoes and coconut milk and mix.
5. Put a lid on the deep fryer.
6. Broil for 4 minutes on the highest setting.
7. Let go naturally rather than quickly.
8. Uncover the fryer and mix in the kale. Blend.
9. Serve.

Nutrition:

Calories: 105 | Protein: 9.3 g. | Fat: 10 g. | Carbs: 25 g.

396. Fresh Veggy Stew

Preparation Time: 5 minutes
Cooking Time: 7 minutes
Servings: 4

Ingredients:

- White mushrooms: 1 cup, sliced
- Leeks: 2, white and very light green parts only, chopped
- Sweet onion: 1, chopped
- Fresh basil for garnishing
- Celery: 1, sliced
- Torn kale leaves: 2 cups
- Olive oil: 2 Tbsp.
- Ground black pepper
- Yukon gold potatoes: 3, chopped
- Salt: ½ tsp. plus more as needed
- Small eggplant: 1, chopped
- Garlic: 3, cloves, minced
- Dried oregano: 1 tsp.
- Roma tomatoes: 3, chopped
- Vegetable stock: 4 cups
- Carrot: 1, chopped

Directions:

1. Choose sauté on the airfryer and pour in oil.
2. Include aubergines, mushrooms, celery, carrots, onions and leeks. Stir-fry for 2 minutes.
3. Put in the garlic.
4. Fry for another 30 seconds.
5. Put in the salt, oregano, broth, tomatoes and potatoes.
6. Put a lid on the deep fryer.
7. Broil for 7 minutes on the highest setting.
8. Let go naturally and then quickly.
9. Uncover the fryer and mix in the kale.
10. Season to taste and adjust the seasonings.
11. Serve.

Nutrition:

Calories: 115 | Protein: 10 g. | Fat: 12 g. | Carbs: 28 g.

397. Creamy Celery Soup

Preparation Time: 5 minutes
Cooking Time: 15 minutes
Servings: 4

Ingredients:

- 1 cup celery leaves, chopped
- 1 cup celery stalks, chopped
- 1 small onion, chopped
- 2 cups fresh spinach, chopped
- 2 garlic cloves, minced
- 1/2 teaspoon black pepper, (finely ground)
- 2 tablespoon butter
- 2 cups heavy cream
- 1 tablespoon mint leaves, torn
- 1 tablespoon lemon juice
- 1 teaspoon salt

Directions:

1. Position the hot air fryer on a dry surface in your kitchen. Lift the top lid and switch it on.
2. Locate the "SAUTE" cooking function and press it; Add the butter and let it get hot.
3. Put the onions, garlic and celery stalks in the pot and sauté, mixing, until softened, about 2 minutes.
4. Pour in the celery leaves and spinach; taste and cook, stirring, for 2-3 minutes.
5. Pour in the cream; gently stir to mix well.
6. Shut the top lid to create a sealed chamber; ensure the safety valve is in the locked position.
7. Locate and press the "MANUAL" cooking function; adjust the timer to 5 minutes with the default pressure mode set to "HIGH".
8. Leave the pressure to develop in order to cook the ingredients.
9. After the cooking time has elapsed, push the "CANCEL" setting. Find and press the cooking function "QPR". Use this setting to release the internal pressure quickly.
10. Open the lid slowly, stir in the mint and lemon juice. Remove the cooked recipe into serving plates or bowls and enjoy the keto recipe.

Nutrition:

Calories: 85 | Protein: 7.1 g. | Fat: 8 g. | Carbs: 18.6 g.

398. Buttery Garlic Cauliflower Soup

Preparation Time: 10 minutes
Cooking Time: 10 minutes
Servings: 4

Ingredients:
- 3 cups low-sodium chicken broth
- ½ cup unsweetened coconut milk
- 8 cups cauliflower florets
- 4 cloves garlic, minced
- 1 teaspoon ground sage
- 1 teaspoon butter
- Pepper to taste
- 1 large onion, chopped
- ½ teaspoon salt

Directions:
1. Choose the sauté setting and heat the butter. Stir in the onion and fry until clear, about 3-5 minutes. Put in the garlic and sage and cook for 1 minute. Next, add the cauliflower, chicken stock, salt and pepper and mix well.
2. Push Cancel to reset the cooking instructions. Cover the lid and set the pressure release to Seal. Choose the Pressure Cook or Manual setting and adjust the cooking time to 10 minutes at high pressure.
3. When the time is up, let the appliance rest for at least 10 minutes; the pressure will naturally release. Next, change the pressure release to venting to allow the last of the vapour to escape.
4. Lift the lid and blend the soup with a hand blender or in a stand mixer. Whisk in the unsweetened coconut milk and flavour with salt and pepper.

Nutrition:
Calories: 171 | Protein: 8.8 g. | Fat: 9.2 g. | Carbs: 18.1 g.

399. Low-Sodium Pumpkin Soup

Preparation Time: 10 minutes
Cooking Time: 5 minutes
Servings: 4

Ingredients:
- Pepper to taste
- Salt to taste
- 1 onion, chopped
- 2 tablespoons curry powder
- 1/8 teaspoon cayenne pepper (optional)
- 1½ cups unsweetened coconut milk
- 4 cups low-sodium pumpkin puree
- 1 tablespoon tamari
- 1 teaspoon lemon juice
- 2 tablespoons butter
- 4 cups vegetable broth
- Optional: ¼ cup roasted pumpkin seeds for serving

Directions:
1. Choose the Sauté setting on the Airfryer and heat the butter. Next, add the onion and fry for 3-4 minutes until translucent.
2. Include the curry powder and cayenne pepper (if using) and mix until it becomes fragrant for 1-2 minutes. Add the vegetable stock and the cup of water. Mix in the pumpkin puree and tamari. Add salt and pepper to taste.
3. Push Cancel to reset the cooking instructions. Cover the lid and turn the pressure release to seal. Choose the Pressure Cooking or Manual setting and adjust the cooking time to 5 minutes at high pressure.
4. Then put the appliance aside for at least 10 minutes; the pressure will relieve naturally. Then turn the pressure release to Vent to let the last of the pressure steam escape.
5. Lift the lid and puree the soup with a stick blender or in a stand mixer. Whisk in the unsweetened coconut milk and add salt and pepper to taste.
6. Scoop into bowls and garnish with roasted pumpkin seeds, if desired.

Nutrition:
Calories: 340 | Protein: 5.8 g. | Fat: 24.9 g. | Carbs: 30.9 g.

400. Spaghetti Chicken Soup

Preparation Time: 10 minutes
Cooking Time: 6 minutes
Servings: 4

Ingredients:
- 1½ lbs. boneless skinless chicken breasts
- 4 oz. whole wheat spaghetti, broken in 1-inch pieces
- 2 lemons, juiced
- 2 medium carrots, peeled and sliced
- 6 stalks celery, sliced
- 8 cups fat-free chicken broth
- 1 teaspoon dried thyme
- 3 cloves garlic, roughly chopped
- Pepper to taste
- 1 bunch kale, stemmed and roughly chopped, to yield 1.5 cups
- 1 tablespoon olive oil
- 1 medium onion, chopped
- Salt to taste
- Optional: lemon wedges for serving

Directions:
1. Choose the sauté setting and heat the olive oil. Next, add the onion, garlic, carrots and celery and sauté for 4-6 minutes. Include the chicken stock and thyme. Add salt and pepper to taste. Put in the chicken breasts and stir well.

2. Push Cancel to reset the cooking instructions. Cover the lid and switch the pressure release to seal. Choose the soup setting and adjust the cooking time to 6 minutes at high pressure.
3. Then put the appliance aside for at least 10 minutes; pressure will relieve naturally. Then turn the pressure release to Vent so that the very last of the steam can escape.
4. Remove the lid, remove the chicken and shred it. Then add the chopped spaghetti and stir; boil for the time indicated on the packet. Put the chicken back into the pot and mix in the kale and lemon juice. Scoop into bowls and serve with an extra squeeze of lemon, some olive oil or freshly ground pepper.

Nutrition:

Calories: 388 | Protein: 45 g. | Fat: 7 g. | Carbs: 35.1 g.

401. Simple Balsamic Onion Soup

Preparation Time: 5 minutes
Cooking Time: 20 minutes
Servings: 4

Ingredients:

- 1 teaspoon salt
- 3 tablespoons unsalted butter
- 6 cups beef broth
- 2 large sprigs fresh thyme
- 2 tablespoons balsamic vinegar
- 3 large yellow onions, halved and then thinly sliced

Directions:

1. Choose the sauté setting and heat the butter.
2. Put in the onions and stir constantly until they have completely cooked down and caramelised. This may take 20-30 minutes or longer, it depends on the onions and the heat of your fryer. What you want to achieve is a deep caramel colour. If the onions start to turn black around the edges, use the "Adjust" button to lower the heat to "Less".
3. When the onions have caramelised, then add the balsamic vinegar, red wine vinegar, stock, thyme and salt and scrape any browned bits off the bottom of the pan.
4. Push Cancel to reset the cooking instructions. Cover the lid and set the pressure release to Seal. Choose the Soup setting and adjust the cooking time to 10 minutes at high pressure.
5. Then put the pot aside for at least 10 minutes; the pressure will naturally relieve. Then turn the pressure release to Vent to let the last of the vapour escape.
6. Crack open the hot air fryer and dispose of the thyme stems. Add salt and pepper to taste and serve warm.

Nutrition:

Calories: 151 | Protein: 5.5 g. | Fat: 9.4 g. | Carbs: 11.5 g.

402. Buttery Apple & Broccoli Soup

Preparation Time: 5 minutes
Cooking Time: 5 minutes
Servings: 4

Ingredients:

- 1 large apple, peeled, cored, and diced
- Pepper to taste
- 4 cups vegetable broth
- 1 cup unsweetened coconut milk
- 2 shallots, chopped, about 3 tablespoons
- Salt to taste
- 1 large head broccoli, cut into florets
- 3 medium leeks, white parts only (frozen is fine!)
- 2 tablespoons butter
- Optional: ¼ cup coconut cream
- Optional: ¼ cup walnuts, toasted

Directions:

1. Choose the sauté setting and heat the butter. Next, add the leeks and shallots and sauté, stirring constantly, until softened, 4-6 minutes. Pour in the broccoli and apple and sauté for a further 5-6 minutes. Put in the vegetable stock and stir well.
2. Touch Cancel to reset the cooking instructions. Cover the lid and switch the pressure release to Seal. Choose the Pressure Cook or Manual setting and adjust the cooking time to 5 minutes at high pressure.
3. Then put the appliance aside for at least 10 minutes; the pressure will naturally relieve. Then turn the pressure release switch to Vent to let the last of the steam escape.
4. Lift the lid and blend the soup with a hand blender or in a stand mixer. Mix in the unsweetened coconut milk and flavor with salt and pepper.
5. Scoop into bowls and decorate with toasted walnuts or a sprinkle of coconut cream.

Nutrition:

Calories: 259 | Protein: 6.8 g. | Fat: 14.3 g. | Carbs: 32.3 g.

403. Swiss Chard Cumin Stew

Preparation Time: 10 minutes
Cooking Time: 8 minutes
Servings: 2

Ingredients:

- 1 bunch Swiss chard (about 12 oz)
- 1 teaspoon salt
- 1 medium onion, diced
- 2 cups vegetable broth
- 2 tablespoons olive oil
- 1 teaspoon ground coriander

- 1 tsp cumin seeds, or 1 tsp ground cumin
- 2 medium sweet potatoes, peeled and in ½ inch cubes
- ½ teaspoon turmeric
- 1 tablespoon fresh ginger, peeled and minced
- Optional: lemon wedges for serving

Directions:

1. Set to sauté and heat the olive oil. Combine the onion and fry until clear, 3-5 minutes. Add the cumin seeds now, if you are using them, and roast for 1-3 minutes until fragrant. If not, add the ground cumin in the next step.
2. Put in the sweet potato, ground cumin (if using), ginger, turmeric, coriander and salt and cook for 3-4 minutes. Pour in the vegetable stock and add the chard. If needed, add more salt and pepper.
3. Push Cancel to reset the cooking instructions. Cover the lid and turn the pressure release to Seal. Choose the Pressure Cook or Manual setting and adjust the cooking time to 8 minutes at high pressure.
4. Then put the appliance aside for at least 10 minutes; the pressure will be naturally released. Then turn the pressure release to Vent to allow the last of the steam to escape.
5. Fill into bowls and serve warm with a squeeze of lemon juice, if desired.

Nutrition:

Calories: 308 | Protein: 6.2 g. | Fat: 14.4 g. | Carbs: 42.6 g.

404. Chili Lentil Soup

Preparation Time: 10 minutes
Cooking Time: 10 minutes
Servings: 4

Ingredients:

- 1 teaspoon salt, plus more to taste
- cups beef broth
- 1 cup green or brown lentils
- ¼ teaspoon cinnamon
- 1 tablespoon cumin
- Pepper to taste
- 1 teaspoon garlic powder
- 1 teaspoon chili powder
- 1 tablespoon olive oil
- 3/4 lb. ground turkey
- 1 small onion, chopped
- cloves garlic, minced

Directions:

1. Choose the sauté setting and warm the olive oil. Put in the onion and garlic and sauté until fragrant, 2-3 minutes. Put in the minced beef and add the cumin, garlic powder, chilli powder, salt, cinnamon and pepper. Fry until the meat is browned well and starts to brown.
2. Pour in the beef stock and scrape off any browned bits from the bottom of the pot. Include the lentils and mix well.
3. Push Cancel to reset the cooking instructions. Shut the lid and switch the pressure release to Seal. Choose the Soup setting and adjust the cooking time to 10 minutes at high pressure.
4. Then put the appliance aside for at least 10 minutes; the pressure will discharge naturally. Then turn the pressure release to Vent to let the last of the steam escape.
5. Crack open the fryer and taste; continue to add more salt and pepper to taste. Scoop into bowls and server with a little olive oil or freshly ground pepper.

Nutrition:

Calories: 364 | Protein: 31.3 g. | Fat: 12 g. | Carbs: 32.2 g.

405. Galric Fish Balls Soup

Preparation Time: 6 minutes
Cooking Time: 10 minutes
Servings: 5

Ingredients:

- 2 minced garlic cloves
- 2 tbsps. butter
- 1 lb. ground salmon
- 2 cups hot water
- 2 beaten large eggs

Directions:

1. Mix the butter, garlic, eggs and salmon in a bowl. Add a seasoning of pepper and salt.
2. Use your hands to combine the mixture and form small balls.
3. Put the fish balls in the freezer to solidify for 2 hours or until frozen.
4. Fill the hot water into the hot air fryer and add the frozen fish balls.
5. Add pepper and salt to the mixture.
6. Put the cover on and check that the vent is set to "Seal".
7. In "Manual" mode, put the timer on for 10 minutes.

Nutrition:

Calories: 199 | Protein: 13.3 g. | Fat: 19.4 g. | Carbs: 0.6 g.

406. Coconut Chicken Breast Soup

Preparation Time: 6 minutes
Cooking Time: 15 minutes
Servings: 3

Ingredients:

- 3 boneless chicken breasts
- 4 cups water
- 1 bay leaf
- 2½ tsps. turmeric powder

- ½ cup coconut milk

Directions:
1. Put all the ingredients in the hot air fryer.
2. Mix everything well to mix everything together.
3. Place the lid on and check that the vent is pointing to "Seal".
4. Switch to "Poultry" mode and put the timer on for 15 minutes.
5. Perform a natural pressure release.

Nutrition:

Calories: 599 | Protein: 46.8 g. | Fat: 61.4 g. | Carbs: 3.8 g.

407. Shredded Chicken Stew

Preparation Time: 6 minutes

Cooking Time: 15 minutes

Servings: 6

Ingredients:
- 1 minced onion
- 1 chopped celery
- 2 tbsps. coconut oil
- 4 beaten eggs
- 5 cups shredded chicken

Directions:
1. Select the "Sauté" button on the Airfryer and start heating the oil.
2. Sauté the onion and celery for 2 minutes or until it becomes fragrant.
3. Next, include the chicken and 4 cups of water.
4. Season with pepper and salt to taste.
5. Place the lid on and ensure that the vent points to "Seal".
6. Touch the "Poultry" button and put the time to 10 minutes.
7. Perform natural pressure release.
8. As soon as the lid is open, push the "Sauté" button and let the soup simmer.
9. Very carefully, add the beaten eggs one by one and simmer for another 3 minutes.

Nutrition:

Calories: 154 | Protein: 9.6 g. | Fat: 12.8 g. | Carbs: 2.9 g.

408. Ginger Kale Soup

Preparation Time: 6 minutes

Cooking Time: 9 minutes

Servings: 3

Ingredients:
- 3 cups water
- 3 tbsps. coconut oil
- 2 cups chopped kale
- 2 beaten eggs
- 1 tsp. grated ginger

Directions:
1. Put all the ingredients apart from the beaten eggs into the hot air fryer.
2. Use pepper and salt for seasoning.
3. Put the lid on and make sure the vent points to "Seal".
4. In "Manual" mode, set the timer to 6 minutes.
5. Perform natural depressurisation.
6. As soon as the lid is open, press the "Sauté" button and let the soup simmer.
7. Add the beaten eggs very carefully, little by little, and simmer for another 3 minutes.

Nutrition:

Calories: 209 | Protein: 6.5 g. | Fat: 20.3 g. | Carbs: 1.7 g.

409. Avocado Flavoured Leek and Salmon Soup

Preparation Time: 6 minutes

Cooking Time: 10 minutes

Servings: 4

Ingredients:
- 2tbsps. avocado oil
- 4trimmed and chopped leeks
- 3minced garlic cloves
- 1 lb. sliced salmon
- 1¾ cup coconut milk

Directions:
1. Put all the ingredients in the hot air fryer.
2. Use pepper and salt to season.
3. Mix to combine all the ingredients.
4. Put the lid on and make sure the vent points to "Seal".
5. Cook in "Manual" mode for 10 minutes.

Nutrition:

Calories: 535 | Protein: 27.3 g. | Fat: 40.9 g. | Carbs: 19.5 g.

410. Asian Coconut Soup

Preparation Time: 6 minutes

Cooking Time: 6 minutes

Servings: 2

Ingredients:
- 1 ½ cups organic coconut milk
- 3kaffir limes
- 2cups water
- 6oz. shrimps
- 1 cup fresh cilantro

Directions:
1. Put all the ingredients except coriander into the deep fryer.
2. Put the lid on and make sure the vent is set to "Seal".

3. In "Manual" mode, set the timer to 6 minutes.
4. Perform natural pressure release.
5. As soon as the lid is open, garnish with the fresh coriander.

Nutrition:

Calories: 517 | Protein: 21.9 g. | Fat: 44.6 g. | Carbs: 15.4 g.

411. Ginger Soup

Preparation Time: 6 minutes

Cooking Time: 12 minutes

Servings: 4

Ingredients:

- 1 lb. sliced halibut
- 1 chopped large onion
- 2cups water
- 2tbsps. minced fresh ginger
- 2tbsps. coconut oil

Directions:

1. Select the "Sauté" button on the Airfryer and heat the oil.
2. Sauté the onion until it is scented.
3. Add the water and the rest of the ingredients. Add pepper and salt to taste.
4. Put the lid on and make sure the vent is set to "Seal".
5. In "Manual" mode, set the timer to 10 minutes.

Nutrition:

Calories: 259 | Protein: 10.9 g. | Fat: 22.8 g. | Carbs: 7.9 g.

412. Onion Salmon Soup

Preparation Time: 6 minutes

Cooking Time: 12 minutes

Servings: 1

Ingredients:

- 3cups water
- 1 salmon head
- 1 sliced onion
- 4tbsps. coconut oil
- 3-inch slivered ginger piece

Directions:

1. Choose the "Sauté" button on the Air fryer and heat the oil.
2. Sauté the onion until fragrant.
3. Pour in the water and add the salmon head and ginger.
4. Apply pepper and salt for seasoning.
5. Set lid in place and ensure vent points to "Sealing."
6. While on "Manual" mode, set timer to 10 minutes.
7. Do quick pressure release.

Nutrition:

Calories: 474 | Protein: 15.3 g. | Fat: 54.4 g. | Carbs: 1.8 g.

413. Chicken Curry Soup

Preparation Time: 7 minutes

Cooking Time: 25 minutes

Servings: 3-4

Ingredients:

- 1 Pinch of Kosher salt
- 3tablespoons of chopped fresh dill
- 2bay leaves
- 1½ bone-in chicken halved breast
- 3Diagonally sliced medium carrots
- 6cups of low-sodium chicken broth
- 2 tablespoons of unsalted butter
- 1 teaspoon of sugar
- 1/3 Cup of jasmine rice
- 3tablespoons of finely chopped fresh mint
- 1 and ½ teaspoons of Madras curry powder
- 1 thinly sliced large onion
- 1 lemon sliced into thin wedges

Directions:

1. Place your chicken, carrots, bay leaf and 1 pinch of salt in your airfryer.
2. Pour in about 3 cups of stock and press to boil over a medium heat.
3. Shut the lid and adjust the pressure to about 10 to 15 minutes.
4. Meanwhile, heat the amount of butter over medium heat in a deep sauce pan.
5. Put in the sugar and the onion with 1 pinch of salt and saute for about 5 minutes.
6. Then add the curry powder and cook for approximately 2 minutes.
7. If the timer beeps, pour in the stock and rice; then increase the heat to high and simmer for 10 minutes
8. Extract the chicken from the broth and shred the chicken meat into small pieces; then return it to the broth.
9. Blend the rice mixture with a blender until smooth, then pour it into the mixture of chopped chicken and broth and let it simmer for about 5 minutes.
10. As soon as the soup is ready, decorate with herbs and serve with lemon.
11. Enjoy your meal!

Nutrition:

Calories: 147.2 | Protein: 16 g. | Fat: 5.1 g. | Carbs: 7.6 g

414. Healthy Salmon Stew

Preparation Time: 6 minutes

Cooking Time: 13 minutes

Servings: 3

Ingredients:
- 3 cups water
- 3 minced garlic cloves
- 3 tbsps. olive oil
- 48oz. salmon fillets
- 3 cups spinach leaves

Directions:
1. Select the "Sauté" button on the Airfryer and heat the olive oil.
2. Fry the garlic until it is fragrant.
3. Add the water and the salmon fillets. Season with pepper and salt.
4. Put the lid on and make sure the vent is set to "Seal".
5. In "Manual" mode, adjust the timer to 10 minutes.
6. Perform a quick depressurisation.
7. As soon as the lid is open, press the "Sauté" button and add the spinach.
8. Let it simmer for 3 minutes.

Nutrition:
Calories: 825 | Protein: 46.1 g. | Fat: 94.5 g. | Carbs: 2.1 g.

415. Coco Tilapia Soup

Preparation Time: 6 minutes
Cooking Time: 8 minutes
Servings: 5

Ingredients:
- 4 tilapia fillets
- 2 cups water
- 1 crushed thumb-size ginger
- 1 cup coconut milk
- 10 peeled and deveined shrimps

Directions:
1. Put all the ingredients in the hot air fryer.
2. Mix in the pepper and salt.
3. Put the lid on and make sure the vent points to "Seal".
4. In "Manual" mode, set the timer to 8 minutes.

Nutrition:
Calories: 238
Protein: 13.6 g.
Fat: 28.8 g.
Carbs: 2.7 g.

416. Egg Soup

Preparation Time: 6 minutes
Cooking Time: 36 minutes
Servings: 2

Ingredients:
- 2 whole eggs
- Salt
- 1 chopped romaine lettuce head
- Pepper
- 1 lb. chicken bones

Directions:
1. Put 2 cups of water and the chicken bones into the hot air fryer.
2. Put the lid on and make sure the vent is pointing to "Seal".
3. Put in "Poultry" mode and set the timer to 30 minutes.
4. Make a quick pressure release.
5. Remove the bones and discard them.
6. Hold down the "Sauté" button and let the soup simmer.
7. As soon as it simmers, gently crack the eggs and scramble for 3 minutes.
8. Put in the lettuce and season with salt and pepper.
9. Simmer for a further 3 minutes.

Nutrition:
Calories: 443 | Protein: 58.3 g. | Fat: 39.2 g. | Carbs: 4.3 g.

417. Kale Soup & Chicken

Preparation Time: 6 minutes
Cooking Time: 20 minutes
Servings: 4

Ingredients:
- 2 chopped celery stalks
- 1 diced onion
- 3 tbsps. coconut oil
- 1 lb. boneless chicken breasts
- 4 cups chopped kale

Directions:
1. Select the "Sauté" button on the Airfryer and bring the oil to the boil.
2. Sauté the onions and celery until they become fragrant.
3. Add the chicken breasts and fry for 2 minutes on each side.
4. Add 3 cups of water and season with pepper and salt.
5. Place the lid on and make sure the vent is set to "sealing".
6. Put in "Poultry" mode and set the timer to 15 minutes.
7. Apply a natural pressure release and open the lid.
8. As soon as the lid is open, push the "Sauté" button and add the kale.
9. Let it simmer for 3 minutes.

Nutrition:
Calories: 303 | Protein: 20.8 g. | Fat: 29.3 g. | Carbs: 2.2 g.

418. Asparagus Soup

Preparation Time: 6 minutes
Cooking Time: 10 minutes
Servings: 4

Ingredients:

- Zest + 1 Tbsp of juice of organic lemon
- 3 tbsp of coconuts oil.
- 1 Sliced or chopped medium sized yellow onion.
- ½ teaspoon of dried thyme
- 5 Cups of bone broth
- 1 Teaspoon of sea salt
- 3 Chopped or minced cloves of garlic cloves.
- 2 Cups of organic sour cream*
- ½ lb of fresh asparagus cut into pieces. (Make sure to remove the woody ends of the asparagus.)

Directions:

1. Get your asparagus, onion and garlic ready. Take all the woody ends off the asparagus spears and discard them.
2. Cut the asparagus into pieces of 1 inch each.
3. Cut the onion into halves and chop.
4. Crush or chop the garlic cloves.
5. Put the ingredients aside.
6. Insert the stainless steel bowl into your hot air fryer without placing the lid on it.
7. Set the fryer to the "sauté" button and then add the coconut oil, onions and garlic. Fry for 5 minutes, stirring occasionally; add the thyme and fry for 1 more minute.
8. Add the stock, asparagus and lemon zest with the salt.
9. Close the lid of the hot air fryer and press the "Manual" button for high pressure.
10. Adjust the pressure timer to 5 minutes and when the timer goes off, include the sour cream and stir; after the hot air fryer has let off the steam, of course.
11. Serve and enjoy

Nutrition:

Calories: 161.2 | Protein: 6.3 g. | Fat: 8.2 g. | Carbs: 16.4 g.

419. Broccoli Creamy Soup

Preparation Time: 6 minutes
Cooking Time: 34 minutes
Servings: 5

Ingredients:

- 2heads broccoli florets
- 4cups water
- ½ lb. chicken bones
- 1 sliced small avocado
- 1 tsp. paprika powder

Directions:

1. Put the chicken bones and water in the hot air fryer.
2. Add pepper and salt to season.
3. Put the lid on and make sure the vent points to "Seal".
4. In "Manual" mode, adjust the timer to 30 minutes.
5. Perform a quick pressure release.
6. As soon as the lid is open, throw away the bones.
7. Mix in the broccoli.
8. Shut the lid again and select the "Manual" button and cook for 4 minutes.
9. Release the pressure quickly.
10. Put all the contents into a blender and add the avocado slices.
11. Blend until smooth and transfer to a bowl.
12. Sprinkle some paprika powder on top.

Nutrition:

Calories: 118 | Protein: 7.3 g. | Fat: 10.3 g. | Carbs: 1.9 g.

420. Turkey and Turmeric Soup

Preparation Time: 6 minutes
Cooking Time: 17 minutes
Servings: 4

Ingredients:

- 1 sliced thumb-size ginger
- 2chopped stalks of celery
- 1 tsp. turmeric powder
- 1 lb. chopped turkey meat
- 3tbsps. coconut oil

Directions:

1. Select the "Sauté" button on the Airfryer and start heating the oil.
2. Mix in the celery, ginger and turmeric powder until fragrant.
3. Pour in the turkey and stir for a further minute.
4. Add 3 cups of water and season with pepper and salt.
5. Put the lid on and make sure the vent is set to "Seal".
6. In "Manual" mode, set the timer to 15 minutes.
7. Perform natural pressure release.

Nutrition:

Calories: 287 | Protein: 22.8 g. | Fat: 24.3 g. | Carbs: 0.8 g.

DESSERTS

421. Mini Cheesecakes

Preparation time: 15 minutes

Cooking time: 10 minutes

Servings: 2

Ingredients:

- ¾ cup erythritol
- 2 eggs
- 1 teaspoon vanilla extract
- ½ teaspoon fresh lemon juice
- 16 oz. Cream cheese, softened
- 2 tablespoon sour cream

Directions:

1. In a blender, add the erythritol, eggs, vanilla extract and lemon juice and pulse until smooth.
2. Add the cream cheese and sour cream and pulse until smooth.
3. Place the mixture into 2 (4-inch) springform pans evenly.
4. Press "power button" of air fry oven and turn the dial to select the "air fry" mode.
5. Press the time button and again turn the dial to set the cooking time to 10 minutes.
6. Now push the temp button and rotate the dial to set the temperature at 350 degrees f.
7. Press "start/pause" button to start.
8. When the unit beeps to show that it is preheated, open the lid.
9. Arrange the pans in "air fry basket" and insert in the oven.
10. Place the pans onto a wire rack to cool completely.
11. Refrigerate overnight before serving.

Nutrition:

Calories 886 | Total fat 86 g | Saturated fat 52.8 g
Cholesterol 418 mg | Sodium 740 mg | Total carbs 7.2 g
Fiber 0 g | Sugar 1.1 g | Protein 23.1 g

422. Vanilla Cheesecake

Preparation time: 15 minutes

Cooking time: 14 minutes

Servings: 6

Ingredients:

- 1 cup honey graham cracker crumbs
- 2 tablespoons unsalted butter, softened
- 1 (453.592g). Cream cheese, softened
- ½ cup sugar
- 2 large eggs
- ½ teaspoon vanilla extract

Directions:

1. Line a round baking pan with parchment paper.
2. For crust: in a bowl, add the graham cracker crumbs, and butter. Place the crust into baking dish and press to smooth. Press "power button" of air fry oven and turn the dial to select the "air fry" mode. Press the time button and again turn the dial to set the cooking time to 4 minutes.
3. Now push the temp button and rotate the dial to set the temperature at 350 degrees f. Press "start/pause" button to start. When the unit beeps to show that it is preheated, open the lid.
4. Arrange the baking pan of crust in "air fry basket" and insert in the oven.
5. Place the crust aside to cool for about 10 minutes.
6. Meanwhile, in a bowl, add the cream cheese, and sugar and whisk until smooth. Now, place the eggs, one at a time and whisk until mixture becomes creamy. Add the vanilla extract and mix well. Place the cream cheese mixture evenly over the crust.
7. Press "power button" of air fry oven and turn the dial to select the "air fry" mode. Press the time button and again turn the dial to set the cooking time to 10 minutes.
8. Now push the temp button and rotate the dial to set the temperature at 350 degrees f. Press "start/pause" button to start.

9. When the unit beeps to show that it is preheated, open the lid. Arrange the baking pan of crust in "air fry basket" and insert in the oven.
10. Place the pan onto a wire rack to cool completely. Refrigerate overnight before serving.

Nutrition:

Calories 470 | Total fat 33.9 g | Saturated fat 20.6 g

Cholesterol 155 mg | Sodium 42 mg | Total carbs 34.9 g

Fiber 0.5 g | Sugar 22 g | Protein 9.4 g

---

423. Ricotta Cheesecake

Preparation time: 15 minutes

Cooking time: 25 minutes

Servings: 8

Ingredients:

- 17.6 oz. Ricotta cheese
- 3 eggs
- ¾ cup sugar
- 3 tablespoons corn starch
- 1 tablespoon fresh lemon juice
- 2 teaspoons vanilla extract
- 1 teaspoon fresh lemon zest, finely grated

Directions:

1. In a large bowl, place all ingredients and mix until well combined.
2. Place the mixture into a baking pan.
3. Press "power button" of air fry oven and turn the dial to select the "air fry" mode.
4. Press the time button and again turn the dial to set the cooking time to 25 minutes.
5. Now push the temp button and rotate the dial to set the temperature at 320 degrees f.
6. Press "start/pause" button to start.
7. When the unit beeps to show that it is preheated, open the lid.
8. Arrange the pan in "air fry basket" and insert in the oven.
9. Place the cake pan onto a wire rack to cool completely.
10. Refrigerate overnight before serving.

Nutrition:

Calories 197 | Total fat 6.6 g | Saturated fat 3.6 g

Cholesterol 81 mg | Sodium 102 mg | Total carbs 25.7 g

Fiber 0 g | Sugar 19.3 g | Protein 9.2 g

---

424. Pecan Pie

Preparation time: 15 minutes

Cooking time: 35 minutes

Servings: 5

Ingredients:

- ¾ cup brown sugar
- ¼ cup caster sugar
- 1/3 cup butter, melted
- 2 large eggs
- 1¾ tablespoons flour
- 1 tablespoon milk
- 1 teaspoon vanilla extract
- 1 cup pecan halves
- 1 frozen pie crust, thawed

Directions:

1. In a large bowl, mix together the sugars, and butter.
2. Add the eggs and whisk until foamy.
3. Add the flour, milk, and vanilla extract and whisk until well combined.
4. Fold in the pecan halves.
5. Grease a pie pan.
6. Arrange the crust in the bottom of prepared pie pan.
7. Place the pecan mixture over the crust evenly.
8. Press "power button" of air fry oven and turn the dial to select the "air fry" mode.
9. Press the time button and again turn the dial to set the cooking time to 22 minutes.
10. Now push the temp button and rotate the dial to set the temperature at 300 degrees f.
11. Press "start/pause" button to start.
12. When the unit beeps to show that it is preheated, open the lid.
13. Arrange the pan in "air fry basket" and insert in the oven.
14. After 22 minutes of cooking, to set the temperature at w85 degrees f for 13 minutes.
15. Place the pie pan onto a wire rack to cool for about 10-15 minutes before serving.

Nutrition:

Calories 501 | Total fat 35 g | Saturated fat 10.8 g

Cholesterol 107 mg | Sodium 187 mg | Total carbs 44.7 g

Fiber 2.9 g | Sugar 36.7 g | Protein 6.2 g

---

425. Fruity Crumble

Preparation time: 15 minutes

Cooking time: 20 minutes

Servings: 4

Ingredients:

- ½ lb. (226.8g) Fresh apricots, pitted and cubed
- 1 cup fresh blackberries
- 1/3 cup sugar, divided
- 1 tablespoon fresh lemon juice
- 7/8 cup flour

- Pinch of salt
- 1 tablespoon cold water
- ¼ cup chilled butter, cubed

Directions:

1. Grease a baking pan.
2. In a large bowl, mix well apricots, blackberries, 2 tablespoons of sugar, and lemon juice.
3. Spread apricot mixture into the prepared baking pan.
4. In another bowl, add the flour, remaining sugar, salt, water, and butter and mix until a crumbly mixture forms.
5. Spread the flour mixture over apricot mixture evenly.
6. Press "power button" of air fry oven and turn the dial to select the "air fry" mode.
7. Press the time button and again turn the dial to set the cooking time to 20 minutes.
8. Now push the temp button and rotate the dial to set the temperature at 390 degrees f.
9. Press "start/pause" button to start.
10. When the unit beeps to show that it is preheated, open the lid.
11. Arrange the pan in "air fry basket" and insert in the oven.
12. Place the pan onto a wire rack to cool for about 10-15 minutes before serving.

Nutrition:

Calories 307 | Total fat 12.4 g | Saturated fat 7.4 g

Cholesterol 31 mg | Sodium 123 mg | Total carbs 47.3 g

Fiber 3.8 g | Sugar 23.7 g | Protein 4.2 g

426. Cherry Clafoutis

Preparation time: 15 minutes

Cooking time: 25 minutes

Servings: 4

Ingredients:

- 1½ cups fresh cherries, pitted
- 3 tablespoons vodka
- ¼ cup flour
- 2 tablespoons sugar
- Pinch of salt
- ½ cup sour cream
- 1 egg
- 1 tablespoon butter
- ¼ cup powdered sugar

Directions:

1. In a bowl, mix together the cherries and vodka.
2. In another bowl, mix together the flour, sugar, and salt.
3. Add the sour cream, and egg and mix until a smooth dough forms.
4. Grease a cake pan.
5. Place flour mixture evenly into the prepared cake pan.
6. Spread cherry mixture over the dough.
7. Place butter on top in the form of dots.
8. Press "power button" of air fry oven and turn the dial to select the "air fry" mode.
9. Press the time button and again turn the dial to set the cooking time to 25 minutes.
10. Now push the temp button and rotate the dial to set the temperature at 355 degrees f.
11. Press "start/pause" button to start.
12. When the unit beeps to show that it is preheated, open the lid.
13. Arrange the pan in "air fry basket" and insert in the oven.
14. Place the pan onto a wire rack to cool for about 10-15 minutes before serving.
15. Now, invert the clafoutis onto a platter and sprinkle with powdered sugar.
16. Cut the clafoutis into desired size slices and serve warm.

Nutrition:

Calories 241 | Total fat 10.1 g | Saturated fat 5.9 g

Cholesterol 61 mg | Sodium 90 mg | Total carbs 29 g

Fiber 1.3 g | Sugar 20.6 g | Protein 3.9 g

427. Apple Bread Pudding

Preparation time: 15 minutes

Cooking time: 44 minutes

Servings: 8

Ingredients:

For bread pudding:

- 10½ oz. Bread, cubed
- ½ cup apple, peeled, cored and chopped
- ½ cup raisins
- ¼ cup walnuts, chopped
- 1½ cups milk
- ¾ cup water
- 5 tablespoons honey
- 2 teaspoons ground cinnamon
- 2 teaspoons cornstarch
- 1 teaspoon vanilla extract

For topping:

- 1 1/3 cups plain flour
- 3/5 cup brown sugar
- 7 tablespoons butter

Directions:

1. In a large bowl, mix together the bread, apple, raisins, and walnuts.
2. In another bowl, add the remaining pudding ingredients and mix until well combined.

3. Add the milk mixture into bread mixture and mix until well combined.
4. Refrigerate for about 15 minutes, tossing occasionally.
5. For topping: in a bowl, mix together the flour and sugar.
6. With a pastry cutter, cut in the butter until a crumbly mixture forms.
7. Place the mixture into 2 baking pans and spread the topping mixture on top of each.
8. Press "power button" of air fry oven and turn the dial to select the "air fry" mode.
9. Press the time button and again turn the dial to set the cooking time to 22 minutes.
10. Now push the temp button and rotate the dial to set the temperature at 355 degrees f.
11. Press "start/pause" button to start.
12. When the unit beeps to show that it is preheated, open the lid.
13. Arrange 1 pan in "air fry basket" and insert in the oven.
14. Place the pan onto a wire rack to cool slightly before serving.
15. Repeat with the remaining pan. Serve warm.

Nutrition:

Calories 432 | Total fat 14.8 g | Saturated fat 7.4 g

Cholesterol 30 mg | Sodium 353mg | Total carbs 69.1 g Fiber 2.8 g | Sugar 32 g | Protein 7.9 g

428. Raisin Bread Pudding

Preparation time: 15 minutes

Cooking time: 12 minutes

Servings: 3

Ingredients:

- 1 cup milk
- 1 egg
- 1 tablespoon brown sugar
- ½ teaspoon ground cinnamon
- ¼ teaspoon vanilla extract
- 2 tablespoons raisins, soaked in hot water for about 15 minutes
- 2 bread slices, cut into small cubes
- 1 tablespoon chocolate chips
- 1 tablespoon sugar

Directions:

1. In a bowl, mix together the milk, egg, brown sugar, cinnamon, and vanilla extract.
2. Stir in the raisins.
3. In a baking pan, spread the bread cubes and top evenly with the milk mixture.
4. Refrigerate for about 15-20 minutes.
5. Press "power button" of air fry oven and turn the dial to select the "air fry" mode.
6. Press the time button and again turn the dial to set the cooking time to 12 minutes.
7. Now push the temp button and rotate the dial to set the temperature at 375 degrees f.
8. Press "start/pause" button to start.
9. When the unit beeps to show that it is preheated, open the lid.
10. Arrange the pan over the "wire rack" and insert in the oven. Serve warm.

Nutrition:

Calories 143 | Total fat 4.4 g | Saturated fat 2.2 g

Cholesterol 628 mg | Sodium 104 mg | Total carbs 21.3 g Fiber 60.7 g | Sugar 16.4 g | Protein 5.5 g

429. Donuts Pudding

Preparation time: 15 minutes

Cooking time: 1 hour

Servings: 6

Ingredients:

- 6 glazed donuts, cut into small pieces
- ¾ cup frozen sweet cherries
- ½ cup raisins
- ½ cup semi-sweet chocolate baking chips
- ¼ cup sugar
- 1 teaspoon ground cinnamon
- 4 egg yolks
- 1½ cups whipping cream

Directions:

1. In a large bowl, mix together the donut pieces, cherries, raisins, chocolate chips, sugar, and cinnamon.
2. In another bowl, add the egg yolks, and whipping cream and whisk until well combined.
3. Add the egg yolk mixture into doughnut mixture and mix well.
4. Line a baking dish with a piece of foil.
5. Place donuts mixture into the prepared baking pan.
6. Press "power button" of air fry oven and turn the dial to select the "air fry" mode.
7. Press the time button and again turn the dial to set the cooking time to 60 minutes.
8. Now push the temp button and rotate the dial to set the temperature at 360 degrees f.
9. Press "start/pause" button to start.
10. When the unit beeps to show that it is preheated, open the lid.
11. Arrange the pan in "air fry basket" and insert in the oven.
12. Place the pan onto a wire rack to cool for about 10-15 minutes before serving. Serve warm.

Nutrition:

Calories 537 | Total fat 28.7 g | Saturated fat 12.2 g

Cholesterol 173 mg | Sodium 194 mg | Total carbs 65.1 g
Fiber 2.3 g | Sugar 32.8 g | Protein 6.5 g

430. Orange Sponge Cake

Preparation time: 50 minutes
Cooking time: 15 minutes
Servings: 6

Ingredients:
- 9 oz sugar
- 9 oz self-rising flour
- 9 oz butter
- 3 eggs
- 1 tsp baking powder
- 1 tsp vanilla extract
- Zest of 1 orange

Frosting:
- 4 egg whites
- Juice of 1 orange
- 1 tsp orange food coloring
- Zest of 1 orange
- 7 oz superfine sugar

Directions:
1. Preheat the air fryer on bake function to 160 f and place all cake ingredients, in a bowl and beat with an electric mixer.
2. Transfer half of the batter into a prepared cake pan; bake for 15 minutes. Repeat the process for the other half of the batter.
3. Meanwhile, prepare the frosting by beating all frosting ingredients together. Spread the frosting mixture on top of one cake. Top with the other cake.

Nutrition:
Calories: 828, | Protein:11.46 g, | Fat: 39.77g, | Carbs: 107.89g

431. Apricot Crumble With Blackberries

Preparation time: 30 minutes
Cooking time: 28 minutes
Servings: 4

Ingredients:
- 2 ½ cups fresh apricots, de-stoned and cubed
- 1 cup fresh blackberries
- ½ cup sugar
- 2 tbsp lemon juice
- 1 cup flour
- Salt as needed
- 5 tbsp butter

Directions:
1. Add the apricot cubes to a bowl and mix with lemon juice, 2 tbsp sugar, and blackberries.
2. Scoop the mixture into a greased dish and spread it evenly. In another bowl, mix flour and remaining sugar.
3. Add 1 tbsp of cold water and butter and keep mixing until you have a crumbly mixture. Preheat the air fryer on bake function to 390 f and place the fruit mixture in the basket.
4. Top with crumb mixture and cook for 20 minutes.

Nutrition:
Calories: 546, | Protein: 7g, | Fat: 5.23g, | Carbs: 102.53g

432. Apple & Cinnamon Pie

Preparation time: 30 minutes
Cooking time: 20 minutes
Servings: 9

Ingredients:
- 4 apples, diced
- 2 oz butter, melted
- 2 oz sugar
- 1 oz brown sugar
- 2 tsp cinnamon
- 1 egg, beaten
- 3 large puff pastry sheets
- ¼ tsp salt

Directions:
1. Whisk white sugar, brown sugar, cinnamon, salt, and butter, together.
2. Place the apples in a baking dish and coat them with the mixture.
3. Place the baking dish in the toaster oven, and cook for 10 minutes at 350 f on bake function.
4. Meanwhile, roll out the pastry on a floured flat surface, and cut each sheet into 6 equal pieces.
5. Divide the apple filling between the pieces. Brush the edges of the pastry squares with the egg.
6. Fold them and seal the edges with a fork. Place on a lined baking sheet and cook in the fryer at 350 f for 8 minutes.
7. Flip over, increase the temperature to 390 f, and cook for 2 more minutes.

Nutrition:
Calories: 140, | Protein: 1.28g, | Fat: 6.33g, | Carbs: 21.19g

433. Chocolate Cake

Preparation time: 40 minutes
Cooking Time: 30 min
Servings: 12

Ingredients:
- ¾ cup white flour

- ¾ cup whole wheat flour
- 1 tbsp. Baking soda
- ¾ tbsp. Pumpkin pie spice
- ¾ cup sugar
- 1 banana
- ½ tbsp. Baking powder
- 2 tbsp. Canola oil
- ½ cup greek yogurt
- 8 oz. Canned pumpkin puree
- Cooking spray
- 1 egg
- ½ tbsp. Vanilla extract
- 2/3 cup chocolate chips

Directions:
1. Mix white flour with whole wheat flour, pumpkin spice, salt, baking soda and baking powder in a bowl, then turn.
2. Mix sugar with oil, pumpkin puree banana, yogurt, egg and vanilla in another bowl, then turn using a mixer.
3. Blend the 2 mixtures, add chocolate chips, turn, set mix into a smeared bundt pan.
4. Put into air fryer and cook at 330°f for 30 minutes. s
5. Allow cake to cool, then cut.

Serve.

Nutrition:

Calories: 244, I Protein: 6.42g, I Fat: 7.3g, I Carbs: 39.35g

434. Berry Crumble With Lemon

Preparation time: 30 minutes

Cooking Time: 20 min

Servings: 6

Ingredients:
- 12 oz fresh strawberries
- 7 oz fresh raspberries
- 5 oz fresh blueberries
- 5 tbsp cold butter
- 2 tbsp lemon juice
- 1 cup flour
- ½ cup sugar
- 1 tbsp water
- A pinch of salt

Directions:
1. Gently mass the berries, but make sure there are chunks left. Mix with the lemon juice and 2 tbsp. of the sugar.
2. Place the berry mixture at the bottom of a prepared round cake. Combine the flour with the salt and sugar, in a bowl. Add the water and rub the butter with your fingers until the mixture becomes crumbled.
3. Arrange the crisp batter over the berries. Cook in the fryer at 390 f for 20 minutes on bake function. Serve chilled.

Nutrition:

Calories: 250, I Protein: 3.2g I Fat: 10.28g I Carbs: 38.09g

435. Vanilla-Lemon Cupcakes With Lemon Glaze

Preparation time: 30 minutes

Cooking Time: 16 min

Servings: 6

Ingredients:
- 1 cup flour
- ½ cup sugar
- 1 small egg
- 1 tsp lemon zest
- ¾ tsp baking powder
- ¼ tsp baking soda
- ½ tsp salt
- 2 tbsp vegetable oil
- ½ cup milk
- ½ tsp vanilla extract
- Glaze:
- ½ cup powdered sugar
- 2 tsp lemon juice

Directions:
1. Preheat the air fryer on bake function to 350 f, and combine all dry muffin ingredients, in a bowl.
2. In another bowl, whisk together the wet ingredients. Gently combine the two mixtures.
3. Divide the batter between 6 greased muffin tins. Place the muffin tins in the toaster oven and cook for 13 to 16 minutes.
4. Meanwhile, whisk the powdered sugar with the lemon juice. Spread the glaze over the muffins.

Nutrition:

Calories: 204, I Protein: 3.6g I Fat: 6.01g I Carbs: 34.06g

436. Handmade Donuts

Preparation time: 25 minutes

Cooking Time: 15 min

Servings: 4

Ingredients:
- 8 oz self-rising flour
- 1 tsp baking powder
- ½ cup milk
- 2 ½ tbsp butter
- 1 egg
- 2 oz brown sugar

Directions:

1. Preheat the air fryer on bake function to 350 f, and beat the butter with the sugar, until smooth.
2. Beat in eggs, and milk. In a bowl, combine the flour with the baking powder. Gently fold the flour into the butter mixture.
3. Form donut shapes and cut off the center with cookie cutters.
4. Arrange on a lined baking sheet and cook in the fryer for 15 minutes. Serve with whipped cream or icing.

Nutrition:

Calories: 370 | Protein: 8.89g | Fat: 11.16g | Carbs: 57.94g

437. Apple Treat With Raisins

Preparation time: 15 minutes

Cooking Time: 10 min

Servings: 4

Ingredients:

- 4 apples, cored
- 1 ½ oz almonds
- ¾ oz raisins
- 2 tbsp sugar

Directions:

1. Preheat the air fryer on bake function to 360 f and in a bowl, mix sugar, almonds, raisins.
2. Blend the mixture using a hand mixer.
3. Fill cored apples with the almond mixture.
4. Place the prepared apples in your air fryer basket and cook for 10 minutes. Serve with powdered sugar.

Nutrition:

Calories: 188 | Protein: 2.88g | Fat: 5.64g | Carbs: 35.63g

438. Almond Cookies With Dark Chocolate

Preparation time: 145 minutes

Cooking Time: 35 min

Servings: 4

Ingredients:

- 8 egg whites
- ½ tsp almond extract
- 1 ⅓ cups sugar
- ¼ tsp salt
- 2 tsp lemon juice
- 1 ½ tsp vanilla extract
- Melted dark chocolate to drizzle

Directions:

1. In a mixing bowl, add egg whites, salt, and lemon juice. Beat using an electric mixer until foamy. Slowly add the sugar and continue beating until completely combined; add the almond and vanilla extracts. Beat until stiff peaks form and glossy.
2. Line a round baking sheet with parchment paper. Fill a piping bag with the meringue mixture and pipe as many mounds on the baking sheet as you can leaving 2-inch spaces between each mound.
3. Place the baking sheet in the fryer basket and bake at 250 f for 5 minutes on bake function.
4. Reduce the temperature to 220 f and bake for 15 more minutes. Then, reduce the temperature to 190 f and cook for 15 minutes.
5. Remove the baking sheet and let the meringues cool for 2 hours. Drizzle with dark chocolate and serve.

Nutrition:

Calories: 170 | Protein: 7.24g | Fat: 0.19g | Carbs: 34.06g

439. Air Fried Banana With Sesame Seeds

Preparation time: 15 minutes

Cooking Time: 10 min

Servings: 5

Ingredients:

- 1 ½ cups flour
- 5 bananas, sliced
- 1 tsp salt
- 3 tbsp sesame seeds
- 1 cup water
- 2 eggs, beaten
- 1 tsp baking powder
- ½ tbsp sugar

Directions:

1. Preheat the air fryer on bake function to 340 f.
2. In a bowl, mix salt, sesame seeds, flour, baking powder, eggs, sugar, and water.
3. Coat sliced bananas with the flour mixture; place the prepared slices in the air fryer basket; cook for 8-10 minutes. Serve chilled.

Nutrition:

Calories: 327 | Protein: 9.73g | Fat: 7.55g | Carbs: 57.33g

440. Vanilla Brownies With Chocolate Chips

Preparation time: 25 minutes

Cooking Time: 20 min

Servings: 2

Ingredients:

- 1 whole egg, beaten
- ¼ cup chocolate chips
- 2 tbsp white sugar
- ⅓ cup flour
- 2 tbsp safflower oil
- 1 tsp vanilla

- ¼ cup cocoa powder

Directions:

1. Preheat the air fryer on bake function to 320 f and in a bowl, mix the beaten egg, sugar, oil, and vanilla. In another bowl, mix cocoa powder and flour.
2. Add the flour mixture to the vanilla mixture and stir until fully incorporated.
3. Pour the mixture into the air fryer baking pan and sprinkle chocolate chips on top. Cook for 20 minutes. Chill and cut into squares to serve.

Nutrition:

Calories: 321 | Protein: 8.56g | Fat: 20.03g | Carbs: 30.78g

441. Cinnamon & Honey Apples With Hazelnuts

Preparation time: 13 minutes

Cooking Time: 10 minutes

Servings: 2

Ingredients:

- 4 apples
- 1 oz butter
- 2 oz breadcrumbs
- Zest of 1 orange
- 2 tbsp chopped hazelnuts
- 2 oz mixed seeds
- 1 tsp cinnamon
- 2 tbsp honey

Directions:

1. Preheat the air fryer on bake function to 350 f and core the apples. Make sure to also score their skin to prevent from splitting.
2. Combine the remaining ingredients in a bowl; stuff the apples with the mixture and cook for 10 minutes. Serve topped with chopped hazelnuts.

Nutrition:

Calories: 1174 | Protein: 22.74g | Fat: 82.57g | Carbs: 106.11g

442. Pan-Fried Bananas

Preparation time: 15 minutes

Cooking Time: 12 min

Servings: 8

Ingredients:

- 8 bananas
- 3 tbsp vegetable oil
- 3 tbsp corn flour
- 1 egg white
- ¾ cup breadcrumbs

Directions:

1. Preheat the air fryer on toast function to 350 f. Combine oil and breadcrumbs in a bowl.
2. Coat the bananas with the corn flour, brush with egg white, and dip in the breadcrumb mixture.
3. Arrange on a lined baking sheet and cook for 8-12 minutes.

Nutrition:

Calories: 162 | Protein: 1.93g | Fat: 5.6g | Carbs: 29.09g

443. Delicious Banana Pastry With Berries

Preparation time: 15 minutes

Cooking Time: 12 minutes

Servings: 2

Ingredients:

- 3 bananas, sliced
- 3 tbsp honey
- 2 puff pastry sheets, cut into thin strips
- Fresh berries to serve

Directions:

1. Preheat the air fryer on airfry function to 340 f and place the banana slices into the cooking basket.
2. Cover with the pastry strips and top with honey.
3. Cook for 10-12 minutes on bake function. Serve with fresh berries.

Nutrition:

Calories: 253 | Protein: 2.02g | Fat: 0.58g | Carbs: 66.38g

444. Easy Mocha Cake

Preparation time: 30 minutes

Cooking Time: 15 minutes

Servings: 2

Ingredients:

- ¼ cup butter
- ½ tsp instant coffee
- 1 tbsp black coffee, brewed
- 1 egg
- ¼ cup sugar
- ¼ cup flour
- 1 tsp cocoa powder
- A pinch of salt
- Powdered sugar, for icing

Directions:

1. Preheat the air fryer on bake function to 330 f and grease a small ring cake pan.
2. Beat the sugar and egg together in a bowl. Beat in cocoa, instant and black coffees; stir in salt and flour. Transfer the batter to the prepared pan.
3. Cook for 15 minutes. Dust with powdered sugar and serve.

Nutrition:

Calories: 377 | Protein: 6.54g | Fat: 28.13g | Carbs: 25.65g

445. Choco Lava Cakes

Preparation time: 20 minutes

Cooking Time: 10 minutes

Servings: 4

Ingredients:

- 3 ½ oz butter, melted
- 3 ½ tbsp sugar
- 1 ½ tbsp self-rising flour
- 3 ½ oz dark chocolate, melted
- 2 eggs

Directions:

1. Grease 4 ramekins with butter. Preheat the air fryer on bake function to 375 f. Beat eggs and sugar until frothy.
2. Stir in butter and chocolate; gently fold in the flour.
3. Divide the mixture between the ramekins and bake in the fryer for 10 minutes.
4. Let cool for 2 minutes before turning the cakes upside down onto serving plates.

Nutrition:

Calories: 428 | Protein: 6.92g | Fat: 35.54g | Carbs: 21.06g

446. Mouthwatering Chocolate Soufflé

Preparation time: 25 minutes

Cooking Time: 18 minutes

Servings: 2

Ingredients:

- 2 eggs, whites and yolks separated
- ¼ cup butter, melted
- 2 tbsp flour
- 3 tbsp sugar
- 3 oz chocolate, melted
- ½ tsp vanilla extract

Directions:

1. Beat the yolks along with the sugar and vanilla extract; stir in butter, chocolate, and flour.
2. Preheat the air fryer on bake function to 330 f and whisk the whites until a stiff peak forms.
3. Working in batches, gently combine the egg whites with the chocolate mixture.
4. Divide the batter between two greased ramekins. Cook for 14-18 minutes.

Nutrition:

Calories: 455 | Protein: 4.64g | Fat: 28.1g | Carbs: 46.38g

447. Maple Pecan Pie

Preparation time: 1 hr 10 minutes

Cooking Time: 25 minutes

Servings: 4

Ingredients:

- ¾ cup maple syrup
- 2 eggs
- ½ tsp salt
- ¼ tsp nutmeg
- ½ tsp cinnamon
- 2 tbsp almond butter
- 2 tbsp brown sugar
- ½ cup chopped pecans
- 1 tbsp butter, melted
- 1 8-inch pie dough
- ¾ tsp vanilla extract

Directions:

1. Preheat the air fryer on toast function to 350 f, and coat the pecans with the melted butter.
2. Place the pecans in the fryer and toast them for 5 minutes. Place the pie crust into the baking pan, and scatter the pecans over.
3. Whisk together all remaining ingredients in a bowl.
4. Pour the maple mixture over the pecans.
5. Set the air fryer to 320 f and cook the pie for 25 minutes on bake function.

Nutrition:

Calories: 2403 | Protein: 19.26g | Fat: 136.07g | Carbs: 278g

448. Tangerine Cake

Preparation time: 30 minutes

Cooking Time: 20 minutes

Servings: 8

Ingredients:

- ¾ cup sugar
- 2 cups flour
- ¼ cup olive oil
- ½ cup milk
- 1 tbsp. Cider vinegar
- ½ tbsp. Vanilla extract
- Juice and zest from 2 lemons
- Juice and zest from 1 tangerine
- Tangerine segments

Directions:

1. Mix in flour with sugar and turn.
2. Mix oil with vinegar, milk, vanilla extract, tangerine zest and lemon juice, then beat properly.

3. Put flour, turn properly, get mix into a cake pan, get in air fryer and cook at 360°f for 20 minutes.
4. Serve with tangerine segments over.

Nutrition:

Calories: 225 | Protein: 3.75g | Fat: 7.58g | Carbs: 34.88g

449. Blueberry Pudding

Preparation time: 35 minutes

Cooking Time: 25 minutes

Servings: 6

Ingredients:

- 2 cups flour
- 2 cups rolled oats
- 8 cups blueberries
- 1 stick butter
- 1 cup walnuts
- 3 tbsp. Maple syrup
- 2 tbsp. Rosemary

Directions:

1. Spray blueberries smeared baking pan and keep.
2. Mix rolled oats with walnuts, flour, butter, rosemary and maple syrup, beat properly, put mix over blueberries, put all in air fryer and cook at 350° for 25 minutes.
3. Allow to cool, slice. Serve.

Nutrition:

Calories: 778 | Protein: 14.16g | Fat: 27.75g | Carbs: 136.5g

450. Blackberries Cobbler

Preparation Time: 15 minutes

Cooking Time: 20 minutes

Servings: 6

Ingredients:

For Filling:

- 2½ cups fresh blackberries
- 1 teaspoon vanilla extract
- 1 teaspoon fresh lime juice
- 1 cup sugar
- 1 teaspoon all-purpose flour
- 1 tablespoon butter, melted

For Topping:

- 1¾ cups all-purpose flour
- 6 tablespoons sugar
- 4 teaspoons baking powder
- 1 cup milk
- 5 tablespoons butter

Directions:

1. For filling: in a bowl, add all the ingredients and mix until well combined.
2. In another large bowl, mix together the flour, baking powder, and sugar.
3. Add the milk and butter and mix until a crumbly mixture form.
4. In the bottom of a greased baking dish place the blueberries mixture and top with the flour mixture evenly.
5. Arrange the baking dish in the center of Instant Omni Plus Toaster Oven.
6. Select "Air Fry" and then adjust the temperature to 320 degrees F.
7. Set the timer for 20 minutes and press the "Start".
8. When the display shows "Add Food" place the baking pan over the drip pan.
9. When the display shows "Turn Food" do nothing.
10. When cooking time is complete, remove the pan from Toaster Oven and place onto a wire rack to cool for about 10 minutes before serving.

Nutrition:

Calories 453 | Total Fat 13 g | Saturated Fat 7.9 g

Cholesterol 34 mg | Sodium 105 mg | Total Carbs 81.7 g

Fiber 4.2 g | Sugar 49.4 g | Protein 6.1 g

451. Glazed Bananas

Preparation Time: 10 minutes

Cooking Time: 10 minutes

Servings: 2

Ingredients:

- 1 ripe banana, peeled and sliced lengthwise
- ½ teaspoon fresh lime juice
- 2 teaspoons maple syrup
- 1/8 teaspoon ground cinnamon

Directions:

1. Coat each banana half with lime juice.
2. Arrange the banana halves onto the greased sheet pan, cut sides up.
3. Drizzle the banana halves with maple syrup and sprinkle with cinnamon.
4. Arrange the baking dish in the center of Instant Omni Plus Toaster Oven.
5. Select "Air Fry" and then adjust the temperature to 350 degrees F.
6. Set the timer for 10 minutes and press the "Start".
7. When the display shows "Add Food" place the baking pan over the drip pan.
8. When the display shows "Turn Food" do nothing.
9. When cooking time is complete, remove the pan from Toaster Oven. Serve immediately.

Nutrition:

Calories 70 | Total Fat 0.2 g | Saturated Fat 0.1 g

Cholesterol 0 mg | Sodium 1 mg | Total Carbs 18.1 g

Fiber 1.6 g | Sugar 11.2 g | Protein 0.7 g

452. Banana Muffins

Preparation Time: 15 minutes

Cooking Time: 25 minutes

Servings: 12

Ingredients:

- 1 2/3 cups all-purpose flour
- 1 teaspoon baking soda
- 1 teaspoon baking powder
- ½ teaspoon ground cinnamon
- ¼ teaspoon ground nutmeg
- ¼ teaspoon ground ginger
- ½ teaspoon salt
- 4 ripe bananas, peeled and mashed
- 2 eggs
- ½ cup brown sugar
- 1 teaspoon vanilla extract
- 3 tablespoon milk
- 1 tablespoon Nutella
- ¼ cup almonds, chopped

Directions:

1. In a large bowl, sift together the flour, baking soda, baking powder, spices and salt.
2. In another bowl, mix together the remaining ingredients except walnuts.
3. Add the banana mixture into flour mixture and mix until just combined.
4. Fold in the almonds.
5. Place the mixture into 12 greased muffin molds evenly.
6. Arrange a sheet pan in the center of Instant Omni Plus Toaster Oven.
7. Place the muffin molds over the sheet pan.
8. Select "Air Fry" and then adjust the temperature to 248 degrees F.
9. Set the timer for 25 minutes and press "Start".
10. When the display shows "Turn Food" do nothing.
11. When cooking time is complete, remove the muffin molds from Toaster Oven and place the pan onto a wire rack for about 10 minutes.
12. Carefully, invert the muffins onto the wire rack to completely cool before serving.

Nutrition:

Calories 223 | Total Fat 6.1 g | Saturated Fat 1.5 g

Cholesterol 45 mg | Sodium 267 mg | Total Carbs 38.3 g

Fiber 2.4 g | Sugar 15.8 g | Protein 5 g

453. Chocolate Muffins

Preparation Time: 15 minutes

Cooking Time: 10 minutes

Servings: 9

Ingredients:

- 1½ cups all-purpose flour
- ¼ cup sugar
- 2 teaspoons baking powder
- ½ teaspoon salt
- 1 cup plain Greek yogurt
- 1/3 cup olive oil
- 1 egg
- 1½ teaspoons vanilla extract
- ¼ cup semi-sweet mini chocolate chips
- ¼ cup walnuts, chopped

Directions:

1. In a bowl, mix well flour, sugar, baking powder, and salt.
2. In another bowl, add the yogurt, oil, egg, and vanilla extract and whisk until well combined.
3. Add the flour mixture and mix until just combined.
4. Fold in the chocolate chips and walnuts.
5. Place the mixture into 9 greased muffin molds evenly.
6. Place the muffins in the center of your Air fryer.
7. Select "Air Fry" and then adjust the temperature to 355 degrees F.
8. Set the timer for 10 minutes and press "Start".
9. When the display shows "Turn Food" do nothing.
10. When cooking time is complete, remove the muffin molds from the machine and place them on a wire rack for about 10 minutes.
11. Carefully, invert the muffins onto the wire rack to completely cool before serving.

Nutrition:

Calories 247 | Total Fat 12.3 g | Saturated Fat 2.8 g

Cholesterol 20 mg | Sodium 155 mg | Total Carbs 28.8 g

Fiber 0.8 g | Sugar 11.3 g | Protein 5.6 g

454. Banana-Choco Brownies

Preparation Time: 15 minutes

Cooking Time: 30 minutes

Servings: 12

Ingredients:

- 2 cups almond flour
- 2 teaspoons baking powder
- ½ teaspoon baking powder
- ½ teaspoon baking soda

- ½ teaspoon salt
- 1 over-ripe banana
- 3 large eggs
- ½ teaspoon stevia powder
- ¼ cup coconut oil
- 1 tablespoon vinegar
- 1/3 cup almond flour
- 1/3 cup cocoa powder

Directions:

1. Preheat the air fryer for 5 minutes.
2. Combine all ingredients in a food processor and pulse until well-combined.
3. Pour into a baking dish that will fit in the air fryer.
4. Place in the air fryer basket and cook for 30 minutes at 3500F or if a toothpick inserted in the middle comes out clean.

Nutrition:

Calories: 75 | Carbohydrates: 2.1g | Protein: 1.7g | Fat: 6.6g

---

455. Blueberry & Lemon Cake

Preparation Time: 10 minutes

Cooking Time: 12 minutes

Servings: 4

Ingredients:

- 2 eggs
- 1 cup blueberries
- zest from 1 lemon
- juice from 1 lemon
- 1 tsp. vanilla
- brown sugar for topping (a little sprinkling on top of each muffin-less than a teaspoon)
- 2 1/2 cups self-rising flour
- 1/2 cup Monk Fruit (or use your preferred sugar)
- 1/2 cup cream
- 1/4 cup avocado oil (any light cooking oil)

Directions:

1. In mixing bowl, beat well wet Ingredients. Stir in dry ingredients and mix thoroughly.
2. Lightly grease baking pan of air fryer with cooking spray. Pour in batter.
3. For 12 minutes, cook on 330oF.
4. Let it stand in air fryer for 5 minutes. Serve and enjoy.

Nutrition:

Calories 589 | Carbs: 76.7g | Protein: 13.5g | Fat: 25.3g

---

456. Bread Pudding with Cranberry

Preparation Time: 15 minutes

Cooking Time: 35 minutes

Servings: 4

Ingredients:

- 1-1/2 cups milk
- 2-1/2 eggs
- 1/2 cup cranberries1 teaspoon butter
- 1/4 cup and 2 tablespoons white sugar
- 1/4 cup golden raisins
- 1/8 teaspoon ground cinnamon
- 3/4 cup heavy whipping cream
- 3/4 teaspoon lemon zest
- 3/4 teaspoon kosher salt
- 3/4 French baguettes, cut into 2-inch slices
- 3/8 vanilla bean, split and seeds scraped away

Directions:

1. Lightly grease baking pan of air fryer with cooking spray. Spread baguette slices, cranberries, and raisins.
2. In blender, blend well vanilla bean, cinnamon, salt, lemon zest, eggs, sugar, and cream.
3. Pour over baguette slices. Let it soak for an hour.
4. Cover pan with foil.
5. For 35 minutes, cook on 330oF. Let it rest for 10 minutes.

Serve and enjoy.

Nutrition:

Calories: 581 | Carbs: 76.1g | Protein: 15.8g | Fat: 23.7g

---

457. Cocoa And Almond Bars

Preparation time: 34 minutes

Cooking Time: 4 minutes

Servings: 6

Ingredients:

- ¼ cup cocoa nibs
- 1 cup almonds
- 2 tbsp. Cocoa powder
- ¼ cup hemp seeds
- ¼ cup goji berries
- ¼ cup coconut
- 8 dates

Directions:

1. Blend almonds in food processor, put hemp seeds, cocoa powder, cocoa nibs, coconut, goji and beat properly.
2. Put dates, beat properly, spray on a lined baking sheet, get in air fryer and cook at 320°f for 4 minutes.
3. Slice into equal segment and allow in fridge for 30 minutes. Serve.

Nutrition:

Calories: 76 | Protein: 2.53g | Fat: 3.86g | Carbs: 11.82g

458. Chocolate And Pomegranate Bars

Preparation time: 2 hours 10 minutes

Cooking Time: 4 minutes

Servings: 6

Ingredients:

- ½ cup milk
- 1 tbsp. Vanilla extract
- 1 and ½ cups dark chocolate
- ½ cup almonds
- ½ cup pomegranate seeds

Directions:

1. Warm pan with milk over medium heat, put chocolate, turn for 5 minutes, remove heat, put half of the pomegranate seeds, vanilla extract and half of the nuts and turn.
2. Put mix into a lined baking pan, spray, spread a pinch of salt, nuts, and remaining pomegranate, get in air fryer and cook at 300° f for 4 minutes.
3. Allow in fridge for 2 hours then serve.

Nutrition:

Calories: 139 | Protein: 2.37g | Fat: 8.17g | Carbs: 13.39g

459. Tomato Cake

Preparation time: 40 minutes

Cooking Time: 30 minutes

Servings: 4

Ingredients:

- 1 and ½ cups flour
- 1 tbsp. Cinnamon powder
- 1 tbsp. Baking powder
- 1 tbsp. Baking soda
- ¾ cup maple syrup
- 1 cup tomatoes
- ½ cup olive oil
- 2 tbsp. Apple cider vinegar

Directions:

1. Mix in flour with baking soda, baking powder, maple syrup and cinnamon in a bowl then turn properly.
2. Mix in tomatoes with vinegar and olive oil in another bowl and turn properly.
3. Blend the 2 mixtures, turn properly, put into round pan, get into the fryer and cook at 360°f for 30 minutes. Allow to cool, divide.

Nutrition:

Calories: 519 | Protein: 3.66g | Fat: 27.44g | Carbs: 66.54g

460. Berries Mix

Preparation time: 11 minutes

Cooking Time: 6 minutes

Servings: 4

Ingredients:

- 2 tbsp. Lemon juice
- 1 and ½ tbsp. Maple syrup
- 1 and ½ tbsp. Champagne vinegar
- 1 tbsp. Olive oil
- 1 lb. (453.592g) Strawberries
- 1 and ½ cups blueberries
- ¼ cup basil leaves

Directions:

1. Mix in lemon juice with vinegar and maple syrup in a pan, boil over medium heat, put oil, strawberries and blueberries, turn, get in air fryer and cook at 310°f for 6 minutes.
2. Dust basil over then serve.

Nutrition:

Calories: 138 | Protein: 1.21g | Fat: 3.95g | Carbs: 26.74g

461. Passion Fruit Pudding

Preparation time: 50 minutes

Cooking Time: 40 minutes

Servings: 6

Ingredients:

- 1 cup paleo passion fruit curd
- 4 passion fruits
- 3 and ½ oz. Maple syrup
- 3 eggs
- 2 oz. Ghee
- 3 and ½ oz. Almond milk
- ½ cup almond flour
- ½ tbsp. Baking powder

Directions:

1. Mix in the half of the fruit curd with passion fruit seeds and pulp in a bowl, turn and slice into 6 heat proof ramekins.
2. Beat eggs with ghee, the rest of the curd, maple syrup, baking powder, flour and milk then turn properly.
3. Share mix into the ramekins also, get in the fryer and cook at 200° f for 40 minutes.
4. Allow pudding to cool. Serve.

Nutrition:

Calories: 214 | Protein: 6.33g | Fat: 9.92g | Carbs: 26.95g

462. Air Fried Apples

Preparation time: 27 minutes

Cooking Time: 17 minutes

Servings: 4

Ingredients:

- 4 big apples
- A handful raisins
- 1 tbsp. Cinnamon
- Raw honey

Directions:

1. Infuse each apple with raisins, spray cinnamon, sprinkle honey, get into air fryer and cook at 367°f for 17 minutes.
2. Allow to cool Serve.

Nutrition:

Calories: 100 | Protein: 0.55g | Fat: 0.33g | Carbs: 26.8g

---

463. Pumpkin Cookies

Preparation time: 25 minutes

Cooking Time: 15 minutes

Servings: 24

Ingredients:

- 2 and ½ cups flour
- ½ tbsp. Baking soda
- 1 tbsp. Flax seed
- 3 tbsp. Water
- ½ cup pumpkin flesh
- ¼ cup honey
- 2 tbsp. Butter
- 1 tbsp. Vanilla extract
- ½ cup dark chocolate chips

Directions:

1. Mix flax seed with water in a bowl, turn and allow for a while.
2. Mix flour with baking soda and salt in another bowl.
3. Mix in honey with pumpkin puree, vanilla extract, flaxseed and butter in third bowl.
4. Blend flour with chocolate chips and honey mix and turn.
5. 5. Measure 1 tablespoon of cookie dough on a lined baking sheet. Do same with remaining dough, get into air fryer and cook at 350° f for 15 minutes. Allow to cool.

Serve.

Nutrition:

Calories: 72 | Protein: 1.94g | Fat: 2.14g | Carbs: 11.36g

---

464. Figs And Coconut Butter Mix

Preparation time: 10 minutes

Cooking Time: 4 minutes

Servings: 3

Ingredient:

- 2 tbsp. Coconut butter
- 12 figs
- ¼ cup sugar
- 1 cup almonds

Directions:

1. Melt butter in pan over medium heat.
2. Put figs, almonds and sugar. Toss, get into air fryer and cook at 300°f for 4 minutes.
3. Share into bowls then serve cold.

Nutrition:

Calories: 186 | Protein: 1.27g | Fat: 8.19g | Carbs: 29.87g

---

465. Lemon Bars

Preparation time: 35 minutes

Cooking Time: 15 minutes

Servings: 6

Ingredients:

- 4 eggs
- 2 ¼ cups flour
- Lemon juice
- 1 cup butter
- 2 cups sugar

Directions:

1. Mix ½ cup sugar with butter and 2 cups flour in a bowl, turn properly, push to the bottom of a pan, get into the fryer and cook at 350°f for 10 minutes.
2. Mix in remaining flour, with the remaining sugar, lemon juice and eggs, beat properly and sprinkle over crust.
3. Put in the fryer at 350°f for 15 minutes still, allow to cool, slice bars. Serve.

Nutrition:

Calories: 660 | Protein: 11.17g | Fat: 37.59g | Carbs: 70.28g

---

466. Pears And Espresso Cream

Preparation time: 40 minutes

Cooking Time: 30 minutes

Servings: 4

Ingredients:

- 4 pears
- 2 tbsp. Lemon juice
- 1 tbsp. Sugar
- 2 tbsp. Water
- 2 tbsp. Butter
- For the cream
- 1 cup whipping cream
- 1 cup mascarpone
- 1/3 cup sugar
- 2 tbsp. Espresso

Directions:
1. Mix 1 tablespoons sugar with pears halves with lemon juice, water and butter in a bowl.
2. Toss properly, move into air fryer and cook at 360° f for 30 minutes.
3. Mix whipping cream with mascarpone, espresso, and 1/3 cup sugar in another bowl, beat properly and allow in fridge till pears are ready.
4. Share pears on plates, spread with espresso cream. Serve.

Nutrition:
Calories: 237 | Protein: 2.12g | Fat: 7.85g | Carbs: 43.19g

467. Sweet Squares

Preparation time: 40 minutes
Cooking Time: 29 minutes
Servings: 6

Ingredients:
- 1 cup flour
- ½ cup butter
- 1 cup sugar
- ¼ cup sugar
- 2 tbsp. Lemon
- 2 tbsp. Lemon juice
- 2 eggs
- ½ tbsp. Baking powder

Directions:
1. Mix flour with butter and sugar in a bowl, turn properly, push to the bottom of a pan, put into the fryer and roast at 350° f for 14 minutes.
2. Mix sugar with lemon peel, eggs, lemon juice and baking powder in another bowl, turn using mixer and sprinkle over baked crust.
3. Bake for 15 minutes still, allow to cool, slice into medium squares. Serve cold.

Nutrition:
Calories: 339 | Protein: 5.34g | Fat: 18.79g | Carbs: 38.32g

468. Cashew Bars

Preparation time: 25 minutes
Cooking Time: 15 minutes
Servings: 6

Ingredients:
- 1/3 cup honey
- ¼ cup almond meal
- 1 tbsp. Almond butter
- 1 ½ cups cashews
- 4 dates
- ¾ cup coconut
- 1 tbsp. Chia seeds

Directions:
1. Mix honey with almond butter and almond meal in a bowl and turn properly.
2. Put coconut, dates, cashew and chia seeds and turn properly still.
3. Pour mix on a lined baking sheet and compress properly.
4. Get it in fryer and cook at 300° f for 15 minutes.
5. Allow to cool, slice into medium bars then serve.

Nutrition:
Calories: 483 | Protein: 8.18g | Fat: 35.96g | Carbs: 39.44g

469. Brown Butter Cookies

Preparation time: 20 minutes
Cooking Time: 10 minutes
Servings: 6

Ingredients:
- 1 ½ cups butter
- 2 cups brown sugar
- 2 eggs
- 3 cups flour
- 2/3 cup pecans
- 2 tbsp. Vanilla extract
- 1 tbsp. Baking soda
- ½ tbsp. Baking powder

Directions:
1. Warm pan with the butter over medium heat, turn till it melts, put brown sugar and mix till it melts.
2. Mix flour with vanilla extract, baking soda, pecan, baking powder and eggs and turn properly.
3. Put brown butter, turn properly and assemble spoonful of mix on a lined baking sheet.
4. Put it in fryer and cook at 340 ° f for 10 minutes.
5. Allow cookies to cool. Serve.

Nutrition:
Calories: 897 | Protein: 10.94g | Fat: 57.82g | Carbs: 83.99g

470. Sweet Potato Cheesecake

Preparation time: 15 minutes
Cooking Time: 4 minutes
Servings: 4

Ingredients:
- 4 tbsp. Butter
- 6 oz. Mascarpone
- 8 oz. Cream cheese
- 2/3 cup graham crackers

- ¾ cup milk
- 1 tbsp. Vanilla extract
- 2/3 cup sweet potato puree
- ¼ tbsp. Cinnamon powder

Directions:
1. Mix butter with crumbled crackers, turn properly, push to the bottom of a cake pan and set in fridge.
2. Mix cream cheese with mascarpone, cinnamon, vanilla, sweet potato puree and milk, and beat properly.
3. Spray mix over crust, set in air fryer, cook at 300°f for 4 minutes and allow in fridge for some hours. Serve.

Nutrition:
Calories: 282 | Protein: 6.13g | Fat: 25.6g | Carbs: 5.83g

471. Peach Pie

Preparation time: 45 minutes
Cooking Time: 35 minutes
Servings: 4

Ingredients:
- 1 pie dough
- 2 lbs. (907.185g) Peaches
- 2 tbsp. Cornstarch
- ½ cup sugar
- 2 tbsp. Flour
- A pinch of nutmeg
- 1 tbsp. Dark rum
- 1 tbsp. Lemon juice
- 2 tbsp. Butter

Directions:
1. Wrap pie dough into pie pan and press properly.
2. Mix peaches with cornstarch, nutmeg, sugar, lemon juice, rum, flour and butter and turn properly.
3. Turn and spray mix into pie pan, put into air fryer and cook at 350°f for 35 minutes. Serve cold/warm.

Nutrition:
Calories: 554 | Protein: 3.49g | Fat: 18.36g | Carbs: 99.21g

472. Special Brownies

Preparation time: 17 minutes
Cooking Time: 23 minutes
Servings: 4

Ingredients:
- 1 egg
- 1/3 cup cocoa powder
- 1/3 cup sugar
- 7 tbsp. Butter
- ½ tbsp. Vanilla extract
- ¼ cup white flour
- ¼ cup walnuts
- ½ tbsp. Baking powder
- 1 tbsp. Peanut butter

Directions:
1. Warm pan with sugar and 6 tablespoons butter over medium heat, turn, cook for 5 minutes, move to a bowl, put salt, cocoa powder, egg, baking powder, vanilla extract, walnuts and flour, turn thoroughly and move into pan.
2. Mix 1 tablespoon butter with peanut butter, warm in microwave for a while, turn properly and sprinkle this over brownies blend.
3. Put into air fryer and bake at 320°f and bake for 17 minutes.
4. Allow brownies to cool, slice. Serve.

Nutrition:
Calories: 284 | Protein: 6.19g | Fat: 20.91g | Carbs: 21.36g

473. Coffee Cheesecakes

Preparation time: 30 minutes
Cooking Time: 20 minutes
Servings: 6

Ingredients:
For the cheesecakes
- 2 tbsp. Butter
- 8 oz. Cream cheese
- 3 tbsp. Coffee
- 3 eggs
- 1/3 cup sugar
- 1 tbsp. Caramel syrup

For the frosting
- 3 tbsp. Caramel syrup
- 3 tbsp. Butter
- 8 oz. Mascarpone cheese
- 2 tbsp. Sugar

Directions:
1. Mix cream cheese with eggs, 1 tablespoon caramel syrup, 2 tablespoons butter, coffee, and 1/3 cup sugar and beat properly, fetch into a cupcakes pan, put into the fryer and cook at 320° f and roast for 20 minutes.
2. Allow to cool and leave in freezer for 3 hours.
3. Mix 3 tablespoons butter with 2 tablespoons sugar, 3 tablespoons caramel syrup and mascarpone, mix properly, scoop mix over cheesecakes. Serve.

Nutrition:
Calories: 425 | Protein: 13.76g | Fat: 30.11g | Carbs: 26.09g

474. Carrot Cake

Preparation time: 55 minutes

Cooking Time: 45 minutes

Servings: 6

Ingredients:

- 5 oz. Flour
- ¾ tbsp. Baking powder
- ½ tbsp. Baking soda
- ½ tbsp. Cinnamon powder
- ¼ tbsp. Nutmeg
- ½ tbsp. Allspice
- 1 egg
- 3 tbsp. Yogurt
- ½ cup sugar
- ¼ cup pineapple juice
- 4 tbsp. Sunflower oil
- 1/3 cup carrots
- 1/3 cup pecans
- 1/3 cup coconut flakes
- Cooking spray

Directions:

1. Mix flour with baking powder, salt, baking soda, allspice, nutmeg and cinnamon in a bowl, then turn.
2. Mix egg with yogurt, oil, sugar, pineapple juice, carrots, coconut flakes and pecans in another bowl, then turn properly.
3. Blend the two mixtures and turn properly, put mix into a spring form pan smeared with some cooking spray, get it into air fryer and cook at 320°f for 45 minutes.
4. Allow to cool, then slice. Serve.

Nutrition:

Calories: 301 | Protein: 5.02g | Fat: 16.84g | Carbs: 34.18g

475. Delicious Maple Plantains

Preparation Time: 5 minutes

Cooking Time: 8 minutes

Servings: 4

Ingredients:

- Salt to taste
- 2 teaspoons avocado oil
- Maple syrup
- 2 ripe plantains, sliced

Directions:

1. Swirl the plantains in oil.
2. Flavour with salt.
3. Broil in frying basket at 400 degrees F for 10 minutes, tossing after 5 minutes.
4. Before serving, sprinkle with maple syrup.

Nutrition:

Calories: 125 | Protein: 1.2 g. | Fat: 0.6 g. | Carbs: 32 g.

476. Coco Bananas

Preparation Time: 10 minutes

Cooking Time: 20 minutes

Servings: 4

Ingredients:

- 3 tablespoons agave nectar
- 4 bananas, peeled and sliced diagonally
- 1 tablespoon coconut oil
- ½ teaspoon cardamom seeds
- Juice of ½ lemon

Directions:

1. Place bananas in a pan that fits your hot air fryer, include agave syrup, lemon juice, oil and cardamom, put in the fryer and cook at 360 degrees F for 20 minutes.
2. Spread bananas and sauce on plates and serve. Enjoy!

Nutrition:

Calories: 210 | Protein: 3 g. | Fat: 1 g. | Carbs: 8 g.

477. Cinnamon & Maple Apples

Preparation Time: 10 minutes

Cooking Time: 20 minutes

Servings: 4

Ingredients:

- ¼ cup maple syrup
- 2 teaspoons cinnamon powder
- 2 cups mandarin juice
- 1 tablespoon ginger, grated
- 4 apples, cored, peeled and cored

Directions:

1. In a saucepan that fits in your deep fryer, combine apples with tangerine juice, maple syrup, cinnamon and ginger, place in the deep fryer and cook at 365 degrees F for 20 minutes.
2. Spread the apple mixture on plates and serve warm. Enjoy!

Nutrition:

Calories: 170 | Protein: 4 g. | Fat: 1 g. | Carbs: 6 g.

478. Vanilla-Choco Bars

Preparation Time: 10 minutes

Cooking Time: 7 minutes

Servings: 12

Ingredients:

- 2/3 cup coconut cream
- 2 tablespoons coconut butter
- 2 tablespoons stevia
- ¼ teaspoon vanilla extract

- 1 cup sugar free and vegan chocolate chips

Directions:

1. Pour the cream into a bowl, add the stevia, butter and chocolate chips and stir.
2. Set aside for 5 minutes, mix well and stir in the vanilla.
3. Put the mixture on a lined baking tray, place in a hot air fryer and cook at 356 degrees F for 7 minutes.
4. Set aside to cool, slice and serve. Enjoy!

Nutrition:

Calories: 120 | Protein: 1 g. | Fat: 5 g. | Carbs: 6 g.

479. Coco-Berry Bars

Preparation Time: 10 minutes

Cooking Time: 6 minutes

Servings: 12

Ingredients:

- ½ cup raspberries, dried
- ½ cup coconut oil
- ¼ cup swerve
- ½ cup coconut, shredded
- ½ cup coconut butter, melted

Directions:

1. Puree the dried berries very well in your food processor.
2. Mix the oil with the butter, Swerve, coconut and raspberries in a bowl that fits in your deep fryer, mix well, place in the deep fryer and cook at 320 degrees F for 6 minutes.
3. Place on a lined baking tray, refrigerate for an hour, slice and serve. Enjoy your meal!

Nutrition:

Calories: 164 | Protein: 2 g. | Fat: 22 g. | Carbs: 4 g.

480. Sweet Chocolate Pudding

Preparation Time: 10 minutes

Cooking Time: 20 minutes

Servings: 2

Ingredients:

- 4 tablespoons stevia
- ½ tablespoon agar
- 4 tablespoons cocoa powder
- 2 tablespoons water
- 2 cups coconut milk, hot

Directions:

1. Combine milk with stevia and cocoa powder in a bowl and stir well.
2. Combine agar with water in a bowl, stir well, add to cocoa mixture, stir and pour into a pudding mould that will fit in your hot air fryer.
3. Place in the deep fryer and cook at 356 degrees F for 20 minutes.
4. Then serve the pudding cold.
5. Enjoy!

Nutrition:

Calories: 170 | Protein: 3 g. | Fat: 2 g. | Carbs: 4 g.

481. Crispy Blueberry Crackers

Preparation Time: 10 minutes

Cooking Time: 30 minutes

Servings: 12

Ingredients:

- 1 cup blueberries
- ½ cup coconut oil, melted
- 3 tablespoons coconut sugar
- ½ cup coconut butter

Directions:

1. In a saucepan that fits your deep fryer, combine coconut butter with coconut oil, raspberries and sugar, toss, place in deep fryer and cook at 367 degrees F for 30 minutes.
2. Place on a lined baking tray, refrigerate for a couple of hours, cut crackers into slices and serve. Enjoy your meal!

Nutrition:

Calories: 174 | Protein: 7 g. | Fat: 5 g. | Carbs: 4 g.

482. Cinnamon Cauli-Rice Pudding

Preparation Time: 10 minutes

Cooking Time: 30 minutes

Servings: 4

Ingredients:

- 2 cinnamon sticks
- ½ cup coconut, shredded
- 2 cups cauliflower rice
- 2½ cups water
- 1 cup coconut sugar

Directions:

1. In a saucepan that fits your hot air fryer, combine water with coconut blossom sugar, cauliflower rice, cinnamon and coconut, mix, place in the fryer and cook at 365 degrees F for 30 minutes.
2. Distribute the pudding into cups and serve cold. Enjoy!

Nutrition:

Calories: 203 | Protein: 4 g. | Fat: 4 g. | Carbs: 9 g.

483. Avocado & Pineapple Pudding

Preparation Time: 10 minutes

Cooking Time: 5 minutes

Servings: 8

Ingredients:

- Sugar to the taste
- 8 ounces canned pineapple, chopped
- 14 ounces milk
- 1 tablespoon avocado oil
- 1 cup rice

Directions:

1. In the hot air fryer, mix the oil, milk and rice, stir, cover and cook on high for 3 minutes.
2. Mix sugar and pineapple, stir, cover and cook on high for another 2 minutes.
3. Separate into dessert bowls and serve.

Nutrition:

Calories: 154

Protein: 8 g.

Fat: 4 g.

Carbs: 14 g.

---

484. Raspberry Jam

Preparation Time: 10 minutes

Cooking Time: 11 minutes

Servings: 2

Ingredients:

- ½ tablespoon butter
- A pinch of cinnamon powder
- Zest from ½ lemon, grated
- ½ pound raspberries
- 1/3 pound sugar

Directions:

1. In your blender, put the blueberries, puree them well, strain them, put them in your pressure cooker, put the sugar, lemon zest and cinnamon, mix, covers and cook in sauté mode for 3 minutes.
2. Pour in butter, mix, covers and cook on high for 8 minutes.
3. Pour into a container and serve.

Nutrition:

Calories: 211 | Protein: 5 g. | Fat: 3 g. | Carbs: 6 g.

---

485. Plum Jam

Preparation Time: 20 minutes

Cooking Time: 8 minutes

Servings: 12

Ingredients:

- 1 teaspoon vanilla extract
- 3 ounces water
- 2 pounds sugar
- 3 pounds plums, stones removed and roughly chopped
- 2 tablespoons lemon juice

Directions:

1. In your hot air fryer, combine plums with sugar and vanilla extract, mix and leave aside for 20 minutes.
2. Pour in lemon juice and water, mix, lid and cook on high for 8 minutes.
3. Separate into bowls and serve cold.

Nutrition:

Calories: 191 | Protein: 13 g. | Fat: 3 g. | Carbs: 12 g.

---

486. Pumpkin Plate

Preparation Time: 10 minutes

Cooking Time: 15 minutes

Servings: 4

Ingredients:

- 3 tablespoons sugar
- 1 teaspoon nutmeg, ground
- 1 teaspoon cinnamon powder
- 2 cups pumpkin flesh, cubed
- 1 cup heavy cream

Directions:

1. Combine the pumpkin with the cream and the other ingredients in a pan that fits your deep fryer, put it in the deep fryer and cook at 360 degrees F for 15 minutes.
2. Separate into bowls and serve.

Nutrition:

Calories: 212 | Protein: 7 g. | Fat: 5 g. | Carbs: 15 g.

---

487. Apple Jam

Preparation Time: 10 minutes

Cooking Time: 25 minutes

Servings: 4

Ingredients:

- 1-pound apples, cored, peeled and chopped
- ½ cup sugar
- ½ teaspoon nutmeg, ground
- 1 cup water

Directions:

1. In a pot suitable for your deep fryer, combine the apples with the water and the other ingredients, stir, put the pot in the deep fryer and cook at 370 degrees F for 25 minutes.
2. Puree a little with a hand blender, distribute into glasses and serve.

Nutrition:

Calories: 204 | Protein: 4 g. | Fat: 3 g. | Carbs: 12 g.

488. Vanilla Pumpkin Cream

Preparation Time: 10 minutes
Cooking Time: 30 minutes
Servings: 4
Ingredients:
- 2 eggs, whisked
- 1 cup pumpkin puree
- 2 tablespoons sugar
- ½ teaspoon vanilla extract
- 1 cup yogurt

Directions:
1. Combine the puree and yoghurt with the other ingredients in a large bowl, beat well, fill into 4 ramekins, transfer to the hot air fryer and cook at 370 degrees F for 30 minutes.
2. Leave to cool and serve.

Nutrition:
Calories: 192 | Protein: 4 g. | Fat: 7 g. | Carbs: 12 g.

489. Sweet Coconut Rice

Preparation Time: 10 minutes
Cooking Time: 25 minutes
Servings: 6
Ingredients:
- 1 teaspoon vanilla extract
- ½ cup raisins
- 3 tablespoons sugar
- 1 cup white rice
- 2 cups coconut milk

Directions:
1. Combine the rice in the pan of the deep fryer with the milk and the other ingredients, put the pan in the deep fryer and cook at 320 degrees F for 25 minutes.
2. Separate into bowls and serve warm.

Nutrition:
Calories: 132 | Protein: 7 g. | Fat: 6 g. | Carbs: 11 g.

490. Vanilla Pears

Preparation Time: 10 minutes
Cooking Time: 15 minutes
Servings: 4
Ingredients:
- 1 egg, whisked
- 14 ounces vanilla custard
- 2 tbsp. sugar
- 2 pears, halved
- 4 puff pastry sheets

Directions:
1. Place the puff pastry slices on a clean surface, place a spoonful of custard in the centre of each, top with pear halves and wrap.
2. Brush the pears with egg, dust with sugar and transfer to the basket of your hot air fryer and cook at 320 °F for 15 minutes.
   1. Place the parcels on plates and serve.

Nutrition:
Calories: 200 | Protein: 6 g. | Fat: 7 g. | Carbs: 6 g.

491. Lemon Bars

Preparation Time: 10 minutes
Cooking Time: 35 minutes
Servings: 8
Ingredients:
- 3 eggs, whisked
- 1 cup erythritol
- 1 and ¾ cups almond flour
- Juice of 3 lemons
- ½ cup butter, melted

Directions:
1. Combine 1 cup of the flour with half of the erythritol and the butter in a bowl, stir well and press into a baking dish lined with parchment paper that will fit in the hot air fryer.
2. Transfer the pan to the air fryer and bake at 350 degrees F for 10 minutes.
3. Meanwhile, in a bowl, combine the remaining flour with the rest of the erythritol and the other ingredients and whisk well.
4. Distribute this over the crust, put the tin back in the deep fryer and bake at 350 degrees F for 25 minutes.
5. Let cool, cut into bars and serve.

Nutrition:
Calories: 210 | Protein: 8 g. | Fat: 12 g. | Carbs: 4 g.

492. Vanilla Sweet Pears

Preparation Time: 10 minutes
Cooking Time: 15 minutes
Servings: 4
Ingredients:
- 4 pears, cored and cut into wedges
- 1 tsp vanilla
- 1/4 cup apple juice
- 2 cups grapes, halved

Directions:
1. Put all of the ingredients in the inner pot of air fryer and stir well.
2. Seal pot and cook on high for 15 minutes.

3. As soon as the cooking is done, let it release pressure naturally for 10 minutes then release remaining using quick release. Remove lid.
4. Stir and serve.

Nutrition: Calories 162 | Protein 1.1 g. | Fat 0.5 g. Carbs 41.6 g.

493. Coconut Apple Compote

Preparation Time: 10 minutes
Cooking Time: 15 minutes
Servings: 6
Ingredients:
- 3 cups apples, cored and cubed
- 1 tsp vanilla
- 3/4 cup coconut sugar
- 1 cup of water
- 2 tbsp fresh lime juice

Directions:
1. Put all of the ingredients in the inner pot of air fryer and stir well.
2. Seal pot and cook on high for 15 minutes.
3. As soon as the cooking is done, let it release pressure naturally for 10 minutes then release remaining using quick release. Remove lid.
4. Stir and serve.

Nutrition:
Calories 76 | Protein 0.5 g. | Fat 0.2 g. | Carbs 19.1 g.

494. Cinnamon Apple & Dates

Preparation Time: 10 minutes
Cooking Time: 15 minutes
Servings: 4
Ingredients:
- 4 apples, cored and cut into chunks
- 1 tsp cinnamon
- 1 tsp vanilla
- 1/2 cup dates, pitted
- 1 1/2 cups apple juice

Directions:
1. Put all of the ingredients in the inner pot of air fryer and stir well.
2. Seal and cook on high for 15 minutes.
3. As soon as the cooking is done, let it release pressure naturally for 10 minutes then release remaining using quick release. Remove lid.
4. Stir and serve.

Nutrition:
Calories 226 | Protein 1.3 g. | Fat 0.6 g. | Carbs 58.6 g.

495. Choco Rice

Preparation Time: 10 minutes
Cooking Time: 20 minutes
Servings: 4
Ingredients:
- 1 cup of rice
- 1 tbsp cocoa powder
- 2 tbsp maple syrup
- 2 cups almond milk

Directions:
1. Put all of the ingredients in the inner pot of air fryer and stir well.
2. Seal pot and cook on high for 20 minutes.
3. As soon as the cooking is done, let it release pressure naturally for 10 minutes then release remaining using quick release. Remove lid.
4. Stir and serve.

Nutrition:
Calories 474 | Protein 6.3 g | Fat 29.1 g |Carbs 51.1 g.

496. Vanilla Cinnamon Peaches

Preparation Time: 10 minutes
Cooking Time: 15 minutes
Servings: 4
Ingredients:
- 4 peaches, cored and cut into chunks
- 1 tsp vanilla
- 1 tsp cinnamon
- 1/2 cup raisins
- 1 cup of water

Directions:
1. Put all of the ingredients in the inner pot of air fryer and stir well.
2. Seal pot and cook on high for 15 minutes.
3. As soon as the cooking is done, let it release pressure naturally for 10 minutes then release remaining using quick release. Remove lid.
4. Stir and serve.

Nutrition:
Calories 118 | Protein 2 g. | Fat 0.5 g. | Carbs 29 g.

497. Original Mug Cake

Preparation Time: 15 minutes
Cooking Time: 13 minutes

Servings: 1

Ingredients:

- ¼ cup self-rising flour
- 5 tablespoons caster sugar
- 1 tablespoon cocoa powder
- 3 tablespoons coconut oil
- 3 tablespoons whole milk

Directions:

1. In a shallow mug, add all the ingredients and mix until well combined.
2. Press "Power Button" of Air Fry Oven and turn the dial to select the "Air Fry" mode.
3. Press the Time button and again turn the dial to set the cooking time to 13 minutes.
4. Now push the Temp button and rotate the dial to set the temperature at 392 degrees F.
5. Press "Start/Pause" button to start.
6. When the unit beeps to show that it is preheated, open the lid.
7. Arrange the mug in "Air Fry Basket" and insert in the oven.
8. Place the mug onto a wire rack to cool slightly before serving.

Nutrition: Calories 729 | Protein 5.7 g. | Fat 43.3 g. Carbs 88.8 g.

498. Sweet Buttery Peaches

Preparation Time: 10 minutes

Cooking Time: 10 minutes

Servings: 2

Ingredients:

- 2 peaches, cut into wedges and remove pits
- ¼ cup butter, diced into pieces
- ¼ cup brown sugar
- ¼ cup graham cracker crumbs

Directions:

1. Arrange peach wedges on air fryer oven rack and air fry at 350 F for 5 minutes.
2. In a bowl, put the butter, graham cracker crumbs, and brown sugar together.
3. Turn peaches skin side down.
4. Spoon butter mixture over top of peaches and air fry for 5 minutes more.
5. Top with whipped cream and serve.

Nutrition:

Calories – 378 Protein – 2.3 g. Fat – 24.4 g. Carbs – 40.5 g.

499. Basic Apple Recipe

Preparation Time: 10 minutes

Cooking Time: 10 minutes

Servings: 4

Ingredients:

- 4 apples, sliced
- 1 tsp apple pie spice
- 2 tbsp sugar
- 2 tbsp ghee, melted

Directions:

1. Add apple slices into the mixing bowl.
2. Add remaining ingredients on top of apple slices and toss until well coated.
3. Transfer apple slices on instant vortex air fryer oven pan and air fry at 350 F for 10 minutes.
4. Top with ice cream and serve.

Nutrition: Calories 196 | Protein 0.6 g. | Fat 6.8 g. Carbs 37.1 g.

500. Sweet Dried Mango Slices

Preparation Time: 10 minutes Cooking Time: 12 hours

Servings: 6

Ingredients:

- 4 mangoes, peel and cut into ¼-inch slices
- ¼ cup fresh lemon juice
- 1 tbsp honey

Directions:

1. In a big bowl, combine together honey and lemon juice and set aside.
2. Add mango slices in lemon-honey mixture and coat well.
3. Arrange mango slices on the air fryer rack and dehydrate at 135 F for 12 hours.

Nutrition:

Calories – 147 Protein – 1.9 g. Fat – 0.9 g. Carbs – 36.7 g.

501. Fried Lemony Raspberries

Preparation Time: 10 minutes Cooking Time: 15 hours

Servings: 4

Ingredients:

- 4 cups raspberries, wash and dry
- ¼ cup fresh lemon juice

Directions:

1. Add raspberries and lemon juice in a bowl and toss well.

2. Arrange raspberries on instant vortex air fryer oven tray and dehydrate at 135 F for 12-15 hours.
3. Store in an air-tight container.

Nutrition:

Calories 68 I Protein 1.6 g. I Fat 0.9 g. I Carbs 15 g.

Tips And Tricks

Air fryers can give you crispier foods that satisfy your cravings, and as we conclude, here are some tips to ensure success while using your air fryer. Here are some great tips for you to get the most out of your air fryer!

1. **Shake it frequently while cooking:** Be sure to open the fryer and shake what you are cooking around as they "fry" in the basket. Smaller foods such as French fries and chips may compress. Even if a recipe does not mention to rotate, shake, or flip, for the best results, make sure to do so every 5-10 minutes.

2. **Do not overcrowd food while cooking:** Make sure you give foods lots of space for the hot air to circulate effectively around what you are cooking. This will give you the crispy results you crave! Also, it is best to work in small batches.

3. **Spray foods:** On occasion, your air fryer will pick up foods that are light and blow them around the fryer. Secure foods you cook with toothpicks!

4. **Check your food's doneness frequently:** One of the best benefits of cooking with an air fryer is that you do not have to worry about how often you open it up to check for doneness. If you are an anxious chef, this can give you peace of mind to create yummy meals and snacks every single time!

5. **Take out basket before removing food:** If you go to invert the air fryer basket when it is still locked tightly in the drawer, you will dump all the fat that has rendered from your food.

6. **Clean the drawer after each use:** The air fryer drawer is extremely easy to clean and quite hassle-free. But if you leave it unwashed, you can risk contaminating future food you cook, and you may have a nasty smell take over your kitchen. Simply clean it after every use to prevent this.

7. **Use the air dryer to dry the appliance out:** After you wash the basket and air fryer drawer, you can pop them back into the fryer and turn on the appliance for 2-3 minutes. This is a great way to dry it thoroughly for your next use!

Conclusion

Hopefully, after going through this cookbook and trying out a some of the recipes, you are now well aware of the flexibility and utility of your air fryer. It is undoubtedly a multipurpose kitchen appliance that is highly recommended to everybody. It gives and our loved ones a palatable and practical atmosphere to enjoy fried foods that are not only delicious but healthy, cheaper, and more convenient. The use of this kitchen appliance ensures that the making of some of your favourite snacks and meals could be carried out in a stress-free manner without hassling around, which invariably legitimizes its worth and gives you value for your money.

This cookbook wants to be your everyday guide to understand the basics of the air fryer because, with all the recipes mentioned in the book, you are rest assured that it will be something that you and the rest of the those around the world will who discovered already the joy of an Air Fryer, will enjoy for the rest of our lives. From now on, you will be able to prepare delicious and flavoursome meals that will not only be easy to carry out but tasty and healthy as well.

However, you should never limit yourself to the recipes solely mentioned in this cookbook, go on and try new things! Explore new recipes! Experiment with different ingredients, seasonings, and other methods! Create some new recipes and keep your mind open. By so doing, you will be able to get the best out of your air fryer.

Use it! The air fryer truly is not an appliance that should stay on the shelf. However, take it out and give it a try when you are whipping up one of your tried-and-true recipes, or if you are starting to get your feet wet with the air frying method.

Regardless of appliances, recipes, or dietary concerns, I hope you have fun in your kitchen. Between food preparation, cooking time, and then the cleanup, a lot of time is spent in this one room, so it should be as fun as possible.

It is just the start. There are no limits to working with the air fryer. There are just so many options to choose from that it won't take long before you find a whole bunch of recipes to use, and before you start to wonder why you didn't get an air fryer much sooner.

An Air Fryer shines when you have the right recipes in place and can use them. It's enough to master 4 or 5 of them to mke your friend try this new healthier way of cooking.

We are pleased that you pursue this Air Fryer cookbook. Happy, healthy eating!

P.J.

INDEX

10-Minute Chimichanga 76
Air Fried Apples 162
Air Fried Banana With Sesame Seeds 155
Air Fried Chicken Kabobs 66
Air Fry Bacon 41
Air Fryer Brussels sprouts 80
Air Fryer Chicken Wings 90
Air Fryer Steak Bites and Mushrooms 79
Almond Cookies With Dark Chocolate 155
Appetizer 37
Apple & Cinnamon Pie 153
Apple Bread Pudding 151
Apple Jam 168
Apple Roll-Ups 17
Apple Treat With Raisins 155
Apricot Crumble With Blackberries 153
Aromatic Baby Potatoes 59
Aromatic Butternut Squash Cream 134
Aromatic Garlic Eggplants 62
Aromatic Lamb Bites 55
Asian Chicken Wings 100
Asian Coconut Shrimp 117
Asian Coconut Soup 145
Asian Salmon 117
Asian Style Pork 95
Asian Style Teriyaki Chicken 105
Asparagus Soup 147
Authentic Mediterranean Calamari Salad 115
Avocado & Pineapple Pudding 167
Avocado Flautas 21
Avocado Flavoured Leek and Salmon Soup 145
Avocado chips 131
BBQ Lime Nachos 62
Baby Spinach Nutty Lamb 54
Bacon Bombs 20
Bacon Wrapped Pork 98
Bacon, Mushroom & Tomato Frittata 22
Bacon-Wrapped Pork Tenderloin 91
Baked Beef 83
Baked Sardines with Sauce 38
Balsamic Brussels Sprouts 130
Banana Bread with Walnuts 33
Banana Muffins 159
Banana Oats 29
Banana-Choco Brownies 160
Barbecue Lemon Chicken 104

Basic Apple Recipe 171
Basil Chicken 82
Basil Cod 120
Bbq Jackfruit Nachos 75
Beef Liver 98
Beef Roll-Ups 87
Beef Soup with Rice 135
Beef and Potato 87
Berries Mix 161
Berry Crumble With Lemon 154
Biscuits Casserole 24
Blackberries Cobbler 158
Blue Cheese & Beets Salad 131
Blueberry & Lemon Cake 160
Blueberry Pudding 158
Bratwurst and Veggies 91
Bread Pudding with Cranberry 160
Bread Rolls 27
Breaded Beef Schnitzel 87
Breaded Chicken bites 103
Breaded Cod Bites 126
Breakfast 15
Breakfast Casserole 15
Breakfast Egg Muffins 16
Breakfast Egg Tomato 28
Breakfast Pizza 19
Breakfast Pockets 21
Broccoli & Sweet Potato 132
Broccoli Creamy Soup 148
Broccoli Muffins 16
Brown Butter Cookies 164
Buffalo Cauliflower Bites 78
Buffalo Yogurt Chicken 103
Buttered Scallops 113
Buttered Shrimp Skewers 109
Buttermilk Fried Mushrooms 81
Buttery Apple & Broccoli Soup 142
Buttery Cod 82
Buttery Garlic Cauliflower Soup 141
Buttery Pesto Salmon 126
Buttery Rosmary Mushrooms 58
Buttery Snow Peas 57
Cabbage & Celery Soup 138
Cabbage Chips 44
Cajun Spiced Salmon 111
Carrot Cake 165

Carrot Small Cakes 32
Carrot Soup with Cashew Sour Cream 139
Carrot Sticks 129
Cashew Bars 163
Celery and Tomato Soup 136
Cheese Air Fried Bake 24
Cheese Pie 17
Cheese Sandwiches 21
Cheeseburger 'Mini' Sliders 89
Cheesy Baked Potatoes 38
Cheesy Beef Sandwiches 64
Cheesy Broccoli 129
Cheesy Cinnamon Pancake 35
Cheesy Jalapeño Poppers 39
Cheesy Pork Rinds 63
Cheesy Potato Soup 133
Cherry Clafoutis 151
Chestnut Turkey Meatballs 102
Chicken In Salsa Verde 96
Chicken Cordon Bleu 84
Chicken Curry 93
Chicken Curry Soup 146
Chicken Curry on Edamame and Asparagus 89
Chicken Meatball Wraps 65
Chicken Omelet 25
Chicken Pita Sandwiches 92
Chicken Popcorn 104
Chicken Soup 133
Chicken Thighs in Soy Sauce 95
Chicken Tikka Kebab 80
Chicken Wings 84
Chicken and Potatoes 85
Chicken À La King 92
Chili Bamboo Shoots 58
Chili Beef 56
Chili Fennel Wedges 58
Chili Lentil Soup 143
Chili Sauce Chicken 49
Choco Lava Cakes 157
Choco Rice 170
Chocolate And Pomegranate Bars 161
Chocolate Cake 154
Chocolate Muffins 159
Cinnamon & Honey Apples With Hazelnuts 156
Cinnamon & Maple Apples 166
Cinnamon Apple & Dates 169
Cinnamon Buns 29
Cinnamon Cauli-Rice Pudding 167

Cinnamon Cream Doughnuts 26
Cinnamon Donuts 34
Cinnamon French Toast 36
Cinnamon flavoured Fries 132
Cinnapple Pork Tenderloins 97
Classic French Fries 45
Classic Lemon Pepper Haddock 118
Coco Bananas 166
Coco Curry Rice Plate 65
Coco Shrimp 121
Coco Tilapia Soup 146
Coco-Berry Bars 166
Cocoa And Almond Bars 161
Coconut Apple Compote 169
Coconut Chicken Breast Soup 144
Coconut-Crusted Chicken Tenders 85
Cod Fillets with Fennel and Grapes Salad 116
Coffee Cheesecakes 165
Coffee Favoured Muffins 34
Conclusion 173
Corned Beef 97
Crab Cakes 122
Crab Dip 109
Creamy Beef Strips 54
Creamy Breaded Salmon 126
Creamy Celery Soup 140
Creamy Chicken 82
Creamy Chicken Asparagus Soup 138
Creamy Mushroom Porridge 31
Creamy Pesto Scallops 127
Creamy Pork Chops 97
Creamy Scrambled Eggs 32
Crispy Air Fried Tofu 81
Crispy Baked Avocado Tacos 81
Crispy Blueberry Crackers 167
Crispy Chicken Sliders 86
Crispy Eggplant 44
Crispy Indian Wrap 72
Crispy Pork Chops 84
Crispy Salt and Pepper Tofu 71
Crunchy Bacon Bites 41
Crunchy Nut Granola 18
Crunchy Pork Egg Rolls 47
Curried Sweet Potato Fries 43
DINNER 60
Delicious Banana Pastry With Berries 156
Delicious Catfish 116
Delicious Cinnamon Pancake 36

Delicious Daily Bean	61
Delicious Maple Plantains	165
Delicious Potato Hash	24
Delicious Rotisserie Chicken	104
Delicious Tomato Soup	137
Desserts	149
Dill Fish Chops	119
Donuts Pudding	152
Dutch Pancake With Shrimp Salsa	91
Easy Crab Cakes	118
Easy Fish Sticks with Chili Ketchup Sauce	120
Easy Jalapeno Poppers	42
Easy Mocha Cake	157
Easy Peasy Pizza	72
Egg Cheddar Muffins	30
Egg Cups	15
Egg Soup	147
Eggplant Bake	82
Eggplant Parmigiana	72
Eggplant stacks	130
English Muffin Tuna Sandwiches	70
Exotic Cornbread	31
Exotic Duck Breasts	50
Exotic Eggplant Recipe	62
Figs And Coconut Butter Mix	162
Fish Dishes	107
Fish Tacos	114
Flounder Fillets	122
Fresh Veggy Stew	140
Fried Chicken	85
Fried Lemony Raspberries	171
Fried Olives	48
Fried Scallops with Saffron Cream Sauce	118
Fried bananas	129
Fruity Bacon Slices+Yogurt Dip	34
Fruity Crumble	151
Galric Fish Balls Soup	144
Garlic Cheesy Meatballs	56
Garlic Duck Breasts	49
Garlic Edamame	37
Garlic Herb Turkey Breast	86
Garlic Lemon Shrimp	122
Garlic Parmesan Chicken Wings	78
Garlic Tilapia	110
Ginger Kale Soup	144
Ginger Soup	145
Glazed Bananas	159
Go-to Easy Cornbread	30
Good'ol steak	93
Grand Air-Fried Coconut Shrimp	123
Great Air-Fried Soft-Shell Crab	124
Green Chiles Nachos	39
Grilled Tilapia with Portobello Mushrooms	114
Ham Wrapped Prawns	113
Handmade Donuts	155
Healthy Angel Cake	35
Healthy Beans Pizza	53
Healthy Broccoli Tots	44
Healthy Chicken & Asparagus	100
Healthy Chicken Thighs	49
Healthy Ratatouille	51
Healthy Salmon Stew	146
Healthy Thyme Mushrooms	130
Herb Zucchini Slices	43
Herbed Lamb Rack	83
Herbed Trout and Asparagus	121
Honey & Vinegar Salmon	128
Honey Minty Lamb	55
Honey and Chicken Drumsticks	88
Honey-Lime Chicken Wings	86
Immune-Boosting Grilled Cheese Sandwich	77
Indian Cauliflower	29
Italian Flag English Muffin	52
Italian Minestrone	136
Italian Spaghetti Squash	131
Japanese-Style Fried Prawns	124
Jicama Fries	130
Juicy BBQ Tofu	96
Juicy Beef & Mushrooms	98
Juicy Spaghetti Squash	131
Jumbo Stuffed Mushrooms	68
Kale Soup & Chicken	147
Kids' Taquitos	77
Korean Lamb Bites	66
LUNCH	49
Lamb & Brussels Sprout	55
Lemon & Orange Grilled Branzini	126
Lemon Bars	163
Lemon Bars	169
Lemon Chicken Breast	87
Lemon Drumsticks	95
Lemon Tuna	107
Lemon and Chicken Pepper	89
Lemon-Pepper Wings	40
Lemony & Spicy Coconut Crusted Prawns	107
Lemony Lentils	60

Lemony Lentils With "Fried" Onions	74
Lemony Parmesan Shrimp	128
Lemony Turkey	101
Lime Baked Salmon	120
Loaded Disco Fries	48
Low-Carb Cheese-Stuffed Jalapeño Poppers	45
Low-Sodium Pumpkin Soup	141
Luscious Lazy Lasagna	73
Madeira Beef Cubes	96
Mahi Mahi with Herby Buttery Drizzle	117
Main Course	68
Mango and Lime Bowl	32
Maple Brisket	64
Maple Pecan Pie	157
Marinated Pork Shoulder	94
Meatball Casserole	83
Mexican Stuffed Potatoes	76
Mind-Blowing Air-Fried Crawfish with Cajun Dipping Sauce	125
Mini Cheesecakes	149
Montreal Fried Shrimp	112
Morning Potatoes	20
Moroccan Style Chicken	105
Mouthwatering Chocolate Soufflé	157
Mozzarella Bean Bake	64
Mozzarella Bread & Eggs	31
Mozzarella Chicken Bake	101
Mozzarella Pepperoni Pizza Bites	41
Mozzarella Rolls	105
Mushroom Leek Frittata	28
Mushroom Pita Pizzas	69
Mushroom Tofu Soup	139
Mushroom and Turkey Stew	82
Mussels & Sausages	95
Mustard Chicken Thighs	101
Mustard Lamb Bites	54
Nacho Chips Crusted Prawns	114
Noodle Soup with Chicken	135
Oatmeal Casserole	25
Olive Oil Sweet Potato Chips	45
Onion Salmon Soup	145
Orange Sponge Cake	153
Orangy Spicy Chicken	102
Oregano Chicken Meatballs	88
Original Mug Cake	170
Original Tuscan Soup	135
Our Daily Bean	75
POULTRY	100
Packet Lobster Tail	108
Pan-Fried Bananas	156
Panko Breaded Cheesy Chicken	67
Paprika Deviled Eggs	40
Paprika Whole Chicken	65
Parmesan Breakfast Casserole	17
Parmesan Cauliflower	39
Parmesan Chicken Meatballs	88
Parmesan Spinach	56
Parmesan Sticks	57
Parsley Catfish	112
Passion Fruit Pudding	162
Pasta With Creamy Cauliflower Sauce	74
Peach Pie	164
Peachy Chicken	50
Pears And Espresso Cream	163
Pecan Crusted Chicken	80
Pecan Pie	150
Pecan-Crusted Catfish Fillets	127
Pepper Egg Bites	18
Pepper Flakes Pork	94
Pepperoni Chips	44
Perfect Breakfast Frittata	28
Perfect Crab Dip	42
Perfect Pork chops	92
Pesto & Tomato Chicken	101
Pesto Gnocchi	70
Pigs in a Blanket	46
Plum Jam	168
Pork Bites with Yogurt Sauce	54
Potato Jalapeno Hash	27
Pumpkin Cookies	162
Pumpkin Plate	168
Quick and Easy Rib Eye Steak	90
Raisin Bread Pudding	152
Ranch Fish Fillets	112
Ranch Kale Chips	43
Raspberry Jam	167
Real Wiener Beef Schnitzel	98
Red Lentils English Muffins	51
Remarkable Fish and Chips with Sauce	123
Ricotta Cheesecake	150
Roast Beef	90
Roasted Almonds	43
Roasted Brussels Sprouts	94
Roasted Grapes with Yogurt	37
Rosti with Salmon	33
Rotisserie-Style, Whole Chicken	86
SOUPS & STEWS	133

Sage Daikon	56	Spinach Muffins	15
Sage Turkey rolls	105	Spinach Quiche	58
Sage and Pear Sausage Patties	20	Spinach Quiche	69
Salmon and Cauliflower Rice	109	Spinach and Artichoke Dip Wontons	47
Salmon and Coconut Sauce	110	Splendid Salmon Patties	123
Salty Baked Almonds	40	Split Pea Soup	134
Salty Green Beans	64	Sriracha Carrot Soup	137
Salty Grilled Corn	64	Steak Nuggets	44
Sausage & Scallion Frittata	23	Steamed Scallops With Dill	92
Sausage Balls with Cheese	41	Stuffed Tomatoes	52
Sausage Burritos	25	Stunning Air-Fried Clams	124
Sausage Cheese Wraps	22	Strawberry French toast	17
Sausage Frittata	26	Sunday Fish with Sticky Sauce	115
Sausage Patties	25	Sweet Asian Style Salmon	119
Sausage and Onion Rolls	38	Sweet Buttery Peaches	170
Sausage, Spinach & Broccoli Frittata	22	Sweet Chocolate Pudding	166
Scrambled Eggs with Pesto & Cheese	32	Sweet Cinnamon Peaches	37
Sea Bass and Fennel.	120	Sweet Coconut Rice	168
Seasoned Salmon	112	Sweet Dried Mango Slices	171
Sesame Bok Choy	63	Sweet Duck Breasts	100
Sesame Chicken	94	Sweet Potato & Tomato Stew	140
Sesame Seed Okra	57	Sweet Potato Cheesecake	164
Sesame Seeds Coated Fish	111	Sweet Potato Tots	42
Sesame Shrimp	109	Sweet Squares	163
Shredded Chicken Stew	144	Sweet and Spicy Montreal Steak	90
Shrimp Croquettes	71	Swiss Chard Cumin Stew	143
Shrimp Scampi	113	Tabasco Shrimp	116
Shrimp Scampi Linguine	115	Taco Salad	61
Shrimp and Green Beans	108	Taco Salad with Creamy Lime Sauce	75
Shrimp and Grilled Cheese Sandwiches	71	Tamale Pie With Cilantro Lime Cornmeal Crust	77
Shrimp and Zucchinis	121	Tangerine Cake	158
Simple Balsamic Onion Soup	142	Tangy Salmon	111
Simple Grilled Chicken	102	Tarragon Chicken	87
Simple Salmon	110	Tasty Air Fried Cod	116
Snapper and Spring Onions	121	Tasty Cinnamon Toast	23
Southern-Air-Fried Catfish	125	Tasty Lobster Tail	127
Soy Sauce Egg Roll	66	Tasty Small Potatoes	53
Spaghetti Chicken Soup	142	Tasty Wrapped Asparagus	129
Special Brownies	164	Tasty meatballs	93
Spiced Nuts	46	Tea Flavoured Chicken	50
Spicy Dry-Rubbed Chicken Wings	79	Tilapia and Salsa	109
Spicy Hash Brown Potatoes	19	Tips And Tricks	172
Spicy Pork Belly	97	Tomato Cake	161
Spicy Shrimp	107	Tomato Filled Eggplants	63
Spicy Sweet Potato Hash	26	Trout Frittata	23
Spicy and Sweet Roasted Nuts	40	Trout and Mint	110
Spinach Dip	42	Trout and Zucchinis	122
Spinach Egg Breakfast	27	Tumeric Indian Wrap	60

Tuna Stuffed Potatoes 108
Tuna Zucchini Melts 70
Turkey Burrito 24
Turkey Pillows 84
Turkey and Turmeric Soup 148
Vanilla Flavoured Strawberry Porridge 31
Vanilla & Berries French toast 35
Vanilla Brownies With Chocolate Chips 156
Vanilla Cheesecake 149
Vanilla Cinnamon Peaches 170
Vanilla Pears 169
Vanilla Pumpkin Cream 168
Vanilla Sweet Pears 169
Vanilla-Choco Bars 166
Vanilla-Lemon Cupcakes With Lemon Glaze 154
Vegan Falafel 52
Vegan Noodle Soup 138
Vegan Soup 139
Vegetable Egg Rolls 68
Vegetable Quiche 28
Vegetables 129
Vegetables Quiche 53
Vegetarian tofu Omelet 33
Veggie Frittata 19
Veggie Plate 96
Veggies on Toast 68
Veggy Corn Soup 134
Veggy Egg Rolls 51
Veggy Pita 52
Vidalia Onion Blossom 46
Wild Rice Soup with Chicken 136
Wondrous Creole Fried Shrimp with Sriracha Sauce 125
Yellow Squash Fritters 69
Za'atar Lamb Loin Bites 55
Zesty Ranch Fish Fillets 119
Zucchini Gratin 16
Zucchini Salad 29

Printed in Great Britain
by Amazon